"This is an exciting book, full of interesting and innovative propositions. Thomas Princen provides a unique perspective on the role of third-party mediators. He sheds new light on the interests that motivate them to attempt to resolve international conflict."
—Janice Stein, *University of Toronto*

Thomas Princen is Assistant Professor of International Environmental Policy at the School of Natural Resources, University of Michigan, Ann Arbor. He has taught negotiation and conflict resolution at Harvard, Princeton, and Syracuse Universities.

The Arab-Israeli Conflict
Volume IV: The Difficult Search for Peace (1975-1988)
Parts 1 and 2

EDITED BY
JOHN NORTON MOORE

Volume IV of *The Arab-Israeli Conflict* is a fundamental research tool for students of the Middle East and for those responsible for U.S. policymaking in that area. It is a successor to John Norton Moore's widely acclaimed three-volume compilation of readings and documents on international law and the Arab-Israeli conflict and to the one-volume abridged edition of that compilation, published by Princeton University Press in 1974 and 1977 respectively. Additionally, Volume IV stands on its own as a documentary history of the period from September 1975 Sinai Accords through the Shultz peace initiative and the Palestinian uprising (Intifadah) in December 1988.

WITHDRAWN

Intermediaries in International Conflict

_____

WRITTEN UNDER THE AUSPICES OF THE
CENTER OF INTERNATIONAL STUDIES,
PRINCETON UNIVERSITY

Intermediaries
in International Conflict

Thomas Princen

PRINCETON UNIVERSITY PRESS

PRINCETON, NEW JERSEY

Library of Congress Cataloging-in-Publication Data

Princen, Tom, 1951–
Intermediaries in international conflict / Tom Princen.
p.   cm.
Includes bibliographical references and index.
ISBN 0-691-07897-1
1. Mediation, International.   2. Pacific settlement
of international disputes.   I. Title.
JX4475.P75   1992
341.5′2—dc20   91-36136   CIP

To my parents, Richard and Jeanne Princen

_____

CONTENTS

FIGURES

PREFACE

THIS STUDY began in the early 1980s with what seemed like fairly straightforward questions. What is this newly rediscovered method of peacemaking called mediation? Is it yet one more tool in the diplomat's bag of tricks—a variation on negotiation—or is there something distinctive about the process and the people who do it? What, in practice, does it actually look like and feel like? Are mediators born or trained? How useful is it in promoting peaceful means of resolving conflicts?

Now, one decade later, although a few patterns and propositions have emerged, the questions only seem to have multiplied. But such is the nature of social science research, especially that in the realm of decision making and policy. One asks questions, begins to get what seems like answers, and then discovers yet more questions. There is no end, no "theory" on the order of relativity or natural selection. But everyone wants to affect policy, to put in one's two bits worth to make the world a little better. So what follows is admittedly tentative, certainly deserving of further theoretical and empirical exploration.

The questions and propositions about intermediary intervention were largely spurred by the recollections of those who have done it. Initially, conversations with two pioneers in domestic environmental mediation—Gerald Cormick and James Arthur—aroused my curiosity. At the international level, Herbert Kelman introduced me to prenegotiations through two of his intensive, problem-solving workshops with Israelis and Palestinians. An anonymous Vatican official who, by spending six years of his ecclesiastical life mediating a dispute over a few obscure islands at the tip of South America and is, therefore, credibly able to claim to be among the most experienced international mediators living, granted me a series of extensive interviews. These revealed what the official accounts and press releases could not: the actual practice of international mediation, the daily grind, the frustrations, the risks, and, in this case, the fleeting glory of a successful outcome. Adam Curle and Joseph Elder, two Quaker mediators with extensive experience in Africa and Asia, acquainted me with a brand of diplomacy recognized by few but valued highly by those entangled in intractable conflicts. Finally, many who sat at one end of the negotiating table or the other shared their insights into the opportunities and the constraints of international mediation. It is from the experience, determination, and wisdom of these practitioners that this book owes its greatest debt and from which I feel most humble as I try to capture the essence of their peacemaking efforts.

Special appreciation goes to three gentlemen who not only labored through a much earlier version—the doctoral dissertation—but, in their own work, served as major intellectual catalysts for this project. They are Howard Raiffa, Herbert Kelman, and Thomas Schelling. In a different context, Dwight Clark, a quiet peacemaker in his own right, deserves particular acknowledgment as he, more than anyone, put me on the track to pursuing in thought and practice a life in tune with the needs of the planet.

Along the way, many others contributed information, insight, comments, and criticism in this endeavor. Among them are Thomas Angelo, Eileen Babbitt, Abraham Ben-Zvi, Jacob Bercovitch, Henry Bienen, Eduardo Doryan-Garron, Richard Falk, Roger Fisher, Louis Kriesberg, James McAdams, Sally Merry, Richard Neustadt, Kenneth Oye, Jeffrey Rubin, Masaru Tamamoto, Saadia Touval, Deborah Welsh, George Williams, and William Wohlforth.

For financial and institutional support, I am indebted to the Center of International Studies at Princeton University where, thanks to a postdoctoral fellowship from the MacArthur Foundation's Program on International Peace and Security, I was able to revise and expand the manuscript considerably over a period of two relatively uninterrupted years. Before that, the United States Institute of Peace supported six months of writing as a visiting scholar at the Program on Negotiation at the Harvard Law School. At the dissertation stage, the John F. Kennedy School of Government at Harvard University with funds from the Pew Charitable Trusts financed research trips to Buenos Aires, Santiago, Geneva, Rome, Washington, D.C., New York, and London and supported many months of writing. The National Institute for Dispute Resolution, the American Academy of Arts and Sciences, and the Program on Negotiation also supported portions of the field research and writing.

For the most part, the arguments and case material in this book have not appeared elsewhere. Earlier versions of the Vatican case can be found in my dissertation and in a teaching case, "Beagle Channel Negotiations," published by the Pew Program at the University of Pittsburgh. Some of the Vatican case analysis can be found in "International Mediation—The View from the Vatican" published in the *Negotiation Journal*, October 1987. An abbreviated version of the Camp David case analysis was published as "Camp David: Problem Solving or Power Politics as Usual" by the *Journal of Peace Research*, February 1991. The quotations in chapter 6 were taken from *Keeping Faith: Memoirs of a President*, by Jimmy Car-

Finally, extended writing and rewriting was impossible without the loving support and encouragement of my wife, Carmencita. And, if the first few years of life are in fact the most important, this book may have already had its greatest impact, namely, on Maria and Paul.

PART ONE

The Nature of
Intermediary Intervention

Chapter One

INTRODUCTION: INTERMEDIARIES IN
INTERNATIONAL CONFLICT

IN THE CLOSING DECADE of the twentieth century, East-West tensions may have eased but international conflict and violence are far from over. Regional conflicts and other so-called minor disputes will continue to attract the attention of major and minor powers alike. Many of these conflicts arise from clashes among newly formed states as in much of the Third World or from religious and ethnic tensions as in the Middle East, the southern Soviet Union, and Sri Lanka. And as in Poland, the Philippines, and Argentina, much of the conflict arises less from external threat than from a struggle for domestic control and economic advancement.

Managing these disputes by force or its threat or by international law becomes increasingly difficult in a system of assertively independent states. Many of these conflicts may retain an East-West dimension but their indigenous sources will remain prominent. Nationalist demands for autonomy and self-determination rooted in ethnic sentiments or economic deprivation make military intervention costly and often counterproductive. But if military intervention is increasingly unattractive, other forms of intervention, forms that rely less on force and more on persuasion and bargaining, become increasingly attractive.

One is the intervention of intermediaries, third parties who intercede for the purpose of influencing or facilitating the settlement of a dispute but who do not impose a solution. They are actors with incentives to be involved but without direct interests in the disputed issues. Relative to the disputants' balance of forces, their domestic politics, and the peculiarities of each side's decision-making processes, their interventions are rarely determining factors in the outcomes of conflicts. But in many conflicts, especially intense conflicts driven by domestic turmoil, intermediaries are not insignificant either. They may provide just enough incentive to settle or, more subtly, just enough change in perceptions and attitudes to tip the balance from a contentious to a cooperative approach to resolving the dispute. The difference they make is not so much between who wins and who loses or how much is gained and lost. Rather, it is between settling early rather than late or between trying one more round at the negotiating table rather than initiating hostilities or between searching for the

preconditions for negotiations rather than getting tied up in the procedures of negotiations. When the difference between violent and peaceful
settlement of a conflict turns on seemingly minor questions of procedure
or saving face, intermediaries can push the parties—sometimes gently
and unobtrusively, sometimes with concrete inducements—toward conciliatory approaches.

THE PREVALENCE OF INTERMEDIARY INTERVENTION

If intermediaries can make a difference, why do we not see more of them?
Does the evening news neglect them or are they just too few and far between to capture our attention? In part, the answer is that the work of
intermediaries cannot compete for the headlines with force reductions or
toppling regimes or trade imbalances, not to mention invasions and the
everyday violence in the world. But, in part, the apparent neglect derives
from what intermediaries do. Few interventions exhibit the drama of
Henry Kissinger's shuttle diplomacy or Jimmy Carter's Camp David negotiations. Many more involve slow and painstaking work with few break-
throughs or outright successes. Much of the work is, by its very nature,
quiet and behind the scenes. Oscar Arias may grab the headlines when he
outmaneuvers the United States in Central America and lands a peace
agreement along with a Nobel Prize. More often, such work is quite un-
eventful. For most of Chester Crocker's tenure as U.S. assistant secretary
of state for African Affairs, his attempts to mediate a settlement in southern Africa merited back-page news, if anything. His eventual success did
make the front pages, but fleetingly. So did a number of other recent
efforts: the cease-fire in the Iran-Iraq war arranged by UN Secretary
General Javier Perez de Cuellar; the commencement of talks between the
Palestine Liberation Organization (PLO) and the United States facilitated
by Sweden; and the Soviet agreement to withdraw its troops from Afghan-
istan as facilitated by UN representative Diego Cordova. Still, these interventions commanded the headlines largely because they involved major
powers or major conflicts.

Lesser known interventions, some regionally prominent, some conducted by major powers, others by minor actors, were, by their frequency
and quite possibly their impact, no less important. Among states, India
arranged negotiations between the Sri Lankan government and rebel
Tamils. Indonesia mediated among the countries of Indochina and between Vietnam and the United States regarding Cambodia. Algeria successfully mediated several hostage crises including the taking of U.S. embassy personnel in Iran. Both Saudia Arabia and the Soviet Union have
mediated talks between Iraq and Turkey over water issues. Saudia Arabia
and the Soviet Union mediated an agreement among Syria, Turkey, and

Iraq to restore water flow to Iraq after Syria constructed a dam on the Euphrates River. Even Cuba, known for its military interventions in Africa, mediated in the Iran-Iraq war and has conducted talks between factions of the PLO. As for nonstate actors, in the Soviet Union, the popular fronts of Latvia, Lithuania, and Estonia established talks between Azerbaijan and Armenia. In Nicaragua, Cardinal Miguel Obando y Bravo mediated talks between the Sandinista government and U.S.-sponsored rebels while Mennonite officials mediated talks between the Sandinistas and the Moskito Indians. In El Salvador, the auxillary bishop of San Salvador, Gregorio Rosa Chavez, served as a mediator in the first substantive negotiations to end the civil war there. Quakers have served as message carriers and conciliators in the India-Pakistan conflict, Northern Ireland, Zimbabwe, the Nigerian civil war (see chap. 9) and, most recently, the Sri Lankan civil war. Catholic Church officials mediated between the Polish Communist government and the Solidarity labor union. And in a rare instance of interstate mediation by the Vatican, Pope John Paul II intervened to avert a war between Argentina and Chile and then achieved a settlement through formal mediation at the Vatican (see chap. 8). Private individuals have also participated as intermediaries, often to facilitate official interactions. Journalist John Scali carried messages between the United States and the Soviet Union at the height of the Cuban missile crisis. Educator Brian Wedge interceded in the Dominican Republic after the U.S. invasion of 1965 to establish a dialogue and break a stalemate between the competing sides. Academics like John Burton and Herbert Kelman have facilitated talks among leaders of Cyprus, Israel, the PLO, Argentina, and Great Britain. Most recently, former U.S. President Jimmy Carter held talks between the Ethiopian government and Eritrean rebels.

Although the level of success and impact varies considerably in these cases, the fact is that intermediaries are ubiquitous actors in the management of modern international conflicts. A number of studies suggest the extent. In ten disputes in Latin America from 1925 to 1945, 35 countries served as intermediaries; and after 1945, in just 13 disputes there were 63 mediation attempts.[1] In 77 major conflicts between 1919 and 1965, 49 involved mediators, and in a different study researchers found that 255 of 310 conflicts between 1945 and 1974 had some form of official mediation (by a regional or international organization).[2] Although definitions of "mediation" may vary, intermediaries clearly are prevalent in modern international conflict. This is even more true when unofficial and behind-the-scenes intermediaries are added to the picture.

Intermediaries are not unique to twentieth-century diplomacy, of course. The practice can be traced back to the earliest times. Until the nineteenth century, mediation was an informal process often crossing over into arbitration when practiced by monarchs and popes.[3] In the Congress of Vienna of 1815 and the Congress of Paris of 1856, compulsory mediation was legally introduced to impose the duty of collective intervention by the great powers. Mediation was also provided for in nineteenth-century treaties between greater and lesser powers, often between a European power and a lesser state of Asia. In practice, mediators intervened to prevent a disruption of the balance of power or to restore a balance. Conducted by great powers or by concerts of powers in conferences or congresses, mediation, consequently, was another form of coercive intervention, one in which interested parties were sometimes excluded.[4]

Contemporary intermediary interventions differ from those of the past in at least two respects. First, before the twentieth century, only states intervened as mediators and only powerful states at that.[5] Today, as suggested above, small states, international organizations, and a variety of transnational actors intervene regularly. They do not change the balance of power nor do they impose solutions, but they do intervene in the affairs of states to effect change. What may be most distinguishing is that they must gain the parties' acceptance, something a European concert of powers had little concern for. Second, influence by intermediaries large and small, state and nonstate, entails more subtle processes than the use or threat of force. It may involve offers of aid (or threats to withhold aid) or simply the appropriation of decisions about negotiating procedures. However contemporary intermediaries influence protagonists in a dispute resolution process, their impact depends not solely upon their position as a great power but upon their position of being in the middle.

This book, then, is an attempt to characterize the peculiarities of this position and to lay out what is distinctive about intermediary intervention as a method of international conflict management and, more generally, as a decision-making process. It is too easy to view intermediary intervention as either an adjunct to the real negotiation—a convenience for the negotiators or a technical corrective for imperfect negotiating—or as a loose form of an essentially legal process—like adjudication or arbitration but without the decision-making authority. To do so misses important features of the intervention, especially the relationship between the intermediary and the disputants and the impact that has on the disputants' interactions. These features must be considered explicitly to assess the potential and the limitations of the process.

As a first approximation, intermediary intervention can be thought of as one of three forms of negotiation. Some negotiations are direct and bilateral. Others are multilateral where one member "mediates" in the sense of bringing others together to form a coalition. In such coalitional bargaining, all parties in multilateral negotiations are potential mediators. But they are not "in between"; they are not intermediaries. Negotiations with a third party who is not a direct party to the negotiations is what I term intermediary intervention and is the subject of this book.[6]

The Function of Intermediaries in International Conflict Management

Why are intermediaries so prevalent in international conflict management? One reason relates to the twin tendencies in international affairs toward decentralization on the one hand and institutionalization on the other. With no central authority, states act on the basis of self-help. At the same time, they coordinate their expectations by creating institutions, whether formal organizations or, more informally, regimes and conventions.[7] Institutions are feasible when dealing with ongoing relationships and issues that recur, such as those in trade disputes or alliance politics. Disputes that are essentially one-time affairs, however, cannot be institutionalized. Japan and the Soviet Union, for example, have never signed a peace treaty owing to their failure to agree on the ownership of a few islands off the coast of Hokaido. This is a one-time affair; once a treaty is signed, it is unlikely to arise again. Its management, therefore, cannot be institutionalized. It can be viewed as one of many items in the ongoing relationship between Japan and the Soviet Union and, as such, decisions on this issue will cast a shadow over future issues. But future issues are unlikely to be of the same sort, that is, a territorial question. Rather, they will be over trade or fishing or a military build-up. Thus, a regime is not about to be created to handle territorial disputes when there is only one foreseeable dispute of this nature. Nor will the two parties create a regime to resolve all future issues to which this territorial issue is presumably casting a shadow. That is what diplomacy under normalized relations is about. The resolution of this dispute is best viewed, therefore, as a one-shot, single-play game in which all the usual bargaining dynamics manifest.[8]

So where do intermediaries come in? The answer parallels that of the question, Why international institutions? Disputing parties negotiate more effectively if they have converging expectations over the set of norms and procedures governing their negotiations and if information is as complete as possible. This is true whether negotiations are highly formalized as in trade negotiations under GATT or informally arranged, ad hoc and one-time affairs as in territorial disputes. As elaborated in chapter 3, the intermediary's unique position in the bargaining relationship affords it the ability to, one, encourage expectations to converge around its proposals and, two, to pool information.[9] The intermediary, in short, serves as a regime surrogate in disputes where institutionalization is impractical.[10]

A second reason intermediaries are prevalent in managing contemporary international conflict is because the international system and diplomatic practice have changed dramatically since the nineteenth century. In the classical, European great power system, relations were managed by less than a half-dozen states. Diplomats, many with familial ties, were part of an elite corps of professionals who operated on the basis of a common set of norms and principles. Members of this "career caste"[11] conducted not just the affairs of their own states, but saw as their duty to manage the system, as well. Negotiations were facilitated by mutual expectations to be accommodative and flexible. And because negotiators were only accountable to a monarch or an emperor and public opinion and mass media were minor concerns, they could operate in secret and with each other's confidence. As a result, when a negotiator needed a concession or wanted to explore a novel idea, he (they were all men) could do so without losing face or risking exploitation. He also had little reason to fear being branded "soft." Appeasement was still an honorable term and a common practice. In short, negotiators, although charged with advancing their own states' interests, enjoyed an environment where communication was relatively effective and agreements were expected to meet all sides' interests.[12]

Modern diplomacy is not so tidy. With the proliferation of international actors, both state and non-state, and the expansion of issues, negotiations are necessarily more complex.[13] One result is that procedural disagreements have become much more common. Craig and George note that "the tenacity with which one side or the other argues over seemingly minor procedural matters has taken on new dimensions in an age when passionate ideological and other differences have displaced the cultural homogeneity that facilitated diplomatic processes in the European system."[14]

In addition, official negotiations are conducted as much by heads of state and politicians as by professional diplomats. As such, they are continually subjected to the pressures of public opinion and domestic politics in their own countries. Gaining favor at home becomes the first priority, not reaching mutually accommodative agreements. The mass media play a prominent role so that grandstanding and tough talking become the dominant mode of discourse. The result is that public pronouncements are directed more to constituencies back home than to negotiators across the table; they neither speak to each other nor do they genuinely listen. In short, effective communication and realistic empathy[15] are rarities in modern international negotiations. In Robert Jervis's words: "In almost no interactions do two adversaries understand each other's goals, fears, means-ends beliefs, and perceptions. Empathy is difficult and usually lacking. . . . The fine-tuning of policies and the subtle bargaining tactics that would be called for in a world of clear communication cannot work in our world."[16]

These developments in diplomacy have important implications for understanding the contemporary role of intermediaries. First, all negotiators know that confidentiality and truthfulness are essential to getting good agreements. But they also know they cannot simply reveal their values and intentions and expect reciprocation without exploitation. Negotiating unavoidably involves a combination of cooperation and competition, of revelation and concealment, of truthfulness and deceit. The negotiators' dilemma is to reconcile these competing tendencies to get agreement while protecting and advancing their states' interests.

In the classical period, negotiators were able to reconcile these competing tendencies in part because they were protected as members of an elite club. They spoke the same language (literally and diplomatically), and they expected that a concession made now would be one reciprocated later. Conducting negotiations in secret, they were accountable not for every public statement but only for the final agreement and, then, only to a single leader. Communication could be relatively direct and open. Consequently, they had little need to take face-saving or communication-enhancing steps. In modern diplomacy, by contrast, negotiators are vulnerable. They can be easily eliminated (through dismissal, election, or coup) if a significant constituency feels a legitimate state interest has been sacrificed or if an opportunity for gain has been foregone. Caught in this bind, modern negotiators often turn to third parties. They do so, however, not to have a solution imposed or justice applied or joint gains discovered but to have a settlement—that is, a favorable settlement—promoted.

Leaders seek third parties—whether formal organizations like the United Nations or ad hoc groups like the Contadora Group in Central America or, more informally, a variety of major powers and minor actors—as legitimating agents. Third parties are expected to persuade the other side of one's rightful position and, when compromise is necessary, persuade one's constituency of the necessity of the concession. They are expected to be trustworthy or, at least, more trustworthy than one's opponent. They are expected to put pressure on the other side and refrain from doing so against oneself. They are expected to clarify one's position for the other side even if the reverse is deemed unnecessary (the other side's position is well known, not to mention, unreasonable). Given all this, they are expected to be "neutral" or "impartial" or, at least, to act to preserve one's expected—and deserved—outcome.

Leaders choose third parties, in short, to save face at home and abroad,

to pressure the other side, to convey clearly their own messages, and to
ensure their idea of "fairness." The increasing employment of intermediaries is, therefore, in part reflective of two problems of modern diplomacy. When confidentiality is essential but encumbered by demands for
an open and accountable government or by the manipulations of opposing
internal factions playing to public opinion, third parties can provide privacy. The third party is not a domestic constituent requiring accountability nor is it subject to the pressures of domestic public opinion (at least not
to the publics of the disputing parties). And it is not an opponent to whom
all overtures must be made guardedly. It may be an ally but it must pass
a special test to serve as an intermediary—it must be acceptable to the
other side. The role an intermediary plays and the effect it has on a dispute, consequently, are heavily conditioned by the twin questions of gaining entry and of gaining party acceptance, issues taken up in chapters 4
and 5.

The second problem of modern diplomacy is communication. The irony
of technological advances is that, for all the information available and its
instantaneous, global transmission, leaders' communications are wrought
with misunderstanding and misperception.[17] Whether deterring an attack
or negotiating an end to hostilities, clear communication is not easy.[18] As
a matter of strategy, threats and promises are credible only if clearly conveyed; likewise, motivations and intentions are assessable only if lines of
communication are open. As a matter of accommodation, both sides must
know each other's minimal needs and, to realize joint gains, its relative
valuations of disputed issues. But to reveal the information necessary to
deter attack, enhance realistic empathy, or reach a compromise solution
is risky. If one's opponent does not exploit the information, one's hardline
constituencies will. Strategic interaction and domestic politics and public
opinion make agreement, especially at a deep level that addresses basic
needs, difficult to achieve (see chap. 3). Leaders in conflict seek out third
parties, therefore, to gain—and, possibly, to reveal—information necessary for settlement. This is not to say that such leaders seek harmony and
friendship. They still want to prevail. But at a minimum, they seek multiple paths to settlement, one of which is to negotiate and, when that is
difficult, to employ third parties to facilitate that negotiating.[19]

A disputing party may accept an intermediary to gain information and
promote communication (if only one way), but the actual effect of an intermediary intervention may be quite a different matter. Logically, intermediaries can not be as "neutral" or "impartial" as parties expect since
evenhandedness to one is bias to the other. Moreover, their impact is not
as simple as legitimating a position, a concession, or pressuring the other
side. Being in between, intermediaries must find ways of pressuring both

sides while alienating neither.[20] The process may be as straightforward as increasing the benefits of agreement or increasing the costs of no agreement. More often, the process is subtle, involving the careful use of proposals for both procedure and substance. One effect is to counter the propensity of modern negotiations to get tied up in seemingly minor procedural questions (see chapter 3). In addition, clarifying messages for one side necessarily entails corrections and reinterpretations of perceptions by both sides. As a result, intermediaries may promote the one-way communication sought by a disputant but, since they operate in between, they also facilitate two-way communication. In the process, disputing parties may inadvertently gain a greater understanding of the other side's needs and fears and maybe even their willingness to change and to accommodate. That this occurs is not necessarily because the intermediary is committed to improved communication (let alone because the disputants are) but merely because the intermediary operates "in between." Consequently, an important function of this book is to explore the effect of intermediaries on the interactions of disputing parties. As suggested, what leaders may seek from the third party—intelligence for improved strategic analysis, say—may inadvertently result in a better assessment of goals and fears, beliefs and perceptions. This, in turn, may lead to an enhanced appreciation for the possibility of change and, concomitantly, the possibility of achieving a mutually acceptable, negotiated agreement.

The unexpected effects of an intermediary intervention may entail more than unexpected benefits for the disputing parties, however. By virtue of being in the middle, intermediaries gain information which they can use to promote their own idea of a good settlement or, simply, to promote their own interests. These topics are explored in chapters 2 and 3.

In this book, then, I portray intermediary intervention in terms of the *intermediary's impact on the disputants and their interaction.* Some intermediaries promote direct interaction, some detract from it. Moreover, as will be seen in chapter 2, some intermediaries are better at enhancing the disputants' direct interaction—what I call "neutral" mediators—while others are better at making agreement more attractive—what I call "principal mediators." Neither is "better" as each has its distinctive advantages. Understanding these advantages is critical for understanding the impact of the intervention and, in the end, for predicting the outcome of an intervention. The purpose of this book is not, therefore, to generate a laundry list of activities intermediaries can perform. Nor is it to categorize their various functions. Rather, the aim of this study is to identify the peculiar effects of intermediary intervention—however subtle and unanticipated—and to show how they may lead to agreement.

INTERMEDIARY INFLUENCE AND THE STUDY OF INTERNATIONAL
RELATIONS AND NEGOTIATION

Intermediaries may appear to do little more than convene meetings or
carry messages but, in most cases, they eventually find ways to urge parties to come to agreement. Some intermediaries base their influence on
promises and threats, others on changing the parties' mode of interaction.
But in one form or another, they have an impact, one peculiar to the
position of being "in between."

Thus, another way to view the contribution of this book is in terms of
influence in international politics. Classic notions of power—military and
economic resources—and concepts of interests and intentions can partially account for the impact of an intermediary's intervention. A powerful
third party can change behavior by using or threatening to use its power
resources, and disputing parties may respond by signing an agreement
between themselves. This is the classical form of intervention and remains
important to this day. Both the Nixon–Kissinger and the Jimmy Carter
interventions in the Middle East in the 1970s fit this model, as does
India's intervention in Sri Lanka in the 1980s. Attempts by regional organizations like the OAU or the OAS are similar in that they try to rally the
collective weight of neighboring countries to condemn one or both sides
in a regional dispute.[21]

Overall, power-based interventions are important elements in the management of international disputes. But just as force and its threat become
increasingly limited in a unilateral context, so too does coercion become
limited in an intermediary context. As will be seen in the Camp David
case of chapter 6, few U.S. presidents can risk their political futures (not
to mention those of their party and key constituencies) the way Jimmy
Carter did. It becomes increasingly important, therefore, to understand
the impact of other forms of intervention, especially those of the many
"powerless" intervenors. It also becomes important to understand the extent to which even the "powerful" actors can facilitate rather than coerce
settlements between disputing parties. Most important from a policy perspective, it is essential to understand the trade-offs entailed in choosing
between a powerful actor with powerful interests and a minor actor with
little or no interests in the disputed issues. When, for example, would the
United States be best advised to intervene in, say, the Middle East or
Central America to compel parties to come to agreement and when would
the United States be better off encouraging other intervenors? When do
the resources of a major power aid in getting agreement and when do they
hinder it? What are the peculiar advantages of a major power and what are
those of a lesser international actor? What difference does it make if the
conflict is a territorial dispute to increase power or a territorial dispute to

preserve a group's national or ethnic identity? In short, how does influence vary with the kind of intervenor, the nature of the conflict, and the issues at stake?

Unfortunately, existing work on international relations and negotiation offer little help in answering these questions. In the study of international relations, third party involvement has been taken from the perspective of alliance politics or international law and organization.[22] But little attention has been paid to third parties as intermediaries, that is, to those who intervene neither as an alliance partner nor with a legal mandate. In part, this is because modern theories of international relations have emerged in response to relations between the superpowers and their competition for spheres of influence. In a Cold War, bilateral context, intermediaries have been quite irrelevant. No European power, not Japan or China, could intervene effectively between the superpowers. The UN, despite its mandate for resolving disputes, has been rendered impotent when it comes to the rivalry between the United States and the U.S.S.R. and their clients.

But as the earlier examples illustrate, when the context is other than superpower relations, intermediaries are strikingly active. So if third parties are indeed important in many, if not most, disputes around the world, then theories derived to account for nuclear power rivalry are inadequate for explaining the interventions of third parties. This is especially true for the interventions of intermediaries where force or its threat is less relevant than the art of negotiation. It would seem, then, that the fast growing negotiation and dispute resolution field would be of help.

In recent years, books, articles, and workshops have proliferated on negotiation and mediation.[23] Much of this work is interpersonal or derived from the labor relations model of negotiation. A dominant concern is to find an alternative to the American propensity towards litigation and other contentious means of dispute resolution. As such, it is highly prescriptive and domestically oriented. Extrapolations to the international setting often ignore the context of the international system and the parties' (including the mediator's) domestic politics. When mediation is brought into the discussion, it is generally with the purpose of saying what the mediator can do to help negotiators overcome their difficulties. A list of techniques for overcoming barriers to effective negotiation is presented. In so doing, these approaches tell us little about intervention when the intermediary and the disputing parties do not follow the prescriptions. They do not tell us about the impact of an intervention other than to show how mediators can educate negotiators or convince them to be better attuned to the benefits of agreement.

Put differently, popular approaches to negotiation focus on the needs and perspectives of the disputants, ignoring those of the intermediary.

They do not tell us what it means for the intermediary to be "in between."
They do not tell us what it means to be involved yet not be a party to the
dispute, to accept the charge of getting an agreement yet have no decision-making authority, to have interests yet be removed from the parties'
interests in the disputed issues. They do not tell us what it is like to initiate a decision-making process which, unlike adjudication or legislation or
executive management, is ill-defined and for which the role must be negotiated continuously. They do not tell us how the intermediary's learning
and bargaining processes determine the intermediary's ability to
influence disputants.

The focus of this book, then, is on how intermediaries learn, how they
develop their role, and how they function in the context of both the international system and domestic politics. Neither prevailing theories of international relations nor popular prescriptive approaches to negotiation
adequately explore the essence of the intermediary's role, that is, what it
means to be "in between." To treat intermediary intervention as just another form of power politics or as a technical solution to the difficulties of
negotiating misses the special nature of the process.

In this book, I use two different, yet complementary, methods to explicate the peculiar role of intermediaries in international conflict.[24] First,
I put myself in the shoes of the intermediary and ask what it means to
enter into someone else's dispute. What difference does it make if I am a
powerful player on the world scene or just a private individual? What
impact can I expect given the nature of the dispute and the disputants?
What are my primary sources of influence? What difference does it make
if I enter at an early or late stage of the dispute? How can I urge parties to
move toward agreement or, at a minimum, to keep them at the table?
How can I bargain with the disputants first to gain their acceptance and
then to establish my preferred role?

In the second part of the book, I use these questions and the resulting
propositions to analyze four case studies. The intention is not just to test
the hypotheses of the first part but to refine them and expand on them. So,
for example, whereas the deductive approach requires an assumption of
unitary actors, in the case studies I explore the role of domestic politics
both for the disputing parties and for the intermediary. The deductive
propositions provide a useful baseline for understanding the cases but I
draw on other concepts to develop a fuller understanding.

The cases are selected to meet several criteria. First, they are clear-cut
instances of intermediary intervention; that is, the third party intervenes
without direct interests in the disputed issues and attempts to bring the
disputing parties together. As noted earlier, they are not primarily direct
negotiations nor multilateral negotiations where the possibility of coalition building makes all actors potential "mediators." Second, the cases

provide enough variation to test in a preliminary way the propositions of Part I. For example, chapter 2 postulates that powerful mediators detract from disputants' interactions while relatively powerless ones contribute to them. Since the intermediaries range from the United States (in two distinct historical periods) and the British, to the OAU and the Commonwealth Secretariat, to the Vatican and the Quakers, enough variation exists to test provisionally the postulate. Third, sufficient data exists to develop and analyze the cases from the intermediary's perspective. One case, the Beagle Channel, is entirely original and researched with the perspective of the intermediary in mind. For the other three—Camp David, Portsmouth, and Nigeria-Biafra—excellent histories and memoirs exist to allow an emphasis on the intermediary perspective.

Of course, the selection is not ideal. Data sources, types of conflict, region, and historical period vary considerably. A study of UN or United States or Middle East interventions might have allowed for better control of one or more variables. But it is the question that drives the empirical research and here I am less interested in one actor's performance or one region's history of third party involvement. My aim is to understand the distinctiveness of the process and the specific effects of the interventions; not just how many wins and losses there were, nor who got agreement and who did not, but how disputants' interactions were affected by the intervention. It is comparative in the sense that I strive to understand these effects as they vary with different kinds of intermediaries.

The benefit of choosing a few cases with considerable detail available on the intermediary's perceptions and decisions is that questions of intermediary effect can be explored in depth. Where, for example, the unitary actor assumptions of Part I fail to generate propositions that account for domestic politics, the cases raise such questions. The price is that the propositions of Part I can only be tested in a preliminary way and correlative inferences in the statistical sense cannot be made.[25] Consequently, the empirical work of parts 2 and 3 should be viewed as primarily an extension of (or complement to) the theory-building effort of part 1. Together they complement each other and meet the necessarily limited aim of this study: to generate analytically useful questions and propositions from which further testing and refinement can occur.

Finally, it is occasionally noted in social science inquiries that few theories are without policy implications and few theorists are without policy agendas. As for policy implications, I have alluded to some already and more will emerge in the succeeding chapters. As for my policy agenda, it is to provide realistic grounds for accommodating a wide range of instruments in the conduct of foreign policy and conflict management generally. I especially wish to see serious attention given to means of influence other than force and its threat. At the same time, my aim is to take a critical look at dispute resolution and especially the effects of intermediaries; I do not view negotiation and mediation as panaceas to the world's problems nor as necessarily superior means of managing conflicts.

Conclusion

This book attempts to characterize a peculiar *role* in international affairs, one that has received considerable descriptive attention but little analytic scrutiny. In part, this is a study of a national role, one that K. J. Holsti found was much neglected in our preoccupations with East-West relations and alliance politics.[26] Nations, he concluded, perceive themselves as performing more than bloc leader, bloc follower, and balancer roles. Many see themselves performing collaborative roles, one of which is mediating. To understand the essential nature of the mediating role, which Holsti does not explicate, one must go beyond the traditional roles and the traditional focus on power, interests, and rationality. At the same time, the analyst must avoid the temptation of requiring altruism for cooperation to occur. So where institutionalists look for interactions that resemble repeated games to explain cooperation, in this study, I look at the facilitating role of intermediaries in conflicts that may be better modeled as single-shot games. The analytic challenge, therefore, is to explain facilitation as more than altruistic behavior and yet other than traditional power politics. I approach this by developing a sense of the tensions a mediating actor faces and the bases of influence it develops when power is not enough to move disputants toward agreement. Moreover, for both empirical and theoretical reasons, I seek to incorporate the interventions not just of states but of nonstate actors as well.

This book, then, is an exploration of dispute resolution in the context of intermediary intervention. It examines the peculiar nature of influence experienced by those acting "in between" disputing parties. It is an attempt to explain what it means to the disputing parties to have someone in the middle and what it means to the intermediary to try to bring the parties together. Unlike much of the prescriptive work on mediation, this is not a how-to-do-it book. It is theoretical in the sense of developing a conceptual framework and a set of propositions for understanding the essential nature of intermediary interventions. It is policy oriented in the sense of providing a basis from which to distinguish third parties and their particular effects on a dispute. Thus, if this book is successful, it will augment conventional notions of influence, and it will help a policy maker decide whether to employ a third party and, if so, what kind. A leader's choice, contrary to the assumptions embedded in the foreign policies of states who rely primarily on unilateral, coercive means, is not obvious. In a world of 160 some states and a multitude of nonstate actors, a world where the causes of conflict are complex and cannot be reduced to a simple balance of power calculus, and a world where national groups of all sizes and locations resist conventional power plays, intermediary intervention provides a subtle, although not necessarily determining, means of managing conflicts and promoting settlements.

Chapter Two

THIRD PARTIES: PRINCIPALS AND NEUTRALS

THIRD-PARTY INTERVENTION—especially mediation—has received little attention in the study of international politics.[1] Modern theories of international relations, especially of security relations, evolved out of the Cold War period following World War II. The dominant paradigm has been deterrence with related theories of containment and tacit bargaining. These theories have emerged in response to East-West tensions, especially the relations between the United States and the Soviet Union. In the context of superpower relations, their orientation has been bilateral; third parties are largely irrelevant. No European power, not Japan or China, can dictate terms to the superpowers on arms control, human rights, or trade. And the United Nations has been rendered impotent when it comes to the rivalry between the United States and the Soviet Union or their clients.

By contrast, when one looks at other contexts, for instance, regional or civil conflicts, third parties are strikingly active. Many of these conflicts involve, at one time or another, intervenors from big and small states, from international organizations, and from private groups as varied as multinational corporations and religious figures. To illustrate, in the Iran-Iraq conflict, the UN's celebrated ceasefire agreement of 1988 was preceded by United Nations attempts as far back as 1974 to settle the dispute over the Shatt al-Arab waterway. In the late 1960s, Saudi Arabia, Kuwait, and Jordan each tried to mediate between the two countries. Earlier, Iran and Iraq appealed to the League of Nations to settle the matter. And, much before that, in the nineteenth century, Great Britain and Russia at various times facilitated discussions between Persia and the Ottoman Empire, gave legal interpretations to previous treaties, and attempted to impose a solution on the parties. Great Britain also fought a war with Persia in 1865 and occupied the eastern side of the Shatt al-Arab in collaboration with the Ottomans. Interspersed throughout all these third-party interventions, the two sides engaged in many direct, bilateral attempts to settle their differences, including negotiations and, of course, armed conflict.[2]

Similar patterns of third-party involvement can be seen in numerous border and intercommunal disputes in Latin American, Asia, and Africa.[3]

For example, in the Beagle Channel dispute between Argentina and Chile, the OAS, the UN, an arbitration panel of International Court justices, the United States, a variety of neighboring countries, several European countries, the two national churches and, finally, the Vatican, performed third-party roles of varying kinds and importance. Similarly, in the Nigerian civil war, the OAU, Great Britain, numerous African neighbor states, and various religious and humanitarian groups intervened to try to resolve the communal conflict (see chap. 9).

If third parties are indeed important in many, if not most, disputes around the world, then theories derived to account for nuclear power rivalry are inadequate for explaining the interventions of third parties. This is especially true for nonforce interventions such as mediation. This is one reason, then, for developing a conceptual framework for comparing third-party interventions.

A second reason is to fill a gap in the fast-growing field of dispute resolution and negotiation. Typically in this literature, mediators are brought into the discussion of negotiation techniques when the disputants find direct negotiations ineffective. A laundry list of steps the mediator can take is generated. Throughout, the implicit assumption is that mediators are apolitical, disinterested entities who enter a dispute just to facilitate agreement. Moreover, with an emphasis on technique, mediators are assumed to be essentially alike. In contrast, I start with the assumption that mediators have their own interests, that fundamental differences exist among mediators, and that a mediator's bargaining relationship with the disputants is critical for understanding its impact on a dispute.

In this chapter, then, I use differences in the parties' interests in the disputed issues and differences in bargaining capabilities to argue that two kinds of mediators can be identified in international conflict management—the "principal mediator" and the "neutral mediator." Although these differences cannot tell the whole story, they do provide structural distinctions that lead to insights about process distinctions. The principal-neutral dichotomy, in turn, suggests how policy makers might choose among third parties to best manage a conflict.

Third-Party Interests and Capabilities

To be effective, negotiators must assess their own interests and those of their opponents. A mediator is no different. In fact, to distinguish mediator roles, it is critical to distinguish the interests mediators have in the *issues disputed by the principal parties.*

To set the stage, imagine a dispute between two countries over a piece of territory, say, a few islands. The Falklands/Malvinas conflict might serve as a good contemporary example. Both countries claim sovereignty over the islands. Initially (at time t_0), only the two "principal parties," are involved. They have a *direct interest* in the issue in dispute, the islands.

An outsider, a "third party," may consider entering the dispute. If, upon reflection, it elects to remain uninvolved, it is strictly a "neutral party"; it has *no interests* in the issue, the islands. In the early stages of the Falklands/Malvinas conflict, this might have been Peru. If, on the other hand, the third party claims the island, it has a *direct interest* and becomes a principal party or, once it enters at time t_1, a "disputant." It may or may not use force to stake its claim, and its entry need not be acceptable to the original principal parties. Its strategic relationship to each party is the same as that between the original two. It bargains with each of the two using a variety of tactics, some cooperative, some contentious. It may offer incentives or it may threaten harm. Either of the superpowers might have elected to play such a role in the Falklands/Malvinas conflict.

Finally, the third party may have *no interest in the issue*, the islands themselves, but choose to enter the dispute to facilitate or somehow influence a settlement between the principals. To do so, this "intermediary" must be acceptable to the two parties and, I will assume, refrain from the use of force. In this instance, acceptance and entry become issues. (Chap. 4 examines the entry question, chap. 5 the acceptance question.)

The intermediary can be further distinguished by examining the nature of its interests. If the intermediary has no interest in the island but does have *indirect interests*, say, security concerns in the region, it is a "principal mediator." I will assume as well that, if the intermediary has strong indirect interests, it also has the resources to bring to bear.[4] The United States fit this description in the Falklands/Malvinas conflict as exemplified by Secretary of State Alexander Haig's shuttle mediation between London and Buenos Aires. If the intermediary has *no interests whatsoever* in the disputed issues—direct or indirect—but simply wants to facilitate an agreement, it is a "neutral mediator." When hostilities were imminent in the Falklands/Malvinas conflict, Peru, the UN secretary general, Pope John Paul II, and a number of private individuals attempted to play this role. These third-party categories are presented schematically in figure 2.1.

These distinctions can be further illustrated in the Middle East conflict where a major issue in dispute is the status of Israel's occupied territories. The "principal parties," Israel and the Palestinians, have direct interests in the dispute. Some of these interests are conflicting—for example, Palestinian autonomy in the West Bank would mean Israel's loss of Judea and Samaria. Some interests are shared—at a minimum, both parties have a shared interest in avoiding further bloodshed. As long as the conflicting interests prevail, the parties tend to choose unilateral means—for exam-

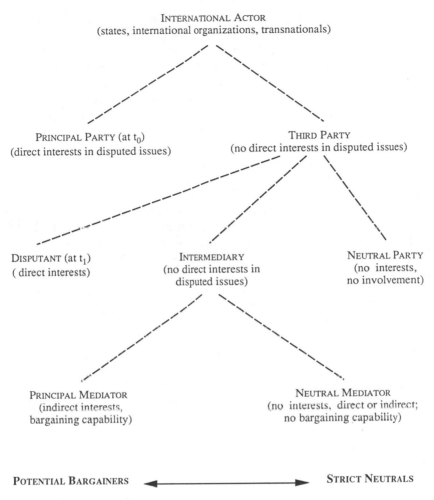

INTERNATIONAL ACTOR
(states, international organizations, transnationals)

PRINCIPAL PARTY (at t_0)
(direct interests in disputed issues)

THIRD PARTY
(no direct interests in disputed issues)

DISPUTANT (at t_1)
(direct interests)

INTERMEDIARY
(no direct interests in
disputed issues)

NEUTRAL PARTY
(no interests,
no involvement)

PRINCIPAL MEDIATOR
(indirect interests,
bargaining capability)

NEUTRAL MEDIATOR
(no interests, direct or indirect;
no bargaining capability)

POTENTIAL BARGAINERS ⟷ STRICT NEUTRALS

Fig. 2.1. Third-Party Intervenors in International Conflict

ple, force. When shared interests gain prominence but not enough entirely to offset the conflicting interests, parties become more inclined toward bilateral means—say, negotiations.

As for third-party roles, Jordan may decide it has a legitimate claim to the West Bank and, as such, would enter the dispute as a fellow bargainer, a "disputant." Its large Palestinian population, its administrative authority in the West Bank (at least until 1988), and its ties with the PLO would all give it bargaining leverage. On the other hand, Jordan may attempt to remove itself entirely from the West Bank issue and be a "neutral."

The United States has no direct interests in the occupied territories but it does have strategic interests in the region as well as a commitment to the survival of the Jewish state. These *indirect* interests may compel the United States to enter the dispute, not as a fellow disputant, but as a "principal mediator." It also has considerable resources—military and economic—to bring to bear. It would bargain for its preferred solution offering positive and negative incentives where necessary.

The Anglican church, desiring peace in the region yet having no interest in the issue of territorial sovereignty, may also enter. Because it has no interests in the occupied territories, direct or indirect, and has insubstantial resources, it cannot bargain with Israelis or Palestinians. It can, however, act as a "neutral mediator." It can carry messages, set up private meetings, or conduct training sessions. It can even convene formal negotiating sessions and have a hand in the drafting of a settlement. At some point, it may even propose a solution and leave the parties with the choice of accepting it or reverting back to the status quo. In all these activities, it influences the interactions between disputants and affects the settlement of the dispute.

Comparing the U.S. role and the hypothetical Anglican church role, the United States may be able to "broker" a settlement. It may be able to make proposals that would be politically untenable for the leadership of either party to propose unilaterally. It may be able to offer inducements to both sides that make agreement more palatable. At the same time, however, as all involved know, in this role the United States must make proposals that protect its interests. It cannot propose measures that increase Soviet presence or that endanger oil supplies.[5] For this reason, both the Palestinians and the Israelis must consider each U.S. move as strategic, one designed primarily to further U.S. interests, not necessarily Palestinian or Israeli interests. The degree to which the United States can foster communication and trust—between itself and each of the parties and between the two parties—is highly constrained by the structural relationship between the third party—that is, the principal mediator—and the disputants.[6] It is a relationship that is primarily strategic: the consequences of what one does depends in part on what the other does and each tries to change the other's choices.[7]

The Anglican church conciliator, by contrast, may be able to open lines of communication, clarify for each side the other's perceptions and intentions, and even suggest steps toward meaningful, direct negotiations. With no obvious interest in the details of an outcome (other than, presumably, that it be a durable peace), and with inconsequential resources to offer or deny, the disputants need have little fear of strategic machinations from the Anglican. As a result, for the disputants to entrust communications to the Anglican or to float a trial balloon for a conciliatory act or to engage in problem-solving exercises is a low-risk enterprise.[8] If at any time they fear they have risked too much, they can back out and disavow participation altogether. The confidentiality the church official can offer and the low profile role the church can assume assure this. The hypothetical Anglican in the Middle East is thus well positioned to facilitate communication but has limited ability to pressure disputants. The conciliator cannot offer inducements or threaten reprisals if concessions are not forthcoming. The church cannot enforce deadlines.[9]

In sum, differences in interests and capabilities distinguish two kinds of intermediaries. The principal mediator has interests in the disputed issues and can bring resources to bear; the neutral has neither but can offer a low-risk environment. The distinction is important for dispute resolution, however, only insofar as it shows how the disputants and, in particular, their interaction, are affected by the intervention. Thus, it is the *target* of the intervention that is critical for understanding not only differences among intermediaries but how their interventions serve to overcome impediments to reaching agreement. These I take up in the next two sections.

THE TARGET OF INTERVENTION

An intermediary targets its intervention either at the nature of the bargain—that is, its structure and its pay-offs to the disputants—or at the nature of the interaction itself—that is, the modes of exchanging information, clarifying perceptions and intentions, identifying interests, recognizing fundamental concerns, exploring options, and so forth. For the principal mediator, a three-way bargain is created whereas for the neutral, a one-way mediation, that is, one-way in the direction of the interaction, is established (see fig. 2.2).[10]

The Principal's Intervention: Three-way Bargaining

A principal mediator bargains with each disputant on those issues in which it has indirect interests, that is, indirect to the disputants' originally disputed issues. At least three bargaining dynamics are possible. The mediator can bargain directly with a disputant to strike a side deal. It can form a coalition with one disputant to compel a concession from the other disputant. Or it can create a three-way, circular bargain in which the mediator makes a deal with one disputant who, in turn, makes a deal with the other disputant who, to complete the circle, makes a deal with the mediator. One effect on the disputants is to expand the alternatives for agreement.[11] In the end, the original dispute may be settled almost as a by-product of these various bargaining combinations.

The principal's intervention, consequently, changes the bargaining dynamics and, fundamentally, the structure of the bargain. The bargain is no longer direct and bilateral; now it is a three-way bargain. Because the

A. Principal Mediator   *B.* Neutral Mediator

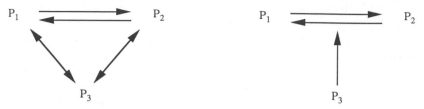

Fig. 2.2. The Target of Intervention. *A.* A principal mediator's (P_3) intervention creates a three-way bargaining structure with the original disputants (P_1 and P_2). As a result, the "pie" is expanded, a recalcitrant party is pressured by a coalition, or, in a circular bargain, joint gains are created and concessions are disguised. *B.* A neutral mediator's (P_3) intervention affects the nature of the disputants' (P_1 and P_2) interaction. With no interests in the disputed issues and no bargaining capabilities, the neutral is constrained to work on only the interaction. As a result, the disputants can use the mediator to pool information, convey intentions, correct misperceptions, and so forth.

mediator is primarily concerned with the dynamics of side-deals, coalitions, and circular deal making, the disputants' bilateral negotiation becomes secondary. Of course, part of what is at issue in the two parallel bargains with the mediator is the issues in dispute between the original disputants. But the focus of the bargaining, the character of the interaction, shifts from direct bilateral bargaining (between disputants) to parallel bilateral bargaining and circular three-way bargaining (among disputants and mediator). Much of the bargaining on the original issues in dispute thus becomes indirect bargaining through the mediator. One consequence of this kind of intervention, therefore, is that it *detracts from the disputants' direct interactions.*

The U.S. role in the Middle East following the October 1973 war epitomizes this kind of intervention and its consequences. The United States bargained separately with Israel and Egypt over military and financial aid. It restored diplomatic relations with Egypt and offered it aid in bilateral deals separate from those with Israel. Egypt offered the United States help with the Saudis in lifting the oil embargo and with the U.S. position vis-à-vis other Arab states. Israel promised disengagement to relax tensions and forestall the possibility of engaging the superpowers directly in the conflict. The bargain was circular in the sense that the United States gave Israel aid, Israel gave Egypt territory, and Egypt gave the United States improved status in the Arab world. Direct bilateral negotiations between Israel and Egypt were averted and even outright discouraged.[12]

So what is the effect of a principal's intervention? It changes disputants' incentive structure. It changes the magnitude of the outcome or the consequences of not agreeing or the sequence of achieving agreement. The entire intervention game is to rearrange payoffs.[13]

For many disputes, rearranging payoffs and detracting from direct encounters is exactly what is needed to overcome an impasse. For example, when the bargaining range is small, the third party expands it. Or, when concessions are especially hard to make for, say, domestic reasons, the three-way bargaining serves to disguise concessions (a circular bargain looks good for all) or to give negotiators a face-saving way out (if the other two form a coalition against me, I can claim that my only choice is a concession or no agreement).

The Neutral's Intervention: One-way Mediating

A neutral mediator cannot bargain with disputants. It has neither the interests nor the capacity. For three-way bargaining, this is a liability. It cannot strike a side deal with the disputants nor form a coalition of two against the third. Nevertheless, whereas the inability to bargain can be a liability in a three-way game, it can be an asset in one-way mediating. That is, if the target of intervention is not to change payoffs by bargaining with the disputants but to affect the disputants' ongoing interaction, and, if the mediator can demonstrate that it is doing no more than working to change that interaction, not on making separate deals, then a different dynamic is established. Under these conditions, the focus of attention in the intervention is the disputants—or, more precisely, the *disputants' interaction*, that is, their relationship, their communication, their mutual perceptions, and, of course, their mode of bargaining.[14]

This is something a principal mediator cannot do readily. It may claim to be solely concerned with the disputants' interaction, with helping *them* resolve *their* dispute. But the undeniable fact is that a principal mediator has interests in the dispute (albeit, indirect) and the capabilities to influence its settlement. It is there to bargain; it has more to do than just help out. Moreover, everyone knows it. The principal mediator can protest to the contrary, but words are not enough. When push comes to shove, the principal mediator, because it has recognized interests and capabilities, will opt to promote its own interests in its dealings with the disputants. It cannot prove otherwise.[15] It is, first, a fellow bargainer, equivalent to another disputant. It cannot escape this reality.

A neutral mediator is different. By its very nature, by the structural relationship between it and the disputants, by its "weakness" in bargaining resources, the neutral can credibly demonstrate its lack of interest (even indirect) in the issues in dispute. As such, it can do nothing *but* work on the disputants' interaction. This is not to say the neutral is free of bias or that it can avoid having a favored solution in mind.[16] The neutral's structural relationship only constrains its ability to bargain with each disputant. It is, most importantly, a constraint that does more than limit; it also affords opportunities.

Specifically, a neutral's constraint allows the mediator credibly to commit itself to one objective, getting agreement—possibly a fair, durable, efficient agreement—but only agreement between disputants, not a side deal, too. In turn, the neutral's constraint allows the disputant to use the mediator as a "pool of information"[17] without risk that that information will be used against it on an issue of interest to the mediator (a risk that is unavoidable in all bargaining relationships among principals); it allows the disputant to accept interpretations and proposals from the mediator without prejudice to other deals with the mediator; it allows the disputant to "play" with an idea, explore a new method, brainstorm a list of options without fear that those ideas will be used against it; it allows a disputant to let off steam and then recoup and use the encounter to understand better the effects of its own actions on the other. In short, the neutral's constraint enables it to influence the disputants' interactions in relatively risk-free ways. This is something a disputant cannot do on its own and something it cannot induce from other interested actors. Only one removed from the strategic interaction inherent in a bargaining relationship has such opportunities.

In sum, distinctions between mediators' interests and capabilities lead to distinctions between their intervention effects. These distinctions suggest that each kind of intermediary had its own set of advantages and limitations. A "principal mediator" like the United States in the Middle East can "bargain"; it has benefits to offer and benefits to deny; it can threaten harm. It can rearrange payoffs to create an acceptable zone of agreement. But it can neither play the role of a full-fledged protagonist nor one of a neutral facilitator. The "neutral mediator," on the other hand, cannot offer inducements or threaten reprisals. It can, however, open lines of communication, encourage joint problem solving, and build trust between disputants, all with little risk to the disputants.

So which is better, a principal mediator with clout or a neutral mediator with trust? A "realist" might argue that only parties with substantial power can be effective international mediators. Nation-states respond to power such that if a third party wishes to see a settlement between two disputing parties, it must be able to bring substantial resources to bear. A "liberal internationalist," on the other hand, would view power politics as the problem, not the solution. Conciliators, those who can improve understanding, are the most effective mediators.

I take the view that neither the principal mediator nor the neutral mediator is the "right" kind of international mediator. Each has its distinctive advantages in managing conflicts. Although a principal's intervention detracts from the disputants' interaction and the neutral's contributes to it, both, in their own ways, can lead to agreement. To see how movement toward agreement can be achieved, it is necessary, finally, to examine how the intermediary's target of intervention affects impediments to resolution.

IMPEDIMENTS TO REACHING AGREEMENT

For the principal mediator, the target of intervention is *payoff structure* and the intervention objective is to *enhance incentives* for agreement. For the neutral mediator, the target of intervention is the *mode of interaction* and the intervention objective is to *create realistic empathy*. These are best understood in terms of three major forms of impediment to effective negotiating: insufficient incentives, psychological bias, and conflictual norms of interaction.

Insufficient Incentives

One party may view an agreement as no better than the status quo (or the best alternative). Or it may feel it can get a better outcome by waiting. Or, with great uncertainty in the proposed agreement itself, it may prefer the alternative that is a sure thing (even if undesirable). In these situations, a principal mediator can make agreement more attractive. The principal can enhance incentives, that is, "expand the pie"; it can arrange a credible deadline so a better outcome in the future is unlikely; or it can offer an insurance scheme or security guarantee to reduce risk. In all cases, the principal mediator relies on its ability to rearrange payoffs to increase the incentives to agree.[18]

Psychological Bias

In other disputes, incentives may be adequate but decision makers' information-processing capabilities limited. In a complex world, leaders employ "short-cuts to rationality." Established beliefs resist change even with new information; decisions are made on the basis of a single important value dimension; historical analogies to recent important cases weigh heavily; other states are assumed to be more unified and rational than available information indicates; one's benign intentions are assumed to be appreciated by others; and the role of accidents and confusion is discounted. Decision makers consequently fail to appreciate changes in their opponents and in the circumstances of the conflict and they discount an opponent's conciliatory moves. In short, cognitive limitations often result in missed opportunities for agreement.[19]

To the extent these cognitive limitations and misperceptions are a product of inadequate processing of complex information, a third party, being outside the dispute, is in a position to collect information from both sides, make a dispassionate and comprehensive analysis, and correct each party's errors. Both the principal and neutral mediators can serve this role if the problem is, indeed, essentially a technical one. But if information is subject to interpretation, if the diagnosis is not obviously correct once pointed out, then the principal mediator will be more suspect of strategically biased interpretations than the neutral.[20]

Conflictual Norms of Interaction

In normal interactions free of intense conflict, actors take account of each other's behavior and assess their intentions and perceptions. They are aware of changes in the other's situation over time and of the possibility of influencing those changes. In conflictual interactions, however, a different dynamic usually prevails. Herbert Kelman puts it this way:

> The norms that govern interactions between representatives of conflicting parties require each to express their own grievances and to proclaim their own rights as firmly and militantly as possible. If the adversary describes atrocities in which hundreds were killed, they must counter with atrocities in which thousands were killed. If the adversary cites historical claims that go back a hundred years, they must counter with claims that go back a thousand years. . . .
>
> The representatives of conflicting parties engaged in such interactions are judged by their constituencies—and indeed judge themselves—by how well they have been able to advance and defend their positions and how strong a case they have presented. They focus only on what they themselves have to say, not on what the other has to say. There is little attempt, as in more usual interaction situations, to gain understanding of the other's perspective—except perhaps in the crudest strategic terms. Nor are they particularly interested in influencing the adversary; their communications are directed to their own constituencies and to third parties, rather than to the representatives of the other party.[21]

An intermediary can reverse these norms of interaction only if the intermediary itself does not operate under them. For the most part, principal mediators must demonstrate effectiveness to their constituencies. They must show that they are making progress, that the parties are following the mediator's lead, that the mediator's concept of historical and legal rights are adhered to. Most importantly, principal mediators must show that *their* interests are being served. Indeed, in many interventions, the principal mediator stakes out its positions on the disputed issues before even bringing the parties together (see part 2 for two U.S. examples). These pronouncements are clearly aimed more at domestic audiences than at the disputing parties.

The neutral mediator is in a different position. It has little reason to operate under these norms. It has entered the dispute not to express a grievance or proclaim a right or establish a presence. With no interests in the disputed issues—direct or indirect—it does not have to show that it is tough because it has nothing to be tough about. It need not show constituencies that it is protecting or advancing such interests.[22] In fact, in practice, neutrals often have insignificant constituencies or ones who tolerate receiving little information. For many religious groups or academic institutions, for example, it is enough to know that the intervention is for peacemaking or research purposes. (See the Vatican and Quaker cases in part 3 for examples.) Moreover, the risk to the neutral is relatively low; it does not, once again, have major interests of its own in the dispute.

In brief, because a neutral can itself avoid conflictual norms of interaction, it is more likely than the principal to promote alternative norms between disputants. The result will be to improve communication and to enhance understanding of each other's intentions and perceptions, what may be termed "realistic empathy."[23] With such empathy, parties are more amenable to engaging in a joint problem-solving process that addresses underlying interests and needs.

To summarize, the dichotomy between principal and neutral mediators suggests two fundamentally different kinds of intervention. For the principal mediator, the target of intervention is *payoff structure* and the intervention objective is to *enhance incentives* for agreement. For the neutral mediator, the target of intervention is the *mode of interaction* and the intervention objective is to *create realistic empathy*. The relationship between differences in third-party interests and capabilities, the target of intervention, and the intervention objectives, is summarized in figure 2.3.

THE NEUTRAL'S DILEMMA

The principal-neutral distinction also leads to an important insight into intermediary behavior in general. In international affairs, most actors never have to demonstrate who they are or what they are up to. States, in particular, act first to promote their own self-interests. And they do so strategically. Everything they say and do has strategic content. Whether

DIFFERENCES IN INTERESTS AND CAPABILITIES   =>
(principal vs. neutral mediators)

DIFFERENCES IN THE TARGET OF INTERVENTION   =>
(payoff structure vs. mode of interaction)

DIFFERENCES IN THE OBJECTIVES OF INTERVENTION
(enhance incentives vs. create realistic empathy)

Fig. 2.3. Summary of Intervention Effects

the mechanism is force, coercive diplomacy, or negotiation, the consequences of what one does is due, in part, to what the other does. Each must act to anticipate and to change the other's choices. Most important, this is known to all. It does not have to be spelled out nor demonstrated. Strategic behavior is a fact of international life—a fact, that is, for *most* actors—all those toward the left-hand side of figure 2.1: the principal parties, disputants, and principal mediators.

The few that attempt to operate toward the right-hand side—the neutrals and the neutral mediators—shoulder quite a different burden. They must demonstrate convincingly that they are neutral. They must convince others they will not attack with force or strike a deal with one party. This stance is not easy in international relations. There is no overarching authority to guarantee such a position.

In other words, neutrals, unlike other actors in international relations, must demonstrate to others that they are not like most other actors. They must do this visibly and credibly. Often, they must do it day-to-day, repeatedly and continually, for if they do not, the fragile reputation they build can easily crumble. In fact, as I will argue further in the next two chapters and in parts 2 and 3, much of what mediators (neutrals as well as principals with neutral pretensions) do can be understood as attempts to demonstrate neutrality, not, contrary to popular understanding, to promote the disputants' interests by achieving the best solution.

CONCLUSION

The distinction between principal and neutral mediators helps differentiate the target and the effect of an intermediary intervention. Principals act to change disputants' payoffs through their separate bilateral bargains whereas neutrals act to change the nature of interaction. These two kinds of nonforce third parties are, of course, "ideal types" in the Weberian sense; they are unreal constructs designed to "penetrate to the real casual interrelationships."[24] Approximations to these ideal types may exist in real life, but their analytic purpose is to reveal the essential characteristics of the processes intermediaries engage in. My purpose throughout this book is to explore the many ways in which intermediaries can influence others to settle or resolve conflicts. These two categories help by highlighting the difference between influence by conventional means—"power" in the form of military and economic strength, say—and by other means—influence through changes in perceptions and norms of interaction, for example.

As noted, neither is the "right" kind of influence. Depending on the nature of the dispute, each plays its part in bringing disputants closer to agreement. Some may argue, nevertheless, that although both kinds of third-party influence can lead to agreement, they both do not lead equally to *resolution*; only those interventions that address underlying interests and fundamental needs can do that. This may be true, but often the precondition for such interaction is some kind of interim settlement—a ceasefire, a disengagement of forces, an enhancement of defensive armaments, an economic boost.

What this suggests, then, is that the policy choice between principal and neutral mediators is not an either-or proposition. Rather, what the principal-neutral framework suggests is that, for complex disputes that evolve over time, a combination of intermediaries carefully sequenced will be most effective. A neutral may be necessary to initiate secret talks, a principal to effect a ceasefire, a neutral again to convene preliminary negotiations, and, finally, say, a principal to expand the pie enough to ensure agreement.

Chapter Three

THE BASES OF INTERMEDIARY INFLUENCE: RECONFIGURATION, PROPOSAL MAKING, AND INFORMATION POOLING

POPULAR ACCOUNTS of third-party intervention, whether news accounts or the prescriptive mediation literature, often emphasize the variety of tasks intermediaries use to facilitate settlement. They describe the shuttling between parties, the search for the right formula, and the endless drafting of settlement packages. Although technique is certainly important, in this chapter I argue that an intermediary's impact on a dispute is fundamentally a consequence of three attributes of intermediary intervention: the ability to change bargaining dynamics by reconfiguring the structure of the bargain; the ability to precipitate movement through making proposals; and the ability to pool information.

In chapter 2, I dealt with the intermediary's impact on bargaining dynamics in terms of differences between the principal and neutral mediators. Differences in interests in the disputed issues and in bargaining capabilities determined whether the primary target of intervention was payoff structure or disputant interaction. The starting point in this chapter is bargaining structure—that is, the number and nature of issues and parties. The primary effects of intermediary intervention can be seen by considering a fundamental structural concept—bargaining range—and the associated concepts of reservation value and outcome indeterminacy. As will be seen, intermediaries effect structural changes by increasing the number of parties (and, in some cases, the value of exchange); by creating a focal point for bargaining moves; and by controlling information. These changes help account for the evolving role intermediaries typically undergo during an intervention. The underlying assumption here is that structure is a major determinant of behavior. In succeeding chapters—especially in the case studies—I introduce political, institutional, and psychological determinants of bargaining and intervention behavior.

BARGAINING STRUCTURE

The fundamental concept of bargaining structure is *bargaining range*, the set of agreement points that both sides prefer over their no-agreement alternatives.[1] Two features are noteworthy to understand bargaining dynamics. First, the bargaining range is bound by the value of each party's no-agreement alternative, what is often termed the *reservation value*. The bargainer is better off to unilaterally take its no-agreement alternative than to take any agreement worse than the reservation value. One implication is that the better one's *alternative* to agreement, the better one's expected agreement will be.[2]

For bargaining behavior, the concept of bargaining range suggests that each party has an incentive not only to improve its own alternative (what defines increased bargaining "power") but to take steps to lead its opponent to *believe* it has a high-value alternative. Because one party often does not know the other's reservation value (or even have a clear idea of its own), each side tries to influence the other's perception of the true range. For example, one side may claim that its alternative is very favorable and that, unless the other can make an attractive offer, it will take that alternative. Or one side may try to show that the other side's assessment of the first's alternative is unduly optimistic. In both cases, the bargainer tries to shrink the perceived bargaining range to favor itself.[3]

The second feature of a bargaining range that is important for understanding bargaining dynamics is the *indeterminacy of outcome*. Unlike a competitive market in which the forces of supply and demand determine an equilibrium or a courtroom in which a jury renders a verdict, in bargaining there is no single solution. Bargaining is a joint decision-making process in which both parties must agree in order to do better for themselves. With more than one possible outcome in the bargaining range, the parties are inevitably faced with the dilemma of how to agree to a single point when, for each side, some points are to better advantage than others and neither side knows perfectly the other's preferences or its choices. A bargainer quite naturally has an incentive to manipulate information both to discover more about the other side and to influence that side's choices. A bargainer may, for example, try to commit to a favorable point in the bargaining range; threaten to withdraw if a favorable point is not accepted; or seek a mutually recognized point that stands out from the rest, that is, a focal point.[4]

The concept of bargaining range distinguished by reservation values and indeterminate outcomes leads to a useful first-cut definition of bargaining.[5] It is an interdependent decision-making process characterized by both strategic interaction and imperfect information. Oran Young puts it this way:

> Strategic behavior will occur whenever two or more individuals all find that the outcomes associated with their choices are partially controlled by each other. Strategic *interaction*, then, is simply the set of behavior patterns manifested by individuals whose choices are interdependent in this fashion.[6] . . .

As a result, any individual engaged in a situation involving strategic interaction will find it impossible to make accurate predictions concerning the
probable behavior of the relevant other(s). Thus, strategic interaction always
produces an irreducible gap in the information of the individuals involved, a
fact that accounts for the occurrence of uncertainty in the technical sense in
any situation affected by strategic interaction.[7]

With strategic interaction and imperfect information, a bargainer, to do
better for itself and to protect against exploitation, has an incentive to
manipulate the expectations of the other. To do this, the bargainer can
manipulate the other side's understanding of payoffs, the choices of action, or the nature of the strategic interaction itself. The important point
here is that bargaining structure makes strategic behavior unavoidable. If
one side eschews such behavior and reveals its preferences and options
fully, the other side is tempted to exploit it. If both agree to avoid such
tactics, they must still make offers and proposals and, with imperfect information, they can never rule out strategic misrepresentation. In fact,
the ultimate manipulative tactic is to claim that one is not being manipulative and that the other must accept its offer because it can do no better.

In sum, even if one party eschews strategic behavior as a practice, to
protect itself, let alone to exploit the other, it still must assume the other
is acting strategically. Because the bargain is symmetrical in this respect,
each will assume the other is manipulating, and both will have exploitative
and protective incentives to act strategically.

Strategic behavior is not necessarily "bad." Sometimes it can lead to
agreement. If one side makes a binding, credible, well-communicated
commitment to a single point in the bargaining range, the other side is left
with the choice of accepting it or taking the inferior option of its no-agreement alternative. The only rational choice the other party is left with is to
agree. Similarly, if one side proposes a fair division scheme and the other
is unable to come up with an equally "fair" scheme, agreement on the
"fair" point is likely. Strategic play, when the moves are clear, can help
ensure agreement.

There are other times, however, when strategic behavior can thwart
agreement. If both sides make credible commitments—but to different
points—or if both come up with reasonable but conflicting standards of
fairness, a bargaining range with indeterminate solution remains and
stalemate is likely. When emotional reactions are added to a bargainer's
repertoire of behavior, then strategic behavior can engender resentment
and anger such that a rational choice is irrelevant. Before turning to the
effect of an intermediary on strategic behavior, it is first necessary to lay
out two types of bargaining in which strategic behavior occurs.

Bargaining Types: Distributive and Integrative

Bargains can be thought of as either primarily distributive or primarily integrative.[8] In conflicts over territory or sovereignty, for example, what one gains, the other loses; the structure of the bargain is zero-sum or distributive. In economic disputes, creative exchanges among differently valued issues make joint gains possible; the structure of the bargain is integrative. See figure 3.1 for an illustration of these two polar case structures.

Agreement is often difficult in distributive bargains because no single point stands out as an obvious solution. Mutually agreeable standards of fairness rarely exist. Consequently, when one side makes a move toward

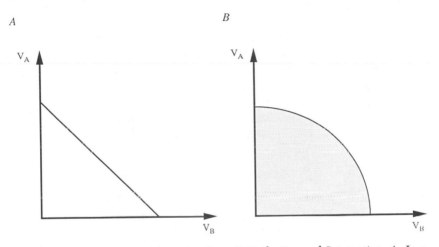

Fig. 3.1. Two, Pure-Case Bargaining Sets: Distributive and Integrative. A. In a *distributive bargain*, all possible agreement points lie along a line. This constitutes the "bargaining set" or "bargaining range." A movement along the line, as when a concession is made, signifies that a gain in value for one side is a loss for the other. If the gain for one equals the loss for the other, the sum is zero and, hence, the term "zero-sum." (Technically, because interpersonal utility comparisons cannot be made, the structure is best termed "constant sum.") There may be an infinite number of possible agreements as depicted in the solid line here, or there may be a finite set of discrete points. B. In an *integrative bargain*, the bargaining set occupies the entire quadrant bound by the axes and the northeastern curve. Any point within the curve is less efficient than some point to its northeast. The curve represents the set of efficient agreement points and is sometimes called the "efficiency frontier." Any movement in a northeasterly direction improves efficiency—that is, at least one side is better off without hurting the other; the bargain, therefore, is termed "integrative." Any movement along or parallel to the curve distributes the gains of the northeasterly moves. Consequently, even in an integrative bargain, there is always a distributive question.

agreement, it can be construed as a concession, a concession that is hard to justify to constituencies and that invites attack from internal opposition groups. Distributive bargains also may be difficult to resolve because there may be few potential points of agreement.

Integrative bargains are generally viewed as easier to resolve than distributive bargains. One reason is that a move that benefits one side need not hurt the other. The parable of the two sisters fighting over an orange illustrates the notion of joint gains. If one sister gets the orange, the other does not; one wins, the other loses. Even if they split the orange, each foregoes half the orange. But when they discover that one sister wants the orange for its juicy part and the other for its rind (to put in a cake), they both do well to separate the pulp and the rind and distribute its parts accordingly.

In most real-life integrative bargains, the solutions are not so clear, of course. Even when joint gains can be discovered, there are usually many points of possible agreement, some of which benefit one side more than the other. To settle on one point over any other is a distributive question and the negotiators are back to the problems inherent in distributive bargains. The determining feature of all bargains, distributive and integrative, is, once again, strategic interaction.

THIRD PARTIES AND THE STRUCTURE OF THE BARGAIN

Given that bargaining structure affects bargaining behavior and, consequently, the likelihood of reaching agreement, how does the structure of the bargain relate to third-party intervention? In a distributive bargain (or, the distributive component of an integrative bargain), the disputants' primary problem is to choose among available agreement points, none of which may have prominence and none of which may be "fair."

Third parties may perform several functions in this regard. Some, say, major powers, may elect to coerce the parties into accepting one point. Others may accept the disputing parties' invitation to make a decision for them and to serve as judges or arbitrators. Short of settlement by force or voluntary adjudication, a third party can enter a distributive bargain to assist, or influence, the parties in their negotiations—that is, to serve as an intermediary. In this role, the third party can provide a sounding board for both sides' positions. It can either separate the parties and shuttle back and forth or bring them together for face-to-face dialogue. It can add incentives for agreement. It can threaten to walk out if agreement is not forthcoming, and so on.[9] These techniques are based on one or more of three elements characteristic of intermediary intervention: reconfiguring the bargain; making a proposal; and pooling information.

Reconfiguration

An intermediary reconfigures the structure of a bargain in one of two ways. First, the number of parties changes from two (a simplification I use throughout this study) to three. Game theorists and sociologists have long worked on the differences between dyads and triads. Here, I only note the coalition-creating effect of changing from two to three partners. This effect is easiest to see with the "principal mediator" but, at some level, it applies to any third party.

When a third bargainer enters a dispute, each of the original two disputants must assess the potential increase in value brought by the third party and, at the same time, the potential loss in value. The third party may offer both disputants a better deal than they could have between the original two. As discussed in chapter 2, this could take the form of two separate bilateral deals or a rotating arrangement in which the first deals with the second who then deals with the third who, in turn, deals with the first. The risk enters with the possibility of being excluded when the third party forms a coalition with the other disputant. Not only might the excluded party miss out on the three-way benefits, it might forego the expected benefits of the original bargain. In this way, an intervention presents not only opportunities, but risks.

The second way in which a third party can reconfigure a bargain is through rearranging the issues themselves, especially, to change the bargain from distributive to integrative. Because conflicts are rarely strictly zero-sum, even though they are often perceived as such, an intermediary can help change the perceived structure. For example, if bargaining has centered on a single issue, the intermediary can disaggregate that issue and find creative ways to trade across subissues to benefit both sides. Or, it can add issues by way of economic or military aid, improved relations, and so forth. By changing issues, the intermediary encourages agreement. Concessions may still be needed, but joint gains are possible, too. When joint gains are made, concessions can be more easily obscured, an advantage for decision makers who must answer to recalcitrant constituencies.

In sum, a third party, by its participation in the dispute, changes the fundamental structure of the bargain. A principal mediator is well disposed to create a three-way bargain or to add resources to expand the bargaining range. Both the principal and the neutral mediators can operate to change the perceptions of the bargaining structure, especially to convert it from distributive to integrative. And, as I will discuss further, both kinds of mediators can reconfigure the bargain by doing no more than being present as an audience.

Proposal

The second characterizing element of an intermediary intervention is the use of a proposal. Although more subtle than reconfiguration, the mere suggestion of a solution can affect negotiations in ways that neither force nor positive or negative incentives can. Whether the disputants accept or reject the suggestion is not as important as the immediate effect on the disputants' bargaining dynamics. This effect is best seen in the context of a simple, single-issue, distributive bargain.

Typically, a distributive bargain is full of maneuvers for claiming as much value as possible. Dickering over the price of a used car or haggling with a rug merchant are well-known examples. Each side knows its bottom line—its reservation value—and each knows that what the other side gets, it does not. Consequently, each party engages in a variety of tactics to settle on a favorable point and claim as much of the fixed value as possible. As discussed above, these moves can usually be construed as attempts to change the perceived bargaining range.

For example, a common tactic is to make an extreme opening bid. Thinking that the eventual settlement point will be roughly halfway between opening bids, the bargainer will make an extreme bid to shift the settlement in a favorable direction. Because bargainers know of this phenomenon, at least intuitively, they must consider all bids to be, in part, strategic. The strategic consideration is necessary not only to gain maximum value for oneself but, importantly, to guard against conceding too much to one's opponent.

Of course, it is not easy to assess a move for its strategic content. The meaning of each move is never clear: Does an apparently extreme bid signal a smaller bargaining range than I originally thought or is it simply a ploy? Does my opponents' final offer mean this is my last chance for an agreement or does it mean we have a lot more bargaining—and a lot more "final offers"—to go? Does my opponents' concession signal weakness or strength? If my opponents' successive concessions are getting smaller and smaller, are they converging on their bottom line (which helps me) or on their preferred outcome (which hurts me)? Is my opponents' attempt to commit to a point in the bargaining range really irreversible and, if not, should I challenge it and risk losing agreement altogether? These questions—and their associated uncertainties—are ubiquitous in distributive bargains (and in the distributive component of integrative bargains).

To help resolve such uncertainties, bargainers quite naturally look for ways to settle on a single point. They may not be particularly concerned about getting a fair solution or even an efficient one. Although each side wants to do best for itself, at a minimum it simply wants to settle on some point where it is better off than having no agreement at all. To do this, bargainers look for bids that have prominence of their own, that is, an agreement point that stands out from the rest. Sometimes this focal point is readily apparent. In selling used cars, the blue book value may anchor perceptions of the "proper" price. In settling a lawsuit out-of-court, a prior award may serve as a common reference point.

In international affairs, however, such standards or precedents may be few. To the extent one side invokes them, the other side may simply ignore them. Moreover, any claim to a "fair" standard or precedent made by one side must still be evaluated for its strategic element: Is my opponent's claim to fairness universally accepted? Are there other "fair" standards? In fact, the natural response to a claim for a fair standard is to find another, equally "fair" standard, but one that is more favorable to one's own side.[10]

In this milieu of strategic moves with uncertain meaning in which all agreement points benefit both sides—although not equally—and yet no point stands out as the obvious solution, negotiators can often lock into incompatible positions. Stalemate results not necessarily because of misunderstanding or a lack of "will" to negotiate but because they cannot readily agree on one point over any other. As a consequence, disputants become receptive to an outside intervention. An intermediary's suggested solution can produce the necessary effect. Like a crystal that catalyzes a reaction among chemicals, the proposal works simply because it comes from the outside. It is effective not because it offers the "best" solution, not because it is fairest or most efficient, but simply because it comes *from outside the realm of strategic moves made by the principal parties.*

The effect of the proposal is easiest to see with the perfectly detached mediator, what I have termed the "neutral mediator." Because the neutral has no interests direct or indirect—in the issues in dispute and because its primary objective is simply to get agreement, all agreement points have equal value to the mediator.[11] Strategic maneuvering to promote one point over another is not necessary because any point will do. Consequently, the parties have little reason to suspect bias. From each party's perspective, before receiving the proposal from the intermediary, there is no reason to expect the intermediary to choose one point over any other. For the parties, the proposal has no strategic content. It is, in other words, truly "neutral."[12]

By this argument, it might appear that only the neutral mediator is positioned to offer nonstrategic, "neutral" proposals. But even the principal mediator, the intermediary whose interests are indirect and separate from the disputants' interests, can make proposals that are fundamentally different from those of principal parties. In the Middle East, for example, the United States, to protect its geopolitical interests, may engage in plenty of strategic maneuvering in its mediation efforts. But if a line has to be drawn in the desert and neither side can concede a kilometer, a mere suggestion from the United States can provide the necessary focal point from which agreement can be reached. It is not the resources or the reputation or the "power" of the United States that matters. The suggestion affects the parties' bargaining because it has prominence, that is, because both sides recognize that the suggestion, at least with respect to this particular issue, lacks the strategic content inherent in the disputants' moves.[13]

This argument does not mean that the proposal will be accepted or that it will be viewed as the best solution by either side. But in a distributive bargain in which no point of agreement is inherently more fair or more efficient (all points except no agreement are efficient in a distributive bargain), a "mere" suggestion can carry weight that the parties' suggestions never can. The intermediary's proposal can "anchor" perceptions.[14] It can appear—or be made to appear to one's constituencies—to be a reasonable solution where none appeared to exist before. It can help parties save face by avoiding the appearance of conceding to the other party's demands. It can serve as the basis of adjustments and exchanges from which agreement eventually can be reached.

So far, I have couched this entire discussion in terms of a proposal for agreement, that is, a substantive proposal. But the argument applies to all questions that must be jointly decided by the disputants—choosing a venue; setting an agenda (which issues in what sequence); establishing norms of behavior; scheduling meetings, recesses, and adjournments; arranging travel (will the parties travel together and, if not, who will arrive first); handling the media (who issues press releases and will they be issued jointly or separately); determining the shape of the table; allocating expenses; preparing food; and so forth. Although many of these decisions appear minor, they can become serious enough to stall a negotiation.[15]

In part, this stalling effect occurs because some of these questions have direct effects on the substantive issues. An agenda, for example, limits the range of issues and how they are considered. Concessions on early issues may be easier for one side, thus forcing the other side to reciprocate with more difficult concessions. Or, if the easy issues are settled first, they cannot be used to create joint gains with the harder issues. Process questions also cause difficulties because parties often consider all moves strategic and potentially linked. Bargainers tend to link each decision, no matter how minor, to subsequent, more consequential matters. Consequently, each decision can assume an importance seemingly out of proportion to the dispute at hand, and each can make or break a set of negotiations. The significance of this observation is that, with so many joint decisions facing disputants, an intermediary has many points of entry in a dispute and, as a result, many points of potential influence. In fact, it

may well be that the nature and timing of proposals are an intermediary's—both the principal's and, especially, the neutral's—most important instruments of influence.

To summarize, intermediaries can precipitate action on all substantive
and procedural issues, from accepting an intermediary itself to proposing
a comprehensive agreement package. Only intermediaries, not the disputants, can make proposals in a nonstrategic way. An intermediary's proposal, therefore, aside from its substantive content, can provide the critical starting point from which movement can begin or a final settlement
can be reached. The important point is that it is not resources or coercive
ability or even negotiating skill that enables a mediator to perform this
function. Rather, it is the fact that both sides know the mediator is di-
vorced from the strategic elements peculiar to disputants and inherent in
their interactions. This is true for distributive bargains and, because they
have unavoidably distributive components, integrative bargains, as well.
Fellow disputants, even "third-party disputants," do not have this ability.
They are not in the middle and, despite their good intentions and claims
to the contrary, they cannot act free of strategic maneuvering. This discussion reinforces the argument in chapter 2 that much of an intermediary's
behavior can be understood as attempts to commit to a "neutral" role
not, contrary to the popular conceptions, to seek efficiencies and fair
outcomes.

Pooled Information

Once involved in a dispute, an intermediary's function tends to progress
from merely providing amenities or conveying messages to making procedural suggestions. The intermediary may eventually convene private cau-
cuses or solicit position statements from each party and seek a formula for
agreement. Whether by design or by chance, the intermediary ends up
with information collected from both sides, information to which neither
side is completely privy. The information may be factual, it may reveal
underlying preferences, or it may be the product of strategic misrepresentation. Whatever its nature, the intermediary is in the unique position of
having information about one side that the other side does not have.

Prescriptive approaches to mediation stress how a third party can use
this jointly held information to craft integrative solutions. When each
party is reluctant to reveal information for fear that the other will exploit
that information (a perfectly legitimate concern), and, as a result, a bargaining range cannot be determined (or, at least, not a sufficiently attractive one), the intermediary is able to pool information from both sides.
For the disputant to reveal such information is relatively unthreatening
because the intermediary need only reveal the feasible set of agreements

or, simply, whether such a set exists, not the information itself. Moreover, it is more likely that the pooled information will be used to identify all possible joint gains when in the hands of a third party than as part of a direct negotiation process with its attendant strategic manipulation.

It is certainly true that pooled information can be used by an intermediary in this way. The prescriptivists tend to ignore, however, another use of such information. That is, because "information is power," what one has and the other does not can be used not only to suggest attractive outcomes but to extract concessions or, say, more information. In short, when an intermediary becomes the sole repository of certain information, information that can directly affect the material interests of the parties, the intermediary begins to acquire means of bargaining with the parties.

This constitutes the third basis of intermediary influence. In addition to reconfiguring a bargain and making a proposal, the intermediary can use pooled information to bargain with disputants. It can offer something to the party it does not have (either the information itself or the resulting potential agreement points) and gain concessions in return. The concessions may be no more than those necessary to reach agreement or they may be concessions needed to advance the intermediary's interests (assuming they extend beyond mere agreement).

The proposition that an intermediary will use pooled information to bargain with disputants and to advance its own interests appears consistent with the principal mediator's role, but what about the neutral mediator? Is there not a contradiction between this proposition and the contention in chapter 2 that the neutral derives its base of influence through its very inability to bargain? Three points are worth considering.

First, the neutral mediator, as developed in chapter 2, does not act to advance the parties' interests over its own as prescriptive approaches to negotiation implicitly assume. Rather, I define a neutral as having *no interests in the disputed issues*, but, as I elaborate further in chapter 4, it may have very strong interests in establishing a reputation as a peacemaker or in simply seeing agreements reached and hostilities avoided.

Second, the argument of chapter 2 is best seen as structural and static; it does not account for *changes* in the intermediary's role over time. Here, then, I am suggesting that when a more dynamic view is taken, when one posits a function unique to intermediary intervention—the pooling of information—it becomes apparent that the intermediary's role can evolve. The more information a mediator has the greater its ability to bargain, and, hence, the more influence it has over the disputants. Even if the intermediary's role begins as little more than setting up a room and serving coffee, it can quite naturally evolve into a role that commands considerable dependency from the parties. The resulting influence entails more than sweetening deals and making proposals; it involves trading on asymmetries in information.

Third, a dynamic view of the intermediary's role suggests that both the neutral and the principal mediators evolve as they participate. The neutral accumulates information that can be used to influence disputants, thus becoming more and more like a principal. It may not offer carrots and sticks, but it can offer (or deny) useful information. The farther down this path the neutral moves, the more it gains in one kind of influence (the use of information) and the more it loses in the other (exploiting its nonstrategic position). As a result, the neutral experiences a tension in role whereas, initially, it is able to gain information *because* it does not bargain with the disputants. The more the neutral accumulates information and moves toward a bargaining mode of intervention, however, the less able it is to elicit such information.

To illustrate, Quaker mediators, among the most "powerless" mediators conceivable, typically carve out a highly restricted intermediary role, often simply providing a meeting place or carrying messages. But once in the dispute, they find they can be increasingly effective using what they have learned of the dispute to suggest steps toward agreement. Traveling to both sides, they can gather information that even the best intelligence officers cannot. As a result, these mediators acquire influence, albeit in a limited form, and use it to meet their objective—say, to reduce the violence. (See part 3, chaps. 8 and 9 for cases in point.)

The principal mediator has a parallel tendency. Where the neutral can elicit information relatively easily, the principal is constrained by its bargaining position. Knowing, nevertheless, that it needs information to promote its interests, let alone those of the parties, the principal initially tries to convince the parties that it is only a "facilitator," not a fellow bargainer. When this fails, the principal mediator resorts to other means to both encourage movement and to elicit information. In fact, the bargaining process, the exchange of offers and counteroffers, can be interpreted as an information-gathering effort as much as an agreement-promoting one. Once the principal moves down this path, it closes off what advantages it may have gained convincing the parties it is a mere facilitator.

To illustrate, Henry Kissinger began his shuttle diplomacy in the Middle East presuming to be a mere message carrier. Soon, however, he was prevailing on both parties with carrots and sticks to make concessions. The resentment he engendered can be interpreted, in part, as a reaction to the shifting roles. (For a similar evolution of role, although possibly less calculated, see Jimmy Carter's effort at Camp David, part 2.)

In sum, pooled information gives an intermediary a third basis of influence. It enables the intermediary both to find integrative solutions and to bargain with the disputants. Because a neutral intermediary's strength derives from its very lack of bargaining capability, the tendency to accumulate information confounds the role by creating a bargaining relationship, albeit a limited one because, without the capabilities and interests, it cannot move all the way toward a principal role. The need to gain information also helps explain why principal mediators typically start out espousing a relatively "noninterventionist" role and then shift to a more conventional bargaining role.

CONCLUSION

An intermediary's basis of influence takes three forms: the ability to reconfigure a bargain; the ability to make a nonstrategic proposal; and the ability to pool information. These follow from the conditions of indeterminacy and strategic interaction (including imperfect information) inherent in all bargaining. They are not the only means of influence but they are the principal means that underlie the techniques mediators employ. So, for example, a standard mediating technique is to separate the parties and shuttle back and forth. The presumed reason is that face-to-face encounters between belligerents are too likely to explode into nasty exchanges of accusations and threats. But by shuttling, mediators also acquire information that both sides do not have. That information can be used to manipulate the parties in a variety of ways, some that meet the parties' interests, some the mediator's interests.

At times, the effect of an intervention can be dramatic, as when a principal mediator reconfigures a bargain by interceding with great resources or by threatening great harm and then emerges from the negotiations with a peace treaty in hand. In part 2, this effect is best exemplified by Jimmy Carter's Middle East interventions. More typically, perhaps, an intermediary's effect on a dispute is subtle or seemingly inconsequential as in the remaining three cases in parts 2 and 3. Merely suggesting a negotiating venue, for instance, seems minor enough in light of great issues like survival or sovereignty. But it is something that disputants cannot propose nonstrategically. And the question of venue—along with the multitude of other questions that must be jointly decided—can be critical enough to make or break a fragile set of negotiations.

Similarly, an intermediary, especially a neutral mediator, may not create a three-way bargain, but its mere presence changes the tenor of the negotiations. The mediator is an audience of sorts. Parties may view it as representative of world opinion;[16] it may embody transcendent values that the parties can appeal to; and so forth. None of these effects is enough to ensure agreement (nor can dramatic interventions necessarily), but they may be just enough to make a difference. Thus, reconfiguration in this way can be subtle as well.

The subtlety—and importance—of an intermediary's effect is analogous to the tipping phenomenon. When balancing a one-ton weight, each ounce is trivial. But the last one is critical. Similarly, each nonstrategic proposal can have little obvious effect. But when strategic behavior prevails in a bargain, when all interaction is manipulative, when trust is rare and escalation constantly a risk, just a bit of nonstrategic behavior in the way of neutral proposals or mere third-party presence may be enough to keep negotiations going. Other factors—shifts in the balance of power or changes in domestic politics—may ultimately determine whether and how settlement is reached. So, although an intermediary's intervention may not be a major causal factor in the settlement of a dispute, it may be a critical factor.

In the case studies of part 2, one may expect to see dramatic interventions with clear-cut results. After all, one might reason, a study of intermediary intervention should demonstrate the great importance of such interventions. In fact, the case studies largely confirm this chapter's conclusion that most interventions are not dramatic. Jimmy Carter's intervention was certainly headline-grabbing. But Theodore Roosevelt's intervention may be more typical where the effects, even of a major power, were more subtle. These effects—whether from reconfiguring, making proposals, pooling information or other actions—in conjunction with the peculiar advantages of acting either as a principal or neutral mediator, account for much of an intermediary intervention's impact.

What these factors do not do, however, is tell about the actual process of intervention. They do not tell what it looks like from the mediator's seat, what are a mediator's major decisions, and how they affect the process. Chapters 4 and 5, then, lay out an intermediary's decision problems. They demonstrate that the static, structural analysis of most of this and chapter 2 does not adequately account for changes in a mediator's role. Most importantly, in chapters 4 and 5 I show that a mediator's role is negotiated, that it is a product of the interactions between disputants and the third party.

Chapter Four

THE INTERMEDIARY'S DECISION PROBLEMS:
ENTRY AND EXIT

IN THIS CHAPTER, I step into the shoes of the intermediary to ask, What does it mean to be in the middle? What is difficult about performing the intermediary's task? What is perplexing? What are the demands disputants and others place on intermediaries? How do these demands conflict? My intention is not to generate a laundry list of what intermediaries can or should do. How-to-do-it works are ample, and detailed descriptive accounts are beginning to emerge in some areas of mediation.[1] Rather, here I portray the intermediary's task as a set of dilemmas or key decision problems. Doing so assumes that to understand intermediary intervention, one must understand intermediary behavior. One must search for what perplexes the intermediary, what confounds the performance of the daily tasks, and what trade-offs the intermediary faces. In particular, it assumes one must understand the difficulties of gaining control over the dispute resolution process and of urging movement.

Questions of control and movement are less important for a third party prepared to use force or one in a position to make a decision for the disputants (that is, an arbitrator or a judge). The user of force must decide when and how much, but the role is clear and party consent is not an issue. The arbitrator already has the parties' consent so the only concern is to make the best decision for the disputants. But for the intermediary, one with no decision-making authority and no ability to use or threaten force, questions of gaining control and urging movement are critical. Unlike in labor-management disputes, mediators in international conflicts generally are not professionals. They are not trained as mediators, and, often, they have never practiced it. Moreover, their position does not dictate when to become involved or how to influence the parties to come to agreement. Typically, international mediators just "wing it." They suddenly find themselves in a position to mediate, and they adopt whatever means are most familiar.[2] One way or another, they must decide *when to enter*, for the timing of entry will affect their ability to bring about an agreement; and, once in the dispute, they must decide *when to exit*, for threatening to leave is a fundamental means of urging agreement when intermediaries have no authority to decide.

Entry and exit, then, are critical decisions for an intermediary. To understand these decisions, it is first necessary to compare the analysis of direct negotiations with the analysis of third-party negotiations—that is, negotiations with an intermediary—and to explicitly account for intermediary interests. The nature of direct negotiations and of intermediary interests constitute the context of the two decision problems. Once these are developed and, in chapter 5, the disputant's decision problems are set out, the stage will be set to examine in detail four examples of intermediary intervention in parts 2 and 3.

DIRECT NEGOTIATIONS

A "first cut" analysis of direct negotiations begins with an assessment of parties, issues, interests, and alternatives. These factors determine the basic structure of the bargain from which specific strategies and tactics can then be expected. As discussed in chapter 3, some negotiations are strictly *distributive*—a concession on the price of a car, for example, is a gain for the buyer and a loss for the seller, whereas other negotiations are *integrative*—trades across differently valued issues, as in many trade disputes, can generate joint gains. For the analyst, such a structural approach is parsimonious. With a little information, one can get a lot of predictive and explanatory mileage. But it is also static. If the structure changes, the mode of analysis does little to explain why the structure—and, hence, the expected tactics—change. In international affairs, understanding change is critical for both descriptive and normative reasons. To explain change in an international setting one must descend the analytic ladder and examine the workings of domestic politics, bureaucracies, and individual decision making.[3]

A "second cut" in the analysis of international negotiations, then, examines characteristics of leadership, economic conditions, the influence of interest groups, and bureaucratic politics. Changes in these factors can lead to changes in national interests and alternatives to agreement. A "third cut" looks more closely at the decision making of individual participants. This third view helps account for change by focusing on interaction processes. That is, a social psychological approach stresses how one side's perceptions of the other side affects its behavior and how this behavior in turn affects the other side's behavior. These two approaches—domestic politics and individual decision making—are developed more fully in the context of intermediary intervention in the case analyses of parts 2 and 3.

INTERVENTION QUESTION

For many students of negotiation and mediation, the preceding framework for analyzing direct negotiations is sufficient to understand the intervention of intermediaries. From their view, when parties in conflict are having trouble negotiating effectively, a mediator can be called in to help them overcome barriers to negotiation. For example, if the parties perceive a distributive bargain and spend all their time exchanging threats and bluffs, a mediator can help them reconfigure the bargain so that it has integrative potential. Or, if both sides see the integrative potential yet do not know how to realize the gains, the mediator can lead them through a problem-solving process to capture those gains.

This view of mediation rests on a fundamental, usually implicit, assumption about mediators—that is, that they are parties whose primary objective is to advance the interests of the disputants. But if, in fact, mediators have their own interests in mind—whether altruistic or self-aggrandizing—the analysis must account for them and thus cannot be considered equivalent to the analysis of direct negotiations. What, then, is the difference?

In one sense, the primary difference relates to analytic purpose. For those who view mediated negotiations as essentially equivalent to direct negotiations, the purpose is to find ways of improving the situation—that is, the *negotiators'* situation. Improvement can mean enhancing existing negotiations, overcoming a stalemate, or preventing or ending hostilities. The starting point is to search through the mediator's bag of tricks to find a way to start or to improve negotiations.[4]

If, by contrast, the analytic purpose is to understand what is distinctive about mediation, what mediators actually do, what is difficult about their task, then the starting point must be different. To perform such an analysis, it is not enough to detail what mediators can do. Rather, one must detail what motives the mediator would have in the first place to intervene. One must first examine, in other words, the *intermediary's interests.* For some, those interests may be patent. Labor mediators, permanent employees of federal or state governments, earn their pay and enhance their professional standing by tackling tough disputes and chalking up agreements. International mediators, however, usually have a complex set of motives relating to their positions in the international system, their national and institutional imperatives, and their individual and organizational goals.

INTERMEDIARY INTERESTS

In most theories of international relations, interests are the bread and butter of political analysis. In the emerging negotiation literature, interests, along with issues and alternatives, are basic analytic ingredients. Curiously, however, in both literatures, when the subject of mediation is broached, interests seem to drop out—interests, that is, of the intermediary.[5] Mediation is treated as an adjunct process. It is a means of facilitating or improving upon a stalled or ongoing conflict management process. It is seen as something that is just added on top, the real stuff being down below. But, in practice, an intermediary does not simply drop in on a dispute, facilitate an interaction, and then exit intact. An intermediary may catalyze a reaction but the intermediary itself is affected in the process. Knowing how it is affected, how its interests may be advanced or impeded, can go a long way toward understanding the nature of intermediary behavior and, hence, mediation as a distinct conflict management process.

If it is important to understand intermediary interests to understand intermediary intervention, how can these interests be conceptualized of? Is it not enough to identify motives like survival or the desire for power and then proceed? In the following, I show that, unlike the international actor who is strictly egoistic in a self-help world and unlike the idealized facilitator who exists only to help others, most mediators have a bit of both motives. What is important is to distinguish between these motives and their effects on the dispute.

Intermediary Interests: A Classification

If, to begin with, one knew nothing about an intermediary, what would be a reasonable first approximation of that intermediary's motives for intervening? That is, lacking specific information about the intermediary's position in world politics, its base of domestic support, or the personal characteristics of the individuals involved, how would one identify the interests of an intermediary, one who, by definition, does not have a direct interest in the issues in dispute? In chapter 2, I classified all intervenors as disputants (with direct interests in the disputed issues) or third parties. Third parties can act either as "principal mediators" with indirect interests in the disputed issues or "neutral mediators" with no interests—direct or indirect—in the disputed issues. Here, I expand the concept of intermediary interests by claiming, first, that all third-party intervenors—disputants, principal mediators, neutral mediators—are self-interested. They may seek concrete gains for themselves or simply the satisfaction of settling a dispute, but they have interests. Most importantly, the specific nature of those interests will determine the kind of intervention and its effectiveness.

Before proceeding, I should clarify what may appear to be a contradiction between the assertion that all mediators should be considered to have interests and that some, the neutral mediators, have none. The neutral mediators have no interests, direct or indirect, *in the issues in dispute between the principal disputants*. They do, however, have interests in the dispute. They may want to see agreement reached, peace realized, or efficiencies gained. They may want to improve their self-images or burnish their reputations as peace makers or as elder statesmen. They may have religious or philosophical reasons for involving themselves. They may be just looking for something to do. Whatever the case, neutral mediators have interests, but they lie outside the issues in dispute and, therefore, are not subject to bargaining with the disputants.

Intermediary's Interests: Public or Private, Extractive or Nonextractive?

An intermediary's interests can be thought of as falling into one of two categories: public or private. Public interests can include a desire to promote peace, stability, and order or to increase general prosperity. The values inherent in these interests pertain not just to the disputants but extend to the larger community.

The second category, private interests, can have two distinct sources. One is the private value an intermediary obtains by entering a dispute, facilitating settlement, and, as a result, enhancing its prestige or sense of worth. A good example is the enhanced international status of the Algerians after their successful mediation of the U.S.-Iran hostage crisis of 1979–1980. Private value can also include linkages to other, unrelated activities.

These public and private interests do not derive directly from the disputants. A third party cannot bargain with one or both disputants to realize the value of these interests. They are realized only when the disputants reach agreement. They are epitomized by the *neutral mediator*.

An example from the business world illustrates these distinctions. A businesswoman intervenes in a hostile takeover battle, receives no compensation for her efforts, but does meet her public interest in stopping a destructive takeover battle. The effort also would meet her private interest by improving her self-image and possibly her business image. That respect may someday rebound to her benefit on other business matters unrelated to this takeover fight.

A second source of private value is that obtained from the disputants themselves. The intervenor may extract some of the surplus value generated in the dispute or gain value directly from one or both of the disputants. In the previous example, the intervening businesswoman could take a commission on the settlement. Alternatively, she could cut a side deal with one or both of the companies or simply establish relations that would lead to future business deals. Notice that in this last possibility—establishing a separate channel with a disputant—the value obtained could be at the expense of one or both of the disputants.

This difference—that is, whether the intermediary obtains value directly from the disputants or simply from getting agreement—expands on the principal-neutral distinction. The principal refers to extractive values and the neutral to public values plus nonextractive values. This suggests that intermediaries can be distinguished not just by their interests in the disputed issues but by whether value can be extracted directly from the disputants or through disputant agreement only. This distinction also helps explain the tensions in intermediary intervention. One tension derives from the tendency of both kinds of mediators to shift roles as discussed in chapter 3. Others are inherent in the entry and exit decisions.

ENTRY DECISION: GAINING CONTROL

An intermediary should enter a dispute early, it is sometimes contended, to facilitate settlement before disputants resort to contentious tactics and risk a damaging escalation. Others argue that a dispute must be allowed to "ripen" or to reach a stalemate before an intermediary should step in. Both contentions make intuitive sense. For example, one could justify the first contention in situations where the disputants have a good relationship or an effective means of communication and where they are roughly balanced in bargaining power. In this case, the parties are likely to be amenable to negotiation and will find an intermediary's assistance useful early in the dispute. By contrast, the second contention may be justified in a situation where a dispute has arisen between parties of disparate abilities and where one disputant feels it can prevail over the other unilaterally. Only when they realize one cannot prevail unilaterally—that is, after the conflict has "ripened"—do they become amenable to negotiation. Because disputes are rarely so clearly delineated, an intermediary still must decide whether to enter early or late. This decision is not so much an either-or choice but a question of trade-offs.[6]

The Decision Problem

To simplify the problem, imagine a continuously escalating (or, deteriorating) dispute, disputants of comparable bargaining power and willingness to accept an intervention, and a single potential intermediary (see fig. 4.1). Deterioration (or escalation) means each disputant's cost of no settlement is worsening over time. Increasing costs may be due to exogenous factors (e.g., a shifting geopolitical alignment) or to self-generated actions (e.g., the use of threats). At some point in an escalating conflict, efforts to jointly settle the dispute appear fruitless and at least one party feels compelled to act unilaterally and contentiously, resulting in an irretrievably destructive escalation.

The intermediary's intervention decision, before a destructive escalation, can be viewed as the weighing of two opposing forces. On the one hand, the longer into the escalating conflict the potential intermediary

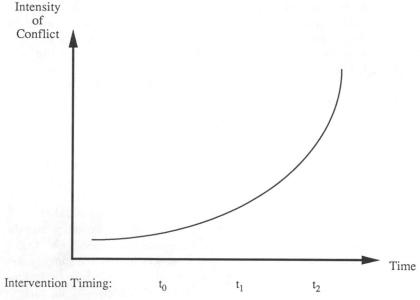

Fig. 4.1. Intervention in an Escalating Conflict. In an escalating conflict in which disputants have comparable bargaining power, the mediator is self-interested and agreement-seeking. To get agreement, the mediator needs control over the dispute resolution process, and the mediator's entry timing affects the likelihood of a successful intervention. That is, because bargaining power increases as one's alternatives to agreement improve and as one's opponent's alternatives worsen, in the *mediator-disputant* bargain over *process*, the later the intervention, the worse the disputant's alternative to mediation. Consequently, the later the intervention, the more control the mediator has over process. Entering early, nevertheless, reduces the chance that the conflict will escalate out of control. Thus, the mediator faces a trade-off: enter early and forestall an escalation out of control but gain little control over process versus enter late and risk uncontrollable escaltion but gain control over process.

waits, the higher the costs (or expected costs) to the disputants and, hence, the better, relatively, becomes their alternative of enrolling an intermediary.[7] On the other hand, the sooner the intermediary intervenes, the less likely it is that the escalating conflict will snowball out of control. Thus, the potential intermediary is faced with *two choices: wait so that the disputants will "need" the intermediary* or *move early so the conflict will not escalate irretrievably*. To assess the trade-offs in this decision it is useful to link entry timing with the eventual intervention process. The crucial link is through the question of *procedural control*, an overriding concern of nearly all intermediaries.

Once involved in a dispute, an intermediary must perform a variety of tasks: provide a site, relay information between parties, construct an agenda, help disputants clarify interests and values, search for innovative solutions, reassure constituencies, manage press relations. Principal mediators may offer concrete incentives as well. To carry out these tasks, the intermediary must gain a certain level of control over the process. That is, the intermediary must have some means of seeing that agreed procedures are adhered to; that confidentiality is maintained; that techniques for overcoming psychological barriers can be employed; that parties can make tentative propositions without commitments; that independent analysis can be conducted; and so forth. Even if the intermediary's interests are entirely public and privately nonextractive, it must gain enough control to employ techniques that encourage more conciliatory moves and fewer contentious moves. Moreover, without a degree of intermediary procedural control, the disputants can easily slip back into the previous means of settlement—say, hostilities.

To illustrate, in the U.S.-Iran hostage crisis, the Algerians were more than mere message carriers. They insisted that all communications between the two countries go through them with no parallel channels. Although the Algerians refrained from making specific proposals for a solution, they did have a hand in the wording and substance of nearly every communication. In effect, they had the final word on what they would transmit.[8]

The Algerians had no "power" in the traditional sense, but they did exercise considerable control over the process. To assess the intermediary's ability to control the process, such control can be construed as a form of intermediary bargaining "power" in which the relevant bargain is not the disputants' bargain but the interactions between the intermediary and each disputant. That is, an intermediary offers the prospect of settlement or, say, the avoidance of hostilities in return for the disputant agreeing to its procedural requirements. Or, as developed in the previous chapter, the intermediary bargains with its pooled information to get parties to accept its suggestions. In any event, the intermediary's bargaining leverage is, as in any bargain, a function of its and its opponent's (in this case, the disputant's) alternatives. Bargaining power increases as one's no-agreement alternative improves or as the opponent's no-agreement alternative worsens.[9] An *intervenor*'s influence over disputants, however, is relative to the dispute resolution processes available to the disputants (e.g., continued stalemate, hostilities, arbitration), not the issues under contention between the disputants. Thus, an intermediary's bargaining power improves as the disputant's alternative to a mediated process worsens.[10] Once the disputants are engaged in a process of mediation, their alternative *to the process* will generally be perceived as the status quo before the intervention. The worse that alternative, the weaker the disputants are *relative to the intermediary* with respect to continuing the process and, by implication, with respect to the techniques and procedures that the intermediary deems necessary to be effective. In escalation, disputants' alternatives are worsening—that is, their *alternatives to a negotiated agreement* are worsening. In the early stages of the conflict, direct negotiation is relatively low risk because it is not equated with conceding. But as the conflict intensifies, threats and violence become more likely. If an intermediary enters early in the dispute, the disputant's alternative to the process with the intermediary, say, mediation, is direct negotiation, a relatively good alternative. But if the intermediary enters late, the alternatives *to mediation* worsen. With respect to the intermediary-disputant relationship, then, the later the intermediary enters, the greater the intermediary's bargaining power, and, hence, the greater its procedural control over the disputant.

To conclude this section, the intermediary's trade-off in the entry-timing question is between assuring involvement and assuring control once involved. That is, if the intermediary enters early, it forestalls an out-of-control escalation but has little procedural control once it sets up a dispute resolution process because the disputants' alternative is relatively good. If the intermediary enters late, it has greater procedural control owing to the disputants' worse alternative, but it risks foregoing any involvement owing to an out-of-control escalation. Put differently, the intermediary's trade-off is between getting in at all and getting in with clout. The timing question, then, can be thought of as an optimization problem between, on the one hand, entering early, in which case the high likelihood of acceptance and low likelihood of uncontrollable escalation are countered by the low level of process influence; and, on the other, entering late, in which case the high likelihood of escalation is countered by the high expected process influence.

EXIT DECISION: URGING AGREEMENT

Once in the dispute, intermediaries face the problem of getting disputants to accept what would appear to be a mutually beneficial solution or simply getting them to move toward agreement. Often, it seems, intermediaries' difficulties lie not so much in the challenges of probing underlying interests or crafting creative, efficient solutions (although these tasks can be daunting as well). Rather, what perplexes intermediaries is being charged with getting a joint decision between disputants and, yet, having no decision-making authority.

To illustrate, in the Vatican mediation of the Beagle Channel dispute, the Pope, despite his moral authority and a well-crafted integrative solution to the conflict, could not get the parties to agree. Even when Argentina had a major change in government and showed an eagerness to settle and when an otherwise acceptable proposal was on the table, it still took months of agonizing negotiating to actually agree (see chap. 8).

If getting movement constitutes a central task (or major difficulty) of intermediary intervention, how would a self-interested intermediary approach this situation? How, putting oneself in the position of an intermediary, would one begin to think about such a perplexing task? As will be seen, answering these questions leads to the conclusion that an intermediary must often depend on the use of a potentially damaging tactic—threatening to exit—to bring disputants to a mutually beneficial solution. It is this threat, however, that becomes the intermediary's fundamental source of influence once the intermediary is fully involved in a dispute resolution process.

To see how an intermediary might deal with disputant intransigence, imagine an intermediary intervention in progress in which all relevant information about the dispute is collected (and known at least by the intermediary if not by both disputants), underlying interests are fully explored (and known at least by the intermediary), and a solution is proposed by the intermediary that appears to improve upon the disputants' no-agreement alternatives and that appears to be fair, efficient, and potentially durable. Imagine also that, despite the value to the disputants of this proposed solution compared to their best alternative, they do not accept it. They might argue, for example, that they need more time, that they want to talk more, that they think an even better solution could be found if they just tried harder.[11] Whatever their reasons, the intermediary considers its proposed solution the best imaginable. And, yet, the disputants still do not budge. Although this situation may appear to be an extreme case, it is not unlike what many intermediaries frequently face in practice. In all of the four case studies of parts 2 and 3, the intermediaries faced a similar problem at some point.

Given the disputants' intransigence, the intermediary has two choices. One, the intermediary can just keep at it, keep urging the disputants to agree, keep searching for more efficiencies. Or, two, the intermediary can leave the dispute.[12] If the exit option is considered, the intermediary may well "suggest" it to the disputants: "I'm sorry. This is all I can do. It is the best solution I can come up with. If you cannot accept this, I'll just have to discontinue the mediation."

What is the nature of this "suggestion" to withdraw from the dispute? In essence, it is a statement to do harm to another unless that person com-

plies with one's desires. But is it a "threat" or a "warning?"[13] Schelling
distinguishes threats and warnings by the statement's implied message
about costs to oneself. If I state that I will hurt you as well as myself, I am
threatening; if I state that I will hurt you but that it will not hurt me, I am
issuing a warning.[14] Thus, the "suggestion" that at some point the intermediary really has no choice and must impose costs on the disputants by
withdrawing the intermediary's services can be viewed as a mere warning. As such, it has no strategic interest. From this perspective, making
such a statement poses no real difficulty for the intermediary because
there is no trade-off to be made, no internal tension to deal with. It is just
a statement of fact. In practice, however, intermediaries do find it very
difficult to issue such statements. These warnings somehow seem incon-
gruous with the intermediary's image of its role.[15] So, to characterize
withdrawal statements as warnings does not help explain the perplexities
and contradictions intermediaries face. An alternative interpretation, one
that accounts for the intermediary's interests, appears plausible in many
situations and generates insights into the nature of the intermediary role.

To interpret the intermediary's "suggestion" to leave as a "warning" is
to assume that only the disputants lose, that the intermediary loses nothing by leaving. The disputants lose because their expected value of an
outcome diminishes as they go from a mediated to a direct negotiation (or
to the best alternative available, which could be continued stalemate, submission to an international agency, or war). The intermediary does not
lose, presumably, because, consistent with the conventional view of the
role of intermediaries, the intermediary is only in the dispute to help the
disputants. Such interventions are primarily technical, not political.

If one makes a different assumption about intermediary behavior—
namely, that the intermediary is a self-interested actor whose primary
objective is to get agreement—the interpretation of the intermediary's
"suggestion" as a warning is found lacking. The following alternative view
of the intermediary's "suggestion" becomes important because it suggests
that an intermediary's strategy may have less to do with finding and stating the facts (e.g., What are your interests? I have no choice but to leave)
and more to do with constraining others'—that is, disputants'—behavior.
In other words, it suggests that under the conditions stated above, an
intermediary's interaction with disputants is a *strategic* one; intermediaries, no matter how powerful or powerless in conventional terms, operate
by finding ways to influence disputants. As discussed in this and previous
chapters, some intermediaries may offer concrete incentives whereas others can only make proposals and use pooled information. In the end, however, all intermediaries have one point of leverage in common: the ability
to deny the benefits of intervention by walking out.

If one assumes the intermediary needs an agreement between the disputants, then the relationship between the disputants and the intermediary is not merely one of the disputant's dependency on the intermediary. The disputants are not the only ones to lose if the intermediary leaves the dispute. If the intermediary leaves, the intermediary loses the potential value of forging an agreement. Because the intermediary forgoes value by leaving, the relationship is one of interdependency, not one-way dependency. And, as discussed earlier, because this value may come from public or private interests or both, it applies to both the neutral and principal mediators.

What this view implies is that the intermediary's "suggestion" to leave the dispute is not a warning at all but a threat in the truly strategic sense. The intermediary's "suggestion," if carried out, would impose costs on both the disputants and the intermediary. Viewed as a threat, then, the intermediary faces the same problem any parent, oligopolist, or military strategist faces: how to make the threat credible. Consequently, in situations where gathering information, exploring interests, and fashioning mutually beneficial solutions is not enough to get agreement, the problem of making strategic commitments becomes an important factor in effective intermediary intervention. It also draws attention to the central dilemma of getting agreement with no decision-making authority, a point I return to shortly.

The intermediary's problem of making credible commitments is intimately linked to the use of deadlines. In any decision-making context—legislative, administrative, or negotiating—when movement is lacking, a standard response is to set a deadline. Deadlines have a way of forcing decisions. But in mediated negotiations, the intermediary has no authority to impose a deadline. So although the intermediary may state that the disputants "must" settle by a certain date, the implicit reply from the disputants is: OK, but if we do not like the outcome we will just keep negotiating. The intermediary has no recourse and the disputants know it. The idea of a deadline loses its decision-forcing effect. The deadline tactic can be used effectively only if the intermediary can commit to that particular time. And, especially for the neutral intermediary with no carrots to offer or sticks to wield, committing to a deadline may mean committing to withdrawing from the dispute.

Two examples illustrate the conclusion that an intermediary often must engage in threats. In the Beagle Channel case, at the very end of the mediation in 1984, when all the conditions for a settlement existed and still the two countries could not agree, the Vatican threatened, as it had done before, to withdraw. But this time its threat was effective because it was credible. To continue would have been onerous for the Vatican given that no better conditions were expected and because no one at this point could accuse the Vatican of not doing everything possible to bring about an agreement. Earlier, the cost to the Vatican of withdrawal would have been severe because the two Catholic countries likely would have reverted to the status quo ante. (See chap. 8.)

A second example can be found in the Algerian mediation of the U.S.-Iran hostage crisis. In late December, Iran insisted that the Algerians, despite their objections, transmit a financial offer that became known in the United States as the "$24 billion misunderstanding." The Algerians nearly withdrew at this point. They were induced to return only when the United States persevered and, presumably, when Iran softened its stance.[16]

One implication of the above argument is that, to the extent threats in the truly strategic sense are required for effective interventions, all the issues of credibility, signaling, perceptions of intentions and interests, and so forth, arise. A second implication is that, under certain conditions, an intermediary's reputation will be crucial. But the requisite reputation will depend less on the usual qualities of being impartial, fair, patient, and so forth, and more on its known ability and willingness to withdraw from a dispute. A third implication is that disputants may want to have an intermediary that, *ex ante*, can commit itself credibly to withdrawing when a party (presumably, the *other* party) is intransigent.

To conclude this section, because one of an intermediary's essential tasks is to get movement and to get disputants to accept a proposal that appears to be in their best interests and because withdrawal is, ultimately, an intermediary's fundamental source of leverage, an intermediary may have to employ threats, a tactic generally considered to hinder effective negotiating. If this is a valid construction of one of an intermediary's essential tasks, then it highlights a paradox of effective intermediary intervention. That is, for the intermediary to lead disputants to a mutually beneficial solution, it may have to employ potentially damaging tactics. The intermediary can find itself employing the very kinds of tactics it is discouraging the disputants from using. By employing such tactics, the intermediary risks tainting an atmosphere of good will, trust, and joint problem solving that it otherwise would have labored to create between the disputants.

Finally, this argument sheds light on a basic contradiction in an intermediary's role: an intermediary is charged with getting agreement but, by definition, it has no decision-making authority. With no authority over the disputants, one way the intermediary can urge them toward agreement is to rely upon what little leverage the intermediary has—the ability to walk out. But, because threatening to exit can engender the very kinds of behavior the intermediary is trying to discourage between disputants, the intermediary experiences an internal, decision-making tension. This tension may well be a major source of the frustration and stress experienced intermediaries talk about.

CONCLUSION

To understand the effects of an intermediary's intervention, it is necessary to understand what it means to stand in the shoes of the intermediary. One must consider not just the intermediary's techniques at the table but the decision problems that bound those techniques—especially the questions of entry and exit. The intermediary's trade-off in the entry-timing question is between assuring involvement and assuring control once involved. If the intermediary enters early, it forestalls an out-of-control escalation but has little procedural control once it sets up a dispute resolution process. If the intermediary enters late, it has greater procedural control owing to the disputants' worse alternative, but it risks foregoing any involvement owing to an out-of-control escalation. With no decision making authority, an intermediary's fundamental source of leverage is to threaten to walk out. The exit tactic is risky, however, because it can engender contradictory behavior by the disputants.

In addition to decision problems, one must account for the motives, objectives, and interests of the intermediary. It is not enough to assume (explicitly or, more commonly, implicitly) either that the intermediary intervenes altruistically or that it does so to enhance its own power. Intermediaries intervene for a variety of reasons, but how those reasons relate to the disputants and the disputed issues ultimately determines the nature of the intervention. Public and nonextractively private interests ensure a limited bargaining relationship with the disputants; this is characteristic of the neutral mediator and, in the case studies, will be most striking in the Quaker mediation of chapter 9. Extractive private interests lead to hard bargaining; this is characteristic of the principal mediator and will be most evident in Jimmy Carter's intervention. The ultimate effect of disputant-mediator relationships will depend, of course, on the position and decisions of the disputants themselves, the topic of the next chapter.

Chapter Five

THE DISPUTANTS' DECISION PROBLEMS: ACCEPTANCE, INITIATION, ROLE BARGAINING

A COMPLETE PICTURE of an intermediary's major decision problems must account for the disputants' major decision problems, at least those relating to the intervention. In this chapter, then, I examine intermediary intervention from the disputants' perspective. This is not to adopt the prevailing prescriptive approach to negotiation in which the focus is on disputants and the tensions experienced by intermediaries are ignored. Rather, the purpose of this chapter is to illuminate further the intermediary's tensions and to do so in terms of the disputants' consideration of a third party. Three disputant decision problems are relevant: initial acceptance of a third party; initiation of the request for a specific intervenor; and bargaining over intermediary control and decision-making authority.[1]

ACCEPTANCE

The Calculation

As a matter of rational choice, two conditions have to be met for an intermediary to be accepted. One, the disputant must expect a better outcome with the intervention than with the best alternative—say, direct negotiations, submission to an international tribunal, stalemate, or hostilities.[2] Two, both disputants *independently* must expect a better outcome with the intervention than without. That is, to gain acceptance of an intermediary, it is not necessary that each side perceive a better outcome for both sides nor that one side expect an improvement for itself and a worsening for the other nor that one side sees itself as doing "better" (by some measure) than the other. The perfectly rational calculation for one side is simply that it expect to do better *for itself* than *its own* best alternative. For an intermediary to gain entry, then, both disputants must see it as such.

If a disputant follows this reasoning, acceptance of a third party would involve no more than a rational calculation to maximize payoffs. Acceptance would occur when both sides' calculations show net benefits. But, of course, parties in conflict do not always calculate rationally. To a protagonist, doing better may mean outdoing the other side. It may mean "getting even" or hurting the other side. It may mean hurting the other side more than one hurts oneself, even if one's best alternative is rationally preferred. A leader under pressure may accept an intermediary just to increase options or to escape an intractable situation. A leader may encourage an intervention to buy time, to gather information about the other side, or to gain favor with the intermediary or other third parties.

In short, disputants may accept a third party for a variety of reasons, only one of which is to establish or improve negotiations. Contrary to those prescriptive approaches that assume mediators just "help" disputants negotiate better, the point here is that disputants need not be disposed to negotiation or any other kind of cooperative effort to accept an intermediary. Moreover, because acceptance ultimately requires a joint decision between disputants, the acceptance question becomes a part of the disputants' bargaining as much as any substantive issue. In fact, questions of which third party to invite, who initiates the intervention, and what role the intermediary performs interact with substantive concerns to make acceptance a complex strategic matter.

In sum, an intermediary can intervene only when both parties accept it. Their grounds for acceptance may be entirely different; they may depend on rational cost-benefit calculations or on the need to escape an untenable position. Their reasons may align with those of the intermediary or they may not. From an analytic point of view, the important point is that acceptance need not depend on shared values or on a convergence of interests. Each party—the intermediary and each disputant—may be able to satisfy its primary interests by satisfying the others' interests, as disparate as they may be. The priest can bring the terrorist and the superpower together and all can come out ahead.

Impartiality

Although far overplayed in much discussion of intermediaries, partiality is an important element in a disputant's acceptance decision. Much of the popular discussion about mediation either implicitly assumes that intermediaries are impartial or it asserts that they *must* be. In fact, many students of negotiation seem to define an intermediary's role in terms of being impartial rather than by the characteristics of being "in between" or by the particular ways an intermediary affects disputants' interactions. So is impartiality critical? Must the intermediary side with neither party or, in some way, with both?[3] Once again, these questions are best addressed from the disputant's perspective.[4]

Stepping into the shoes of a rational disputant, if I am weighing the relative benefits of employing a third party in my dispute, the actor I most want is one whose interests align perfectly with mine and whose capabilities best complement mine. That party is an "ally." Lacking an ally, I would want a third party whose interests at least partially align with mine—an "agent." Lacking either an ally or an agent, I would want a third party whose interests, if they do not align with mine, at least do not align with my opponent's. In other words, an "impartial." The impartial third party is thus only a "third best choice." The reasoning can be pushed a step further.

First, consider that, as a matter of rational calculation, a disputant's fundamental decision rule for acceptance is that the expected outcome of third-party negotiations (that is, with an intermediary, whether a principal mediator or a neutral mediator) be greater than the best alternative (whether direct negotiations, adjudication, stalemate, or war). It is conceivable, then, that a disputant could accept a third party who is clearly biased against it if its expected outcome is still better than the alternative. For example, Egypt, after its war with Israel in 1973, may have viewed the United States as biased toward Israel but accepting the United States as a third party was still better than trying to maintain a tenuous cease-fire and suffering continuing domestic deterioration. Thus, the "fourth best choice" is a "biased party." These third party choices are as follows:

$$\text{ALLY} > \text{AGENT} > \text{IMPARTIAL} > \text{BIASED}$$

Given this preference ranking by a disputant, a host of combinations between two disputants will lead to agreement on a third party. Assuming for the moment that both disputants have the same perceptions of the third party's alignment of interests, it is possible, for example, that a third party will be acceptable if its interests clearly align with one side and, by implication, is biased against the other side. Relaxing the assumption of parallel perceptions, acceptance is possible if each side sees the third party as biased toward itself or even if each side sees third party bias *against* itself. Notice, however, that, in contrast to the popular view, mutually agreed impartiality is only one possibility among many possible combinations.

In sum, impartiality per se is not a necessary condition of acceptance. Each disputant need only view the intervention as benefiting itself and, all else equal, would prefer an impartial third party only if an agent or ally is unavailable or not acceptable to the other side. One may be tempted to argue that, as a matter of prediction, an impartial mediator is more likely to be mutually acceptable. But the foregoing would argue even against that. Assuming that third parties of all kinds are available (not a bad assumption in international affairs where would-be intermediaries are abundant), there is no a priori reason to expect the one combination (mutually perceived impartiality) to have a higher probability of occurrence.

This discussion of impartiality leads to a useful distinction between the terms impartiality and neutrality. Impartiality refers to questions of acceptability whereas neutrality applies to the effect of the intervention on the parties' interaction. This distinction appears more useful analytically than those that equate the two or that simply claim intermediaries *are* impartial and neutral or that intermediaries are never impartial or neutral.

Asymmetric Bargaining Power

The above discussion assumes both disputants are roughly equal in bargaining power. In this situation, one would expect the benefits of an intermediary intervention to be roughly equal because the intermediary likely would employ a fair division scheme that would favor neither side. But if a significant disparity in bargaining power exists—that is, if one side's no-agreement alternative is noticeably better than the other's—then a different dynamic vis-à-vis the intermediary may arise, one that may result in foregone joint gains.[5]

When the bargaining range is markedly skewed toward the more powerful disputant (by definition), the intermediary is inclined to rectify the imbalance and propose a solution that is "fair."[6] But a fair solution from the perspective of the status quo is likely to be different from a fair solution from the perspective of reservation values. If the intermediary chooses a status quo based fairness principle, the solution may, in fact, be less than the powerful side's reservation value. Fearing such a possibility, at least intuitively, the powerful disputant may resist an intervention altogether.

A "fair" solution (that is, status quo based) suggested by an intermediary can thus thwart acceptance. The powerful disputant, aware of the dilemma, may try to convince the intermediary of its true reservation value. Analytically, however, the powerful disputant would face the same problem of commitment any negotiator encounters with its counterpart. One difference that may make convincing the intermediary easier would be the relatively greater willingness to reveal information to an intermediary, especially a neutral mediator, than to a disputant's counterpart. Acceptance may also be facilitated if the disputant chooses an intervenor with a demonstrated interest in simply getting an agreement, not necessarily one committed to getting a "fair" agreement. A high-profile intervenor, one in need of a public success, may be better, in this case, for both disputants than an equity- or efficiency-oriented intervenor.

INITIATION

Once the disputant decides to engage an intermediary, it must then decide how to initiate the intervention. The disputant can appeal directly and unilaterally to the chosen intermediary, seek first the concurrence of the other disputant, or wait for the intermediary to step in unsolicited.

The choice—with all its potential for strategic interpretation (and misin-terpretation)—can significantly affect the disputants' interaction and the likelihood of reaching agreement.

A direct appeal risks creating the image of a coalition between the initi-ating disputant and the intermediary against the other disputant. Rather than a gesture of conciliation, the move is easily viewed as a provocation. It may be less provocative, however, if the initiating party is the weaker disputant. Even so, the second disputant would have to be convinced that the intermediary is the best choice for itself.[7]

A second route for the initiating disputant is to seek the concurrence of the other disputant before approaching the potential intermediary. This approach can be risky as well. If the disputants find it difficult to agree on the issues in dispute, seeking an intermediary adds one more potentially divisive issue to the bargain. Nevertheless, to employ an intermediary, they need not agree on the important dimensions of the intermediary's role. From the individual disputant's perspective, what matters is identi-fying the dimensions important to oneself, finding an intermediary appro-priately located on those dimensions, and then convincing the other dis-putant to accept it. The designation of procedural and decision-making authority can be a subsequent—but, of course, joint—decision (see "Role Bargain" this chap.).

A third possibility is to wait for an intervenor to step in. The strategic implications of accepting an offer to intervene, rather than soliciting an intervenor, is the flip side of the intervenor's entry question discussed in chapter 4. For the disputant, accepting an intervenor early in an escalat-ing dispute confers advantage vis-à-vis the intermediary on the disputant. The disputant can use its relatively favorable alternative as a bargaining lever with the intervenor over questions of process control, decision-mak-ing authority, and so forth. Of course, to the extent an intervention halts the escalation of destructive acts, the disputant will benefit from an early intervention. At the same time, however, an early intervention may de-tract from the disputant's interest in self-determination or in allowing the dispute to "ripen" so that the full benefits of the conflict can be realized. This would be especially important for the weaker party in an asymmetric bargain.

ROLE BARGAIN

Accepting an intermediary into one's dispute raises specific questions about the intermediary's role. Will it serve coffee, draft solutions, offer incentives, or make the final decision for the disputants? Because interna-tional intermediaries mostly operate ad hoc, what they do is as much a joint decision among disputants and the intermediary as acceptance itself. Every question over procedure and decision-making authority is subject to debate and, ultimately, to veto by either disputant. And these questions change as conditions external to the negotiations (e.g., domestic politics, economic and military conditions) change. Consequently, the role bargain is ongoing and fluid. It changes as the dispute changes and as the intermediary and the disputants gain information and skill. Thus, although an intermediary's role is determined first by structure—that is, depending on its interests in the disputed issues and on its bargaining capabilities, it is a principal or neutral mediator—ongoing decisions over the intermediary's procedural control and its decision-making authority are negotiable items.

An appropriate level of intermediary control over procedures depends on the stage of the conflict, the nature of the intervention, and the disputants' interests in the process. To the extent the dispute has escalated, interactions are intense, and disputants are fixed on positions or resist creative solutions, the disputant may want to grant the intermediary considerable control. In the Beagle Channel case, for example, given the parties' distributive view of the dispute, high tensions, and the near-war, it made sense for both parties to agree to the Pope's suggestion for a site— that is, Vatican City, not, say, Montevideo or Geneva—and to accept strict Vatican control over press coverage (see chap. 8).

If, on the other hand, all the ingredients for agreement are in place and only a neutral location with some process facilitation is needed, then the disputants would want to grant only limited intermediary control. This is often the case in environmental or scientific disputes in which technical details need to be worked out and emotions are relatively low. All parties still have strategic concerns: the environmentalists would not want to conduct meetings in the developer's offices. But because neither law nor convention designates a location for such ad hoc negotiations, the services of an intermediary are needed to provide a neutral place and to facilitate the negotiations. In the Portsmouth case, for example, both Japan and Russia insisted that Roosevelt do no more than provide facilities. To reinforce a limited role, Roosevelt did not even attend the negotiations (see chap. 7).

A second consideration in the disputant's role decision is choosing an appropriate level of decision-making authority. Should the intermediary facilitate discussions, make suggestions, formulate settlement proposals, or make a binding decision? If self-determination is a relatively low priority for the disputant and getting agreement a high one, then, all else equal, an arbitrator would be preferred over a mediator. If efficiency and self-determination are highly valued, a mediator with no authority, yet one who could push for creative solutions, would be better suited.

In sum, the disputant faces a trade-off in its acceptance and initiation decisions. By involving a third party, it risks confounding the dispute with potentially divisive issues related to acceptance, initiation, and role definition. It must continually negotiate with the intermediary and with its

opponent over the intermediary's procedural and decision-making authority. On the other hand, by employing an intermediary, the disputant
may gain relief from wrangling over such minor questions. The disputants
may even escape the burden of a final decision if they can agree to grant
that authority to the third party.

CONCLUSION

Disputants accept a third party for a variety of reasons. What they expect
and what they get may be entirely different, however. At a minimum,
they get more bargaining, maybe not over substance, but at least over
process. The initiation of an intervention and the bargain over role become strategic concerns in their own right, especially to the extent they
are linked to substantive isues. Thus, the prescriptivists may delineate
useful functions for the intermediary, but the intervention's actual impact
on the disputants and their interaction is not strictly facilitative. A third
party—whether a third disputant, a principal mediator, or a neutral mediator—is something to contend with. The third party may, in good faith,
promise substantial benefits, but disputants must be aware that accepting
a third party, even a neutral mediator, let alone a principal mediator,
entails trade-offs. Expected benefits may be high but so may be expected
losses (by, e.g., being excluded by a coalition); the disputants may get
help but they also get another party to deal with (procedural questions,
e.g., may be simplified or confounded by the extra party); the intermediary may be well positioned to propose a "fair" solution, but a more powerful party may do better unilaterally (if, say, the status quo is used as the
baseline, not reservation values); soliciting an intermediary unilaterally
may be intended as a conciliatory gesture but perceived as a provocation
or as a sign of weakness; abdicating decision-making authority may accelerate settlement but reduce self-determination.

In short, acceptance of an intermediary entails uncertainty and risk.
Much like the intermediary's continuing decision to remain in the dispute, the disputant must, in some way, calculate continuously the value of
retaining the intermediary. That calculation changes not only with external factors (economic and military conditions, say) but, for reasons discussed in previous chapters, with unanticipated effects (such as the focal
point impact of the intermediary's suggestions) and the evolving, often
increasingly influential role of the intermediary. Intermediary intervention is, then, neither a technical fix for overcoming the difficulties of negotiations nor a short-cut to a solution. But as I have argued earlier and as
the following case studies illustrate, intermediary intervention may provide just enough boost to a dispute resolution process to tip the balance
away from contention and toward cooperation.

PART TWO

Intermediary Intervention
in Practice: Principal Mediators

Chapter Six

CAMP DAVID: JIMMY CARTER MEDIATES BETWEEN ISRAEL AND EGYPT, 1977–1979

ON MARCH 26, 1979, Israeli Prime Minister Menachem Begin and Egyptian President Anwar el-Sadat met in Washington, D.C., to sign a peace treaty between their two countries. U.S. President Jimmy Carter presided over the signing just as he did much of the negotiating that led up to it. For more than two years, roughly half of his single term of office, Carter committed his personal resources and that of his administration to finding peace in the Middle East. His mediation of a settlement was heralded worldwide as a tremendous achievement, settling many outstanding issues and bringing peace to two arch enemies. At the same time, Carter did not achieve a comprehensive solution, try as he might. Much as Henry Kissinger did in his 1973–1975 disengagement negotiations, Carter eventually resigned himself to dropping the most troubling and most intractable issue—the Palestinian question.

The Camp David process raises many questions about U.S. foreign policy, Middle East relations, diplomatic practice, and the effect of domestic politics on international negotiations. In this chapter, I limit my focus to those features of the U.S. role, especially Jimmy Carter's efforts at Camp David, that reveal what it was like *for the mediator* to attempt to reconcile the irreconcilable. Where most treatments of such negotiations analyze the process as a step in a larger game and gloss over the fine details, here I examine those details for the nuances of meaning and interpretation. I deal explicitly with what Carter did as a mediator and what it meant to him—and to the disputants—to be an intermediary, that is, to be "in between."

The pertinent questions, then, are, What effect did the mediator have on the disputants and their interaction? To what extent was this effect due to Jimmy Carter's leadership style and to what extent was it due to his position as U.S. president? How can the movement toward agreement and the eventual peace treaty be explained? In short, this chapter examines those propositions of part 1 that deal with role bargaining and reconfiguring the bargain. Carter's intervention provides a test case of the structural argument of chapter 2 that principal mediators may bargain with disputants but, try as they might, are constrained in their ability to facilitate negotiations. Unlike, say, Kissinger's Middle East diplomacy or Alexander Haig's Falklands/Malvinas mediation where little pretense was made to do anything other that engage in hard bargaining with the protagonists, here Jimmy Carter sincerely tried to do more; he did try to help the disputants solve their problem. Because this case provides considerable detail of specific interactions between mediator and disputants and because it affords an opportunity to understand how a powerful mediator saw his task, this chapter documents the mediator's limitations through, in part, the effects of cognitive biases and conflictual norms of interaction.

The Camp David case provides a rare opportunity to understand how a powerful mediator saw his task. Jimmy Carter's memoirs serve as my primary data base along with the account of one of his aides, William Quandt.[1] I take their renditions at face value, recognizing the natural human tendency to reconstruct events and decisions in a favorable light. With a focus on the above questions, I do not give a comprehensive account of the Middle East conflict or detail all of Carter's negotiations. Numerous accounts exist, of which several are noted. Rather, I dwell on that part of the Carter intervention that shows how he saw his role as mediator as well as how the two disputing parties saw that role.

THE CASE

From the beginning of his presidency in January 1977, Jimmy Carter saw peace in the Middle East as a major foreign policy objective.

> Human rights, Israeli security, Soviet influence, Middle East peace, oil imports—these would be major concerns of our new administration. I struggled with the questions, and sought advice from all possible sources, only to be told by almost every adviser to stay out of the Middle East situation. It seemed that all the proposed solutions had already been tried and had failed. However, I could see growing threats to the United States in the Middle East, and was willing to make another try—perhaps overly confident that I could now find answers that had eluded so many others. (p. 279)

Carter devoted much of his first months in office to familiarizing himself with the complexities of the conflict. He read voraciously on the topic and sought advice from all quarters. He met with leaders in the region and consulted with Congress and the American Jewish community. In the process, he became convinced that something could be done and that something *had* to be done. For him, there was a moral imperative as well as a strategic necessity to act.

In March 1977, Carter publicly outlined his idea of a just settlement. Israel would have to withdraw to the 1967 lines and a homeland would have to be established for the Palestinians in the West Bank and Gaza. Normal relations between Israel and the Arab states would have to be obtained. In short, a comprehensive settlement was the goal, not interim agreements. These goals could be best accomplished, Carter felt, by reviving the Geneva framework and involving all interested parties, including the PLO and the Soviet Union, in an international conference. Carter subsequently launched an initiative to convene the Geneva Conference.

Menachem Begin, elected Israel's prime minister in May 1977, opposed the U.S. initiative. For ideological as well as security reasons, his administration was more committed than any before to retaining Samaria and Judea (the West Bank) as integral parts of a unified and historically justified Jewish state, "Eretz Israel." Moreover, he refused to negotiate with the PLO and was highly suspicious of the Soviet Union. A resumption of the Geneva Conference, he feared, would leave Israel isolated as both superpowers vied for the sympathy of the Arab states. To resist demands to cede the West Bank, he publicly indicated his willingness to return the Sinai, taken in the October 1973 War, to Egypt.

Carter invited Begin to visit him in Washington in July 1977 to lay out a set of principles Carter considered essential for a comprehensive settlement:

First, that our goal was a truly comprehensive peace, one that would affect all Israel's neighbors; second, that it would be based on United Nations Resolution 242; third, that the definition of peace would be quite broad, including open borders and free trade; fourth, that it would involve Israel's withdrawal from occupied territory to secure borders; and fifth, that a Palestinian entity (not an independent nation) should be created. He [Begin] said that he could agree with all of them except the Palestinian entity.

I then explained to the Prime Minister how serious an obstacle to peace were the Israeli settlements being established within the occupied territories. Israeli leaders continued to permit or encourage additional settlers to move into Arab neighborhoods, sending a signal of their apparent intentions to make the military occupation permanent. I reminded Begin that the position of the U.S. had always been that any settlements established on lands occupied by military force were in violation of international law. He listened very closely, but did not respond. (pp. 290–91)

Carter also stressed that the United States had no plan and no preconditions. The important issues would have to be resolved ultimately through direct negotiations. "We have no desire to be intermediaries."[2]

Begin gave a lengthy review of the history of the Arab-Israeli conflict and stressed the danger to Israel if it should ever return to the 1967 lines. He proposed that Geneva be convened only for an opening session, followed by "mixed commissions" to negotiate separate peace treaties, and then reconvened to sign the peace treaties. In short, he rejected any possibility of a comprehensive settlement through multilateral negotiations. He opposed Carter's view of the Palestinian question as a "mortal danger" to Israel but would take it up with the cabinet.[3] In private talks, Begin told Carter he was making tentative plans to meet directly with Egyptian President, Anwar el-Sadat. Finally, Begin made a brief appeal for military assistance but did not push the matter.

Sadat, in his April 1977 meeting in Washington and in subsequent meetings with U.S. officials, also expressed misgivings about Geneva and the U.S. initiative. He doubted, first, that the interests of all Middle East participants could be reconciled in such a conference. He did not want to jeopardize agreement on the Sinai in a multilateral forum where every party expected to come out with major gains. In addition, his distrust of the Soviet Union was aggravated by U.S.-Soviet secret talks that led to a joint statement on the Middle East in October 1977. These concerns contributed to Sadat's search for alternatives, which began with secret, direct talks with Israel in September 1977 and culminated in his trip to Jerusalem in November 1977.

Sadat's Jerusalem visit produced, by all accounts, a "psychological breakthrough" in the Middle East conflict. It also destroyed any possibility of a U.S.-sponsored Geneva conference. The United States was left with the delicate task of supporting Sadat's conciliatory move, helping him fend off criticisms from his Arab allies and, at the same time, remaining on good terms with Jordan and Saudi Arabia as oil embargoes were a not-so-distant memory. These concerns led the United States to urge Sadat not to make a separate peace with Israel and to urge Israel to reciprocate Sadat's bold initiative.

Subsequent negotiations, some bilateral, some with U.S. participation, revolved around two sets of issues. One set included time schedules for Israel's withdrawal from the Sinai (which Begin expressed his willingness to carry out in their meeting of December 16), security and arms limitation arrangements, the fate of Israeli settlements in the Sinai, and the pace of the normalization of Israeli-Egyptian relations. The second was the Palestinian question and the future of the West Bank and Gaza.

After several weeks of intensive, bilateral talks between the two countries, Begin, before submitting his proposals to his cabinet or to Sadat, took them to Jimmy Carter. He sought not U.S. mediation but U.S. endorsement, which he got. In fact, according to then Foreign Minister Moshe Dayan, at this time Begin's "goal [was] direct face-to-face negotiations [with Egypt], without intermediaries, and under no foreign patronage."[4] Having consulted with Washington, Begin then traveled to Ismailiya on the banks of the Suez Canal to deliver his proposals to Sadat on December 25, 1977. Sadat reacted coolly, countering with a proposal to issue a declaration of principles, which Begin rejected. The two leaders then agreed to set up two joint committees, one military and the other political, to agree on principles. These and a multilateral conference hosted by Egypt failed to make progress. Shortly after the Ismailiya talks, Israel began work on four new settlements in the Sinai Penninsula.

While the direct bilateral efforts were taking place, the United States worked to soften Saudi and Jordanian criticism and served as an intermediary between Egypt on the one hand and Saudi Arabia and Jordan on the other. At the invitation of Israel and Egypt, the United States participated in the political committee talks that broke down in January 1978. But as relations between Israel and Egypt deteriorated, the United States intensified its efforts to break the deadlock, including a public campaign to mobilize U.S. domestic support for Carter's position on settlements and withdrawal. Some of Carter's aides suggested moving toward a strategy of collusion with Sadat to bring pressure on Begin. Carter was disinclined to use such techniques but when movement became increasingly unlikely, Carter entertained the idea of a more active role.

> Whenever we seemed to be having some success with the Arabs, Begin would proclaim the establishment of another group of settlements, or make other provocative statements. This behavior was not only very irritating, but it seriously endangered the prospects for peace and Sadat's status both in Egypt and within the Arab world. The repeated Israeli invasions or bombings of Lebanon also precipitated crises; a stream of fairly harsh messages was going back and forth between me in Washington and Begin in Jerusalem.
>
> Secretary of State Vance spent a lot of time in the two countries trying to keep the negotiations going, but his was a difficult and thankless task. At a banquet in Israel attended by Cy and the Egyptian negotiating team, Prime Minister Begin's opening remarks offended the Egyptians. President Sadat ordered the withdrawal of all Egyptians from Israel and threatened to conclude the peace talks altogether. I called to urge him to leave his negotiators in Jerusalem, but he refused. (pp. 304–5)
>
> We were not making progress, and Sadat was letting us know that he was preparing to renounce the talks with Israel because of his growing embarrassment and frustration. We cast about for some action to be taken, and for the first time discussed the possibility of inviting both Begin and Sadat to Camp David to engage in extensive negotiations with me. (p. 305)

First, however, Carter invited Sadat to Washington in February. Sadat expressed his bitterness toward Begin after the Ismailiya talks and said he was convinced Begin did not want peace. He was prepared to call off all further talks. Subsequently, Dayan, Weizman, and, finally, in March 1967, Begin came to Washington. Carter recounts his conversation with Begin:

He was "wounded in the heart" when his December plan [offering to withdraw from the Sinai] had first received words of praise which had later faded away. That Sadat's visit to Jerusalem was only a grand gesture; that Egypt wanted an independent Palestinian state and total withdrawal. I told him this was absolutely not true. I knew for a fact. And if my presumption was correct, what would he be willing to do to achieve peace? The answer, in effect, was nothing beyond what he had already promised.[5]

Carter then outlined six points that would require policy changes by Israel, and Begin responded with what became known as the "six noes." Carter was exasperated:

Again, I was prepared to withdraw from the Middle East issue altogether. It would be a great relief to me, and I certainly had my hands full with other responsibilities. . . . it was clear to everyone on both sides of the table that, unless he changed his positions, Begin was becoming an insurmountable obstacle to further progress.

This was a heartbreaking development, and I began to inform the congressional leaders who supported Israel about our failure, being careful to describe the positions of Sadat and Begin as accurately as I could, checking each point with my personal notes. Some of them met with Prime Minister Begin and confirmed "the six no's." They, too, were discouraged.[6]

Little transpired in the coming months. Trips by Vice-president Walter Mondale and Secretary of State Cyrus Vance produced nothing. In July, Sadat announced publicly that there would be no further negotiations and demanded that the Israeli military team leave Egypt.

Although failure of his peacemaking efforts seemed inevitable, Jimmy Carter nevertheless viewed continued deadlock as a threat to U.S. interests. Suspended negotiations would lead to renewed tensions and, quite possibly, war in the region and another oil embargo. What is more, the last extension of the term of the UN peacekeeping force was about to expire. A new initiative, although necessary to break the deadlock, was risky especially in light of domestic pressures to abandon the entire effort.

I was really in a quandary. I knew how vital peace in the Middle East was to the United States, but many Democratic members of Congress and party officials were urging me to back out of the situation and to repair the damage they claimed I had already done to the Democratic party and to United States-Israeli relations. It seemed particularly ironic to be so accused, when I was trying to bolster our relations with Israel and strengthen its security. . . . (pp. 315–16)

There was no prospect for success if Begin and Sadat stayed apart, and their infrequent meetings had now become fruitless because the two men were too personally incompatible to compromise on the many difficult issues facing them. I finally decided it would be best, win or lose, to go all out. There was only one thing to do, as dismal and unpleasant as the prospect seemed—I would try to bring Sadat and Begin together for an extensive negotiating session with me. (p. 316)

The site would be Camp David, the presidential retreat in the forested mountains of Maryland. Both Begin and Sadat agreed enthusiastically to the Camp David invitation but no one expected much to be accomplished.

All of us wanted to minimize expectations, citing clarification of the issues as our objective. I had something much more substantive in mind, but had a lot of work to do before my ideas would be clear.

I told Cy to send messages to many of the world leaders, brief and noncontroversial, asking for their support. We'll ask the religious leaders to set aside a week of special prayer. . . . We will use every influence we have at Camp David to make it successful, and not put a time limit on how long we stay there. We will have no press contact. . . . We will have to keep Sadat and Begin convinced before they get here that they must make concessions and negotiate freely. They both agreed not to have negative statements issued between now and the convening of the meeting. (Diary, August 10, 1978)

After our original decision to go to Camp David, I was deluged with warnings from my closest advisers and friends. . . . No one, including me, could think of a specific route to success, but everyone could describe a dozen logical scenarios for failure—and all were eager to do so. I slowly became hardened against them, and as stubborn as at any other time I can remember. (p. 317)

Carter's press aides complained bitterly about his decision to exclude the press. But for Carter, this was a last-ditch effort for which any personal political gain was of minor concern.

I felt that in going to Camp David we would be burning our bridges, that the meeting was an all-or-nothing gamble, and that what the press might report during the negotiating session was no longer important to me. It was imperative that there be a minimum of posturing by Egyptians or Israelis, and an absence of public statements, which would become frozen positions that could not subsequently be changed. (p. 318)

The meetings were held in the secluded environs of Camp David. The mass media were indeed excluded, and all sides were requested to refrain from discussing the negotiations with the press. The atmosphere of the meetings was informal. There was no protocol for table seating at meals or for dress. Carter wore faded blue jeans and the delegates were encouraged to dress as they pleased. Dayan wore khaki slacks but the Egyptians were quite formal, although ties were not common.

Although Carter expected the conference to take about three days, he was prepared to remain until they reached agreement—that is, at least until they signed an agreement for peace between Egypt and Israel with an agenda for implementation during the succeeding months. There were no regular working hours. Many of the meetings took place in the evening, especially with the Israelis, and went into the early hours of the morning. Jimmy Carter set the tone for hard work and long hours. Dayan:

> President Carter was indefatigable. Apart from the long hours of consultation with his aides and hard bargaining with the other delegations, he spent much time preparing himself for such meetings by trying to master every detail of the subjects under negotiations.[7]

The summit began on Tuesday, September 5, 1978 with the Egyptian delegation the first to arrive. Carter asked Sadat to talk immediately, and Sadat obliged by laying out his thoughts and plans. He indicated he would be flexible on all issues but land and sovereignty. Carter told him he would delay suggesting any of his own proposals until after he and Begin had a chance "to explore all their differences."

Two hours later, Carter received Menachem Begin.

> I had wanted to generate an atmosphere of informality from the beginning, but in his attitude and words, Begin approached the initiation of talks in a very thorough and methodical way. His questions were not about substance; he was concerned about the daily schedule, the procedures to be followed, the time and place of meetings, how a record of the proceedings would be kept, how many aides would be permitted on each side, and so forth. . . . I responded that my preference was to meet privately and separately with him and Sadat first, and then the three of us could decide how best to proceed.[8]

Carter asked both sides to refrain from relaying to the outside world any information about negotiating positions or successes and failures as the talks progressed.

> There is no doubt in my mind that success would have been impossible if we had explained our own opinions or goals to the press each day. It would have been difficult to be flexible, with every necessary change in position being interpreted as a defeat for one or more of the negotiating parties.
>
> I discovered later that there had been an additional restraint on unauthorized conversations: both the Egyptians and the Israelis had naturally assumed that we were tapping their telephones. However, this was not the case. (p. 331)

The evening of the first day, Carter again met with Begin.

My first goal that evening was to put him at ease and assure him there would be no surprises. I described my understanding of Israel's special problems and positions, and emphasized again the importance of our meeting. I told him we had plenty of time. We were isolated at Camp David and could remain so as long as necessary to reach agreement. We should not depend on referring problems to our subordinates to solve at a later time. I assured him that we would have no bilateral secrets, and that I would not give to Sadat nor to him any official United States proposals without discussing the unofficial drafts first with both sides.

Where we could not reach a final agreement on an issue at Camp David, I said, we should carefully define what differences remained, so that we would not later have to start at the beginning of the debate. I reserved the right, and had the duty, to put forward proposals, and might on occasion merely adopt either the Egyptian or the Israeli position if I believed it to be best. I would not be timid, but would not deal in surprises, I assured him again. Begin insisted repeatedly that the Israelis see any American proposal before it was presented to Sadat, and claimed that he had an official commitment from President Ford that this procedure would be followed. I assumed that my approach would not violate that commitment.

I spelled out to Begin the advantages of a good rapport between him and Sadat during the days ahead. I believed that as they got to know each other, it would be easier for them to exchange ideas without rancor or distrust. Yet in fact, for the last ten days of negotiation leading up to our final agreement, the two men never spoke to one another, although their cottages were only about a hundred yards apart. (pp. 332–33)

Begin then outlined his views, stressing the crucial issue of Israeli security. He discussed Sinai, UN Resolution 242, the West Bank, and so forth. On each topic, Begin established Israel's position which was either resolute or would have to be dealt with in future negotiations. On the Palestinian question, for example, Begin promised "full autonomy" but would not elaborate on what exactly that ambiguous term meant.

In general, the conversation was discouraging. I had hoped that Begin would bring some new proposals to Camp David, but the Prime Minister simply repeated almost verbatim the old Israeli negotiating positions. There were few indications of flexibility, but at least I made it clear that we wanted final decisions at Camp David and that we were going to put forward our positions forcefully. He agreed with this—without apparent enthusiasm. . . .

With Begin's permission, I had taken very careful notes, to ensure accurate transmission of his views to President Sadat the next day. (p. 337)

The next morning, Carter relayed Begin's views to Sadat, who responded by noting that Begin was bitter and inclined to look back into history rather than to deal with the present and the future. Sadat, by contrast,

> promised to go to extremes in being flexible, in order to uncover the full meaning of Begin's positions, and stated that if our efforts at Camp David should be unsuccessful, then when the equitable Egyptian proposal were made known, they would bring the condemnation of the world on the Israeli leader. (pp. 338–39)

Sadat then presented Carter with an opening proposal, one that took extreme positions on some issues and shocked Carter. Sadat assured Carter he could make modifications, but he asked Carter not to reveal them at this early stage in the negotiations. Despite the harshness of the written proposal, Carter was encouraged by Sadat's indicated flexibility.

That afternoon, Carter brought Sadat and Begin together for direct talks. As for his function, Carter

> decided to play a minimal role during these first sessions, so that the two leaders could become better acquainted and have a more fruitful exchange. I knew what they had to say—I could have recited some of the more pertinent passages in my sleep. (p. 343)

The two began by sharing their expectations for the meeting and the issues to be discussed. Begin wanted to deal with the Sinai and avoid the West Bank and Palestinian questions. Sadat was determined to address all three issues, and Carter supported him in his rejection of a separate agreement. Begin and Sadat also disagreed on linkages between Sinai withdrawal and West Bank autonomy. Where Begin saw months of technical details to be worked out, Sadat saw the immediate possibility of a comprehensive framework for peace. With these preliminary remarks, Sadat presented his proposal, which Begin promised to read carefully.

Thursday morning, the third day, Carter met with Begin and his aides for a vigorous, often heated, discussion of Sadat's proposal. Then Begin and Sadat met again privately with Carter. This time, the cordiality of the previous day dropped by the wayside.

Begin began by discussing Sadat's proposal, vigorously refuting one point after another. The discussion became tense and heated when they argued about who defeated whom and, especially, when they turned to the question of land. Then Sadat, according to Carter,

> leaned forward in his chair, pointed his finger at Begin, and exclaimed, "Premier Begin, you want land!" Sadat reminded us that the disputed phrase was

extracted directly from United Nations Resolution 242, which all of us agreed to be the foundation of our peace efforts. He was fervent in condemning "the Israeli settlements on my land."

All restraint was now gone. Their faces were flushed, and the niceties of diplomatic language and protocol were stripped away. They had almost forgotten that I was there, and there was nothing to distract me from recording this fascinating debate.

Begin repeated that no Israeli leader could possibly advocate the dismantling of the Sinai settlements, and he added that four other conditions would have to be met before the Sinai could be returned to Egypt.

Begin had touched a raw nerve, and I thought Sadat would explode. He pounded the table, shouting that land was not negotiable, especially land in the Sinai and Golan Heights. Those borders were internationally recognized. He pointed out that for thirty years the Israelis had desired full recognition, no Arab boycott, and guaranteed security. He was giving them all of that. He wanted them to be secure. "Security, yes! Land, no!" he shouted. . . . he must terminate the discussions if Begin continued to prove that he wanted land.

Begin was calmer than Sadat. He responded that he had already demonstrated his good will by changing a long-standing policy of his government concerning the Sinai land between Eilat and Sharm el-Sheyk. His predecessors had been determined to keep this land, and he was offering it back to Egypt, which was very difficult for him. (p. 351)

For Carter, this was a "fruitless discussion." The topic shifted to Lebanon and democracy, and then Sadat raised the question of trust. He, according to Carter,

said that the warm feelings he had developed during his visit to Jerusalem had been destroyed because "minimum confidence does not exist anymore since Premier Begin has acted in bad faith."

I [Carter] replied that this mutual feeling of bad faith was something I would like to correct, that they were both honorable, decent, and courageous men, and that I knew both of them well. Respect was warranted on both sides, but misunderstandings had to be cleared away. I used as an illustration the most irritating example, Sadat's statement in Jerusalem, "My forces will not exceed the Mitla and Gidi passes." Begin had misinterpreted what he meant, and had subsequently inferred that Sadat was not a man of his word. Sadat then felt that Begin did not trust him, and resented it deeply. We discussed this point for fifteen confusing minutes. . . .

I acted as a referee and put them back on track, and on occasion explained what was meant when there was an obvious misinterpretation. (p. 353)

Carter concluded the meeting by reciting a long list of questions and

problems left outstanding. In his view, the meeting was largely unpro-
ductive:

> We had accomplished little so far except to name the difficult issues. There
> was no compatibility between the two men, and almost every discussion of
> any subject deteriorated into an unproductive argument, reopening old
> wounds of past political or military battles. (p. 355)

In their next meeting that afternoon, Begin repeated his desire to turn
matters over to technical officials to work out before approval by the heads
of state. Sadat saw this as a waste of time, arguing that they needed specific guidance from the leaders and that such matters should be settled
here at Camp David. Each leader then expressed the sacrifices he had
made and the clear signals he had given to indicate his country's profound
desire for peace. But when the discussion turned to Sinai settlements,
Sadat announced angrily that a stalemate had been reached and that he
saw no reason to continue. Carter:

> I was desperate, and quickly outlined the areas of agreement and the adverse
> consequences to both men if the peace effort foundered at this point because
> of the differences we had just discussed. I emphasized the United States' role
> in the Middle East, and reminded them that a new war in this troubled
> region under present conditions could easily escalate into another world war.
> I asked them to give me at least one more day to understand as best I could
> the positions of the two delegations, to devise my own compromise propos-
> als, and to present my views to both of them. I pointed out to Prime Minister
> Begin that if the only cause for his rejection of the peace effort was the Sinai
> settlers, I did not believe the people of his nation or the Knesset would agree
> with him. It was my belief that he could sell this action to his people if he
> would let the settlers leave Egyptian territory.
>
> He disputed this, saying that there was *no way* he could sell a dismantling
> of the Israeli settlements to his government or to his people. . . . To move
> the settlers would mean the downfall of his government—an outcome he was
> willing to accept if he believed in the cause. But he did *not* believe in it.
>
> They were moving toward the door, but I got in front of them to partially
> block the way. I urged them not to break off their talks, to give me another
> chance to use my influence and analysis, to have confidence in me. Begin
> agreed readily. I looked straight at Sadat; finally, he nodded his head. They
> left without speaking to each other. (p. 359)

Over the next several days, Carter met with his staff, with the Egyptian
delegation, with the Israeli delegation, and—separately—with Sadat and
Begin. He explored the nuance of each position, seeking an opening for
change. He pushed for flexibility and tried to explain to one side the views

and commitments of the other. But it looked hopeless. "A sense of gloom and foreboding still prevailed, and my personal notes indicate how anxious I was" (p. 364)

Sinai settlements proved a major stumbling block. On this, Begin stated emphatically that he would never personally recommend that the settlements in the Sinai be dismantled. He added, according to Carter, "'Please, Mr. President, do not make this a United States demand,'" (p. 365) and later in the same discussion, "'Mr. President, do not put this in a proposal to us'" (p. 366)

Begin said there had to be two agreements. The most important was between the United States and Israel; an Israel-Egypt agreement was of secondary importance. Carter came to see Israel's preference as working in his favor.

> It was true that the relationship between our two nations was vital to Israel, but I also knew it was a good negotiating tactic by either Sadat or Begin first to reach agreement with me and then to have the two of us confront the third. Sadat had understood this strategy before he arrived at Camp David. Begin was just now beginning to realize the disadvantage of being odd man out. I must admit that I capitalized on this situation with both delegations in order to get an agreement; it greatly magnified my own influence. (p. 366)

As for West Bank settlements, Begin implored Carter not to include them in the discussions nor to mention them in any United States plan.

> I replied that I could not agree that I would produce a plan which excluded the settlements, and asked him bluntly if he objected to our producing a United States proposal at all.
>
> He answered that he did indeed object, that he had always thought it was a bad idea. This was a belated admission of an attitude that had become apparent to us all. Begin went on to say that any United States plan would become the focal point of dissension and disagreement after we adjourned from Camp David, and that there was no likelihood of its being accepted by either the Israelis or the Arabs. . . .
>
> I said, "This atmosphere between the two of you is not conducive to any agreement. We are going to present a comprehensive proposal for peace. It will not surprise either you or Sadat. When it is finished tomorrow, I will present it to you first, and then to the Egyptians. I can see no other possibility for progress." (p. 367)

Carter then informed Sadat of his meeting with Begin and his intention to present a United States proposal. He added,

> The time for the three of us to meet together was over. I would continue to meet individually with the two leaders, back and forth, until the best possible

compromise had been evolved, at which point the three of us, along with our key advisers, would all meet. (p. 368)

Thereafter, Carter and his team met separately with Begin and Sadat. Trilateral meetings did, however, continue at the technical level with lower level officials. Once, Carter spent an entire day negotiating and drafting text with the legal experts of both sides. Weizman and Dayan each met Sadat several times, and other members of the two delegations met directly as well.

Carter personally worked on the proposal, striving to create one fair to both sides and one that would not violate Sadat's two fundamental principles—land and sovereignty over the Golan Heights and Sinai. It would also have to be sold to the Israeli delegation. Delivering the proposal to Begin on Sunday, the sixth day at Camp David, Carter explained that

> this document is not meant for publication. . . . On the settlements, anything acceptable to both you and Sadat is all right with me. My commitment is to continue to try to represent your interests and to negotiate for you with Sadat, and I will help in any way possible, including withdrawing from direct involvement, if that is necessary. (p. 374)

Begin replied that because both Egypt and the United States had given their proposals, he would produce his own because all three should be published. A heated discussion then ensued about several points in the U.S. proposal, especially the reference to UN Resolution 242.

The U.S. proposal, presented to Sadat the next day, was the basis for intense discussion among all participants over the next several days. Moods shifted frequently as obstacles were overcome only to discover new ones. At one point, on the eighth day, Begin presented Carter with a document to end the negotiations. It stated only that the meeting took place and that Israel thanked the United States for its efforts. Undeterred, Carter and his aides continued to try to hammer out a mutually acceptable agreement. But on the tenth day, negotiations became hopelessly stuck on the question of settlements. Having exhausted all conceivable solutions, Carter and his team resigned themselves to failure and prepared a joint statement outlining points of agreement and of difference between the two sides. Even that small achievement was nearly denied, however, when Sadat, after a heated discussion with Dayan, requested a helicopter and packed his bags to leave. Carter:

> It was a terrible moment. Now, even my hopes for a harmonious departure were gone. I sat quietly and assessed the significance of this development—a rupture between Sadat and me, and its consequences for my country and for the Middle East power balance. I envisioned the ultimate alliance of most of

the Arab nations to the Soviet Union, perhaps joined by Egypt after a few months had passed. (pp. 391–92)

Then he went to Sadat:

I explained to him the extremely serious consequences of his unilaterally breaking off the negotiations: that his action would harm the relationship between Egypt and the United States, he would be violating his personal promise to me, and the onus for failure would be on him. I described the possible future progress of Egypt's friendships and alliances—from us to the moderate and then radical Arabs, thence to the Soviet Union. I told him it would damage one of my most precious possessions—his friendship and our mutual trust. (p. 392)

Sadat reconsidered and the U.S. team resumed its search for an acceptable formula for settlement. In the ensuing days, with even more ups and downs, progress was made. Not until the last day, Sunday, a deadline Carter set, was agreement in sight. Even then, a last-minute objection by the Israelis to a letter accompanying the agreement nearly destroyed everything. Sunday evening, the thirteenth day of negotiations, Begin, Sadat, and Carter signed the Camp David accords at the White House.

The accords consisted of two documents, "The Framework of Peace in the Middle East" and "The Framework for the Conclusion of a Peace Treaty between Egypt and Israel." Although these were momentous achievements, a peace treaty still had to be signed. The Camp David accords were the basis for the negotiations to conclude a treaty. In many ways, Carter was to discover, the hard part lay ahead.

With Camp David behind them, the details of a treaty now had to be worked out in full view of the press and domestic constituencies. All three leaders faced significant challenges at home. Begin faced severe criticism especially from within his own party regarding the "full autonomy" promised the Palestinians. Sadat, although secure in his own domestic position, was concerned about Arab reaction. And for Carter, the 1980 election was getting uncomfortably close. Moreover, the Iranian revolution posed new problems in the region.

The Israeli Knesset voted in favor of the accords on September 27, 1978. The next day the United States promised Israel support in building two airfields in the Negev. The U.S. team prepared a draft treaty, and representatives from both sides commenced negotiations in Washington on October 11. Among the many issues left outstanding, Israel wanted access to Sinai oil and wanted a guarantee from the United States should Egypt renege. It also needed help to pay for the withdrawal of troops from the Sinai, a cost that could be as high as $2 billion. For its part, Egypt needed something for the Palestinians lest it be isolated in the Arab world and jeopardize some $2 billion it was receiving from Saudi Arabia.

Carter, anxious to speed up the process, on October 17 personally intervened. When Dayan offered to accelerate the withdrawal, Carter agreed to consider financing it. By October 22, treaty terms were agreed upon and readied for submission to the respective governments. Begin got cabinet support for the existing draft and then announced he was "thickening" settlements on the West Bank. Carter was furious. He wrote Begin, "At a time when we are trying to organize the negotiations dealing with the West Bank and Gaza, no step by the Israeli government could be more damaging." He added, "I have to tell you with gravest concern and regret that taking this step at this time will have the most serious consequences for our relationship."[9] The next day the Nobel Peace Prize was awarded to Begin and Sadat.

Talks resumed in Washington with the Israelis showing increasing interest in U.S. commitments as part of the treaty. Dayan wanted a letter stating how the United States would guarantee the implementation of the treaty. He wanted the United States to assume responsibility for supplying an alternative to the UN forces if these should not be forthcoming and to address matters arising from Israel's withdrawal from the Sinai oil fields. He also wanted to revise and to update all previous U.S.-Israeli memorandums of understanding. Weizman added that Israel's final withdrawal from the Sinai should be made contingent on the completion of the Negev airfields (with U.S. assistance).

At the same time Israel was pressing for greater U.S. commitments, it seemed to be reneging on its commitments to the Palestinians, especially elections in the West Bank and Gaza. In response, Brzezinski urged Carter to reduce aid to Israel by a certain amount for each new settlement and to postpone decisions on aid until Begin accepted a target date for elections.[10] Carter decided Vance should not go to the Middle East as earlier proposed, concluding that Israel indeed wanted a separate peace with Egypt while keeping the West Bank and Gaza permanently. Vance did meet Begin in New York and carried a letter from Carter informing Begin that the peace treaty was now in doubt. In reply, Begin refused to consider a target date for elections or to accelerate withdrawal. In addition, he demanded that U.S. aid for the withdrawal take the form of a grant, not a loan.

Meanwhile, Sadat was becoming increasingly impatient as the Israelis seemed to be backtracking and as the Arab world and many of his advisers stepped up their criticism. To Sadat, Begin was stalling because everyone knew Carter's position was weakening as the U.S. elections got closer.

On November 21, 1978, the Israeli cabinet voted to accept the text of the treaty and annexes but rejected the letter setting a target date at the end of 1979 for elections in the West Bank and Gaza. Begin informed Carter that Israel also wanted to resolve the question of a grant from the United States to cover withdrawal costs and that it needed assurances on oil. As if to make it even more difficult, Egypt now insisted on a presence in Gaza. By early December Carter had to reassess the chances of securing a peace treaty, especially before the U.S. election got into full swing. According to Quandt, "In a somber mood Carter said that if the negotiations failed, he wanted it to be clear that Sadat was not to blame. He wanted to be on Sadat's side. The Israelis would have nowhere else to go in any event" (p. 280). Carter decided to send Vance to the Middle East once again. He told him to press Israel hard, even if that ended up costing him Jewish support and the election.

Vance went first to Egypt and secured Sadat's acceptance of the revised draft. In Israel, Begin seemed to suspect U.S.-Egyptian collusion, reacting angrily to Vance's admission that the United States supported the Egyptian position including Sadat's latest proposals which, in Begin's view, deviated from the Camp David accords. Returning to Cairo, Sadat seemed pleased at Begin's reaction. Stalemate had clearly been reached at the end of 1978.

In early 1979, with the elections approaching and with the fall of the shah of Iran, Carter needed a political success. The only conceivable foreign policy achievement was a peace treaty between Egypt and Israel. In February, Carter asked Begin and Sadat to send representatives to Washington for what became known as "Camp David II." Little was achieved, however, because Israel's representative, Moshe Dayan, was given little authority to negotiate. So Carter asked Begin to come to Washington, but the meeting was disappointing. Carter then decided, in "an act of desperation," to go to the Middle East.

Two days before his departure, the Israeli cabinet approved all of the new U.S. proposals, so Carter had good reason to expect a prompt success. He went first to Egypt where he and Sadat celebrated the close ties between their countries. Carter pledged to get the best possible agreement for Egypt while in Israel. He promised Sadat that once the treaty was signed, he "could plan for a 'massive' government-to-government relationship in the military and economic fields."[11]

Arriving in Israel on March 10, 1979, Carter was shocked to be told by Begin that there was no chance of concluding the negotiations and signing the peace treaty because the Knesset first had to debate the agreement. The ensuing talks were accusatory and bitter. Carter tried to appease Begin by promising a U.S. guarantee of Israel's oil supply and to relax several of Sadat's demands. The U.S. team, including Carter, then labored for hours to try to find language acceptable to Begin. Before the meeting broke up, Carter again pleaded with Begin to try to reach agreement in the next day or so. Begin replied that the sky would not fall if agreement was not reached. After Begin and Carter made speeches to the Knesset, the two teams met again. Begin said that the talks were over and a joint communique should be issued announcing that some progress had been made. Carter ordered his plane to be prepared to return directly to Washington but because it was late in the day, they stayed overnight. Meanwhile, Dayan and Weizman were working the cabinet and came up with some new proposals the Americans could make. The two Israelis also conferred with Begin. That morning Begin agreed to the new proposals and said he would recommend them to the Knesset. Agreement was in hand. Carter flew directly to Cairo and with Sadat announced to the press that a peace treaty would be signed.

The ceremony took place in Washington, March 26, 1979. That day, the United States also signed a memorandum of agreement with Israel guaranteeing the treaty. As for military aid, the U.S. committed $3 billion, of which $800 million would be in the form of grants, to help construct the Negev airfields. The United States also told Israel it was prepared to act positively on a number of weapons systems that had been requested earlier. The United States promised Egypt similar assistance, including military equipment and $1.5 billion in aid over the next three years.

ANALYSIS OF CARTER'S INTERVENTION

To understand Jimmy Carter's intervention in the Israeli-Egyptian conflict, it is necessary to understand how his practice affected the disputants and their interaction. In this section, I examine the three parties' contrasting views of the mediator's role and of the conflict and the steps that facilitated or impeded movement toward agreement.

The nature of an intervention and its effect on the dispute is determined in part by how the parties conceive of the dispute resolution process. For Camp David, the question is, How did the parties—Israel and Egypt as well as the United States—view the bargaining process? Was this yet another example of the United States persuading, cajoling, and, where necessary, pressuring, to get the parties to accept its idea of a Middle East settlement? Was this power politics as usual, hard bargaining where all concerned (including the United States) had major interests at stake? Was each disputing party sticking to its positions while considering what carrots and sticks the mediator might employ if they agreed?

Or was there something different going on here, a different approach that the man Jimmy Carter brought to the conflict? Was the process he advocated, the secluded Camp David negotiations, the emphasis on personal relations, the concern for religious and moral commitments, unlike those pursued in the past? Did Carter create a negotiating environment fundamentally different from that of his predecessors—U.S. presidents and secretaries of state, UN Secretaries General, and others—who had tried to achieve peace in the Middle East? Did Carter elicit underlying interests and increase understanding to the point where agreement was virtually the only rational choice? In short, did President Carter perform chiefly a "principal mediator" role, playing the three-way coalitional bargaining game and trading on U.S. resources to meet U.S. interests? Or did he assume the mantle of "neutral mediator," aiming for improved communication and understanding? To address these questions, I first examine the three parties' views of the intermediary's role.

The Intermediary's Perspective

A peculiar feature of mediation as a decision-making process is that it is fundamentally an ad hoc process, especially in the international realm. More regularized processes include official diplomatic exchange, adjudication, and review and judgment by international organizations. But when an international mediator enters a dispute, more often than not the mediator has little idea of what to do or what to expect. Unlike conventional diplomacy or adjudication, there are few guidelines and even fewer rules. A mediator steps in between with little more than a prayer and a hope of bringing the two sides together.

Lacking a formal role definition, a mediator naturally starts with what he or she knows best.[12] A retired judge mediating in a corporate "minitrial" adheres to legal precedents and procedures of evidence. A Catholic priest conducts prayers and seeks confessions of sorts. A geopolitical realist like Henry Kissinger engages in secret deals and manipulations. For his part, Jimmy Carter, although president of the most powerful country on earth, initially drew on his problem-solving skills as an engineer and on a set of moral standards as a religious person to guide him as a mediator in the Middle East conflict. In Carter's second presidential debate in 1976, for example, he stated that the Arab boycott of U.S. businesses trading with Israel was a disgrace, "It's not a matter of diplomacy or trade with me; it's a matter of morality."[13] He felt compelled to do what was "right," to protect the rights of all peoples in the Middle East, not just America's staunchest ally, Israel, but, increasingly, Egypt, the Palestinians, and other Arab countries. Above all, he felt compelled to do all possible to bring peace to a troubled region.

> Since I had made our nation's commitment to human rights a central tenet of our foreign policy, it was impossible for me to ignore the very serious problems on the West Bank. The continued deprivation of Palestinian rights was not only used as the primary lever against Israel, but was contrary to the basic

moral and ethical principles of both our countries. . . . We needed to resolve
the underlying problems rather than see continued violence, which threatened to spread beyond the Middle East and even to involve the superpowers. (p. 277)

He believed in the basic goodness of humankind, that conflict could be
overcome if the protagonists understood each other and appreciated each
other's basically good intentions. As Camp David began, he noted that

> there was no compatibility at all between Begin and Sadat on which to base
> any progress. This warmer relationship would have to be created from
> scratch. . . . (p. 328)
>
> I spelled out to Begin the advantages of a good rapport between him and
> Sadat during the days ahead. I believed that as they got to know each other,
> it would be easier for them to exchange ideas without rancor or distrust. (p.
> 333)

What is more, Carter saw conflict in very personal terms. Quandt expresses it this way:

> The idealist in Carter also played a role. The president deeply believed that
> men of good will could resolve problems by talking to one another. At Camp
> David he initially thought he would need only to get Sadat and Begin to-
> gether and help them overcome their mutual dislike. The agreement itself
> would then be worked out by the two leaders in a spirit of compromise and
> accommodation. The depth of their distrust, even hatred, was hard for him
> to understand.[14]

Above all, Jimmy Carter viewed the Middle East conflict as solvable.
Although fully aware of the great difficulties and the few successes of his
predecessors, Carter found the conflict to be fundamentally tractable. It
was a complex problem requiring complex analysis and new ideas, but
once the right formula was discovered, peace would be at hand. To be
sure, the parties might need pushing at times, but once they talked to
each other and saw that the benefits of peace outweighed the expected
outcome of delay, they too would come around.

> In order to achieve a comprehensive peace settlement serious obstacles had
> to be overcome. There had never been any direct communication between
> the governments in conflict except for rare clandestine meetings. . . .
>
> Most previous peace efforts, therefore, had been designed either to end
> one of the frequent military engagements or merely to devise some means by
> which negotiations could begin. The status quo sometimes seemed to suit the
> major protagonists, but I feared it could not be maintained for long.[15]

For a U.S. role, Carter saw both a moral and a political dimension.
First, Carter saw a moral obligation to seek peace. He and his country

owed it to all concerned—the Israelis, the Arab countries, and the Palestinians—to bring peace to the region. With the ever-present threat that
another Middle East war would engage the two superpowers in direct
conflict, world peace demanded a solution. And from the narrower U.S.
perspective, the threats of oil cutoffs and Soviet encroachment in the region were all the more reason to bring an end to the regional conflict.

These concerns, then, constituted Jimmy Carter's initial interests as an
intermediary. The effect of the U.S. intervention on the dispute resolution process was in part a function of these interests, a point I will come to
shortly. The intervention was also due to the mediator's particular approach to getting settlement. Three features of Carter's approach stand
out.

One, Carter saw his function as primarily that of a facilitator. It was
their conflict and they had to resolve it. "I continued to pray devoutly that
they could do so, and was especially thankful for their new independence
from us. . . . We want as much responsibility as possible to be on Begin
and Sadat" (p. 298).

Two, although the job was theirs to do, Carter would have to come up
with the right formula because neither Sadat nor Begin nor any of Carter's
predecessors had done so. In fact, to resolve the apparent contradiction
between encouraging the disputants' independence and finding the right
formula for them, early in his presidency Carter says that

> After meeting with these key Arab leaders, I was convinced that all of them
> were ready for a strong move on our part to find solutions to the long-standing
> disputes and that with such solutions would come their recognition of Israel
> and the right of Israelis to live in peace (p. 288). . . .
>
> I knew that any proposal would be doomed if it originated with us alone or
> bilaterally with either of the other two countries. Acceptable plans must al-
> ways seem to come from joint negotiations. Of course, I also wanted Sadat
> and Begin to keep as much direct responsibility as possible for the success of
> the peace talks. (p. 306)

Thus, Carter viewed the primary task of the facilitating mediator to be
to find a formula while leaving responsibility for agreement to the dispu
tants. Indeed, consistent with his training as an engineer, Carter's first
step as a mediator was to master the facts and then present his solution. In
his first meeting with then Prime Minister Yitzhak Rabin, he led off with
his concept of the principles necessary for a solution. If he saw this as
"mediating," it was not in the sense of eliciting underlying interests and
helping each side explore options. Rather, he appeared to feel that, presented with a reasonable formula, reasonable men could not help but
agree; from there, only the details need be worked out and peace would
be achieved. In other words, he was the engineering consultant building
a bridge across a great chasm separating the principal parties. Only he

could see the project from both sides because the protagonists necessarily had their own parochial views. Consequently, he would develop a mutually acceptable blueprint and then the three of them would proceed to build the bridge. All the two disputants needed to do was give him the necessary information. As it turned out, much to Carter's consternation, they (especially Begin) did not cooperate. On the third day at Camp David, Carter describes his heated conversation with Begin:

> I became angry, and almost shouted, "What do you actually want for Israel if peace is signed? How many refugees and what kind can come back? I need to know whether you need to monitor the border, what military outposts are necessary to guard your security. What else do you want? If I know the facts, then I can take them to Sadat and try to satisfy both you and him. My problem is with the issues that do not really relate to Israel's security. I must have your frank assessment. My greatest strength here is your confidence—but I don't feel that I have your trust. What do you really need for your defense? It is ridiculous to speak of Jordan overrunning Israel! I believe I can get from Sadat what you *really* need, but I just do not have your confidence. . . .
>
> You are as evasive with me as with the Arabs. The time has come to throw away reticence. Tell us what you really need. (pp. 348–49)

A third feature of Jimmy Carter's approach was his aversion to hard bargaining. Before Camp David, for example, Carter reacted adversely to a strategem of collusion discussed by his aides. One of those aides, William Quandt, concluded that, "No doubt Carter felt somewhat uneasy with the strategy of collusion discussed with Sadat in February 1978. It was a bit too manipulative."[16] And when Sadat wanted to open the negotiations with a proposal that would "appease his fellow Egyptians and the Arab world," Carter denounced the strategy as "a waste of time."[17]

For Carter, it seemed, getting a Middle East settlement was a complex problem-solving task. Posturing for the crowd back home, making extreme offers, exaggerating the significance of concessions, and all the other usual tricks of hard bargaining had no place in Carter's concept of the task at hand. Certainly, both leaders would have to be tough to protect their vital interests, but intransigence was not to be tolerated. The stakes were too high to allow such pettiness. Granted, Carter's predecessors may have engaged in such gamesmanship, but his was a different approach, one guided by reason as well as strong moral and religious commitments.[18]

The Disputants' Perspectives

If the above captures the essential nature of Jimmy Carter's concept of the conflict, of U.S. interests, and of his approach to reaching a solution, then how did his actions match up with the disputing parties' concept? Information from the disputants is more scarce; neither Sadat nor Begin wrote such detailed accounts of Camp David. But, on the Israeli side, Moshe Dayan's memoirs appear to be a faithful rendering of the Israeli perspective on U.S. mediation, especially Camp David. Sadat's autobiography completed in 1977 hints at his view of the U.S. role as does the account of his foreign minister, Ismail Fahmy, who resigned over Sadat's decision to go to Jerusalem.[19]

Menachem Begin initially viewed the United States as unnecessary for agreement. Shortly after Sadat's trip to Jerusalem and before Begin's trip to Egypt, Begin's "goal [was] direct face-to-face negotiations, without intermediaries, and under no foreign patronage."[20] Later, after direct negotiations stalled and others (especially, the United States) were pushing for a Geneva conference, Israel welcomed a direct, but limited, U.S. role. The primary U.S. function, from Israel's perspective, was not to establish a "warmer relationship" or to "find solutions." To the extent these were deemed necessary, the Israelis could, and preferred, to achieve them on their own. Rather, the United States could throw its weight behind Israel to guarantee its security should concessions be necessary. When a treaty was at hand, after Camp David, Israel only wanted "the U.S. [to] assume responsibility for there being no abrogation of the treaty we would sign with Egypt. We were concerned that Egypt, after our withdrawal from Sinai, might not honor her obligations."[21]

Regardless of the precise role the United States might play, Israel's primary consideration in all its dealings with the Americans, Dayan stresses, was the Israel-U.S. relationship. And in that, there were risks for Israel. In Dayan's view, the United States deliberately used Israel's dependency on the United States to push for concessions, "They knew how anxious we were to arrive at agreed positions with them, and so they used the tactic of getting us to make step-by-step concessions by trying to give us the impression that if only we would move a little further toward them, all our differences would be resolved" (p. 66).

In other words, from the Israeli perspective, the game was not a matter of giving the United States the responsibility for finding a formula. Rather, it was hard bargaining as usual with the United States. Israel would extract what it could in aid and security guarantees and resist by all stratagems possible U.S. efforts to wrest concessions from itself in its dealings with Egypt. And in this game, when agreement was threatened and Carter's political fortune was on the line, the United States, from Israel's perspective, was not above playing hardball:

> We handed our comments on their proposal to the Americans, they met with the Egyptians, and then they returned to us, this time with the peremptory demand that we agree to their proposed formula. The demand was made with

a note of anger and exasperation, and it was accompanied by the warning to heed the effect on Israel's standing in the world if she were presented—as she would be—as the party responsible for blocking the peace agreement. (p. 168)

In addition, the hard bargaining was not just squeezing concessions from both sides to reach an equitable, compromise agreement. From the Israeli perspective, the United States aligned itself with Egypt. In the negotiations over the terms of the peace treaty after Camp David, Dayan notes that

The Americans did not say it in so many words, but it was evident that they supported Sadat's position, and that was the pattern in our two-day discussions at the State Department. There was much talk and argument, with each side trying to convince the other, but to little effect. The Americans represented Egypt's views, without the authority to change or concede anything, so they kept pressing Egyptian demands upon us; but when we queried them or sought to find some middle ground we were faced by a blank wall. The second party to the negotiations was far away—in Cairo. The American role was to ask not "what," but "how"—not what an agreement on the Palestinian issue should be, but how to get us to accept their stand. True, the Americans were not a direct party to this issue, but they had made up their minds and had a clear point of view on the matter, a view identical with that of the Egyptians. (p. 130)

If Israel saw a U.S. bias toward Egypt, the reverse was also true: Egypt saw an equally strong U.S. bias toward Israel. In his memoirs concluded before Camp David began, Anwar Sadat refers to Israel as "America's stepdaughter," one for whom the United States often sacrificed its own interests to protect and promote those of Israel. After the October War, he hoped this attitude would soften:

I couldn't ask [President Carter] to suspend that "special relationship" [between the United States and Israel], or to stand on my side in opposition to Israel. . . . I found that all I could ask . . . was an end to the *carte blanche* the USA had given to Israel, in the days of the Johnson administration—an end, in other words, to the unconditional support for Israel's actions, whatever these might be.[22]

On the Egyptian side, it appears the bilateral relationship with the United States, the Sinai notwithstanding, was of primary importance, not that with Israel. As a member of the Camp David team, Quandt had the same impression. He recorded in his personal notes on the third day at Camp David that

The Egyptians seem more anxious to identify their positions with those of the United States than to reach any kind of agreement with Israel. . . . At this stage, it would seem that their preferred outcome from Camp David would be agreement between the United States and Egypt, with Israel isolated and under strong American pressure to change positions.[23]

Finally, although Carter may have viewed his role as facilitative and altruistic, at least some of the Israelis and Egyptians did not. Dayan:

> This desire to end the Camp David Conference with an agreement was prompted no less by the wish of the participants, particularly the President of the United States, to register success, than by the urgent political need to bring the Arab-Israeli conflict to an end, or at least to lay the foundations for its solution.[24]

And Fahmy, after Carter told him how little leverage the United States had over Israel and the Soviet Union, wrote, "I was really dismayed to find President Carter so hesitant and so ready to put his personal future above the major issues of war and peace in such a sensitive and strategic area as the Middle East."[25]

In sum, each of the three parties viewed the third party's role in different terms. Carter saw himself as having a moral mandate to achieve peace in the region and viewed the task as complex problem solving. His role was primarily to facilitate, not to confront or to bargain. The Israelis felt they could manage their conflict on their own terms were it not for U.S. insistence on an immediate settlement. Given the United States' stance and its historical propensity to pressure its allies, Israel's task was to extract as much assistance from the United States as possible while resisting concessions wherever possible. Egypt (at least, Sadat) apparently viewed U.S. participation as essential despite its incestuous relationship with Israel. As a consequence of that special relationship, Egypt had to be cautious of every U.S. move. If Sadat played it right, if Carter became dependent on him as much as Nixon did after the October 1973 War, Sadat, too, could extract benefits from the United States beyond mere agreement with Israel. Egypt, in short, viewed the U.S. role as one of potential benefactor in Egypt's bilateral dealings and one of potential dealmaker vis-à-vis Israel. Both sides, it should be stressed, believed its negotiations with the United States were crucial, *not* the negotiations with each other. As predicted in chapter 2, one effect of the intervention of a principal mediator was to detract from the disputants' direct interactions.

Carter's Mediating Practice

These differing views of the third party's role manifested themselves in specific bilateral and trilateral interactions throughout Carter's struggle to settle the Middle East conflict. Two instances stand out: Carter's first encounter with Begin and his initial effort at Camp David to bring Begin and Sadat together for direct talks.

In their first meeting, July 19–20, 1977, Carter asked Begin to assure him that there would be no more settlements on the West Bank. Carter failed to receive a direct response at that time. Begin did respond, however, when he returned to Israel. He responded not with words but with actions, recognizing as permanent some of the settlements on the West Bank.

Carter and others were shocked. They felt they had received Begin's tacit agreement not to pursue settlements. But why the sense of betrayal? Carter had begun his meeting with Begin by laying out his position on virtually all substantive points. Not only did he back up his points with reasoned argument, he noted the adverse consequences of not reaching agreement. In short, he gave every indication that the two—Carter and Begin—were in a game of hard bargaining. In such a game, parties exchange positions and attempt to commit to a favorable position with arguments, promises, and threats. Was not Carter implicitly asking for Begin's next bid? Carter may not have intended it, but in Begin's world, everything is hardball politics, including his dealings with Israel's benefactor, the United States. Communication and understanding and religious belief are fine, but in the Middle East the question is national survival, nothing less. The two were clearly playing different games.

Begin's response with action, not words, was effective because he, unlike Carter, could commit credibly to his position. In effect, Begin was saying: Your position, what amounts to your opening bid because I am a newly elected prime minister, is, among other things, no more settlements. I understand your reasoning, but reasoning is not enough in the Middle East. Actions count, especially actions that cannot be reversed. On that count, with no direct interests in this issue of settlements, you cannot commit your country to your position. I can. My position is that settlements will continue, and they will be permanent. And it is credible because I made the declaration public, the settlements are in place, and they are now legal. On this issue, I can do this. You cannot. Next offer?

If hard bargaining and the exchange of positions was the game—and Carter, at least from Begin's perspective, gave every indication that it was—Begin was just playing it more adroitly at this point. In fact, if Carter was fully into the game he seemed to be promoting, Carter would have cheered Begin's move. Much like a chess player admiring his opponent's clever move, Carter could easily have interpreted the move for what it was (at least in Begin's mind) and proceeded to the next move. Instead, he countered with another "reasonable" offer: "My colleagues and I decided to develop a reasonable proposal . . . hoping that public opinion and the general desire for peace might be decisive."[26] In other words, from Carter's perspective, the public knows that peace transcends all else and when he can finally bring Begin to this realization, agreement will be in hand. Reasonable people may disagree, but a "reasonable proposal" cannot readily be rejected.

Of course, the rules of the game were not as clearly and mutually recognized as in chess. Begin saw politics and hard bargaining; Carter saw facilitation and problem solving. Throughout the Camp David process, it turned out, they bargained as much over the nature of the game as over the substantive issues. What is more, as the next example illustrates, Carter's concept of conflict resolution suffered from its own contradictions.

The second instance illustrating Carter's mode of intervention was Carter's efforts to bring Sadat and Begin together face-to-face in the first days of the negotiations at Camp David. The open sparring and heated exchange were probably predictable. Nine months earlier, at Ismailiya, Egypt, the two leaders reportedly had clashed. This was in part owing to incompatible personalities but also to a long history of distrust and enmity, not only between them personally but between their peoples. The relevant question here, however, is, What effect did Camp David and, in particular, Carter's approach and position have on the two leaders and their interaction, and did it make a difference?

In the "brutally frank" exchange between Sadat and Begin, Carter saw his job to be damage control:

> I acted as a referee and put them back on track, and on occasion explained what was meant when there was an obvious misinterpretation . . . (p. 353).
>
> We had accomplished little so far except to name the difficult issues. There was no compatibility between the two men, and almost every discussion of any subject deteriorated into an unproductive argument, reopening old wounds of past political or military battles. (p. 355)

In other words, for Carter, this "fascinating debate" was the first round of a sparring match; the result, presumably, would be to find a basis for agreement. If the encounter got off track—that is, too emotional—he would intervene. There was a bridge to build and all this emotion, besides being a "waste of time," was obstructing the real work—examining the issues and finding the right formula to satisfy both sides.

Did Carter's view have an effect on the disputants? Was Carter's only choice to cease face-to-face talks between the leaders? Was their encounter a "waste of time?" No data exists from the two leaders on their reaction to Carter's role in this encounter, so these questions cannot be answered definitively. But one can at least interpret the meaning of Carter's actions and, on the basis of alternative concepts of conflict and conflict management, speculate as to the effect on the two leaders.

Carter said he wanted the two leaders to build a "warmer relationship." But based on what?—presumably, amicable negotiations and, finally, agreement. But which was to come first, amicable negotiations or trust building? It could have been that, at the onset of these crucial negotiations at Camp David when, in a sense, the two leaders were forced to come together, their first concern was that each recognize the other's sacrifices, needs, and fears.

Sadat, for example, told Begin that for thirty years the Israelis had desired full recognition, no Arab boycott, and guaranteed security, and he was giving them all of that. He said he had tried to provide a model of friendship and coexistence for the rest of the Arab leaders to emulate. Instead, he had become the object of extreme insult from Israel and scorn and condemnation from the Arab world. He said his initiative had come not out of weakness, but out of strength and self-confidence. He said that the warm feelings of his Jerusalem trip had been destroyed by Begin's bad faith acts on Sinai settlements. In addition, he felt that after all he had done for peace, Begin still did not trust him.[27]

Begin, on the other hand, pointed out that he had already demonstrated his good will by changing a long-standing policy on Sinai land. His predecessors had been determined to keep the land but he was offering it back, which was very difficult for him to do. Moreover, it had also taken courage to invite Sadat and to receive him in Jerusalem—the commanding officer of the nation that had launched a sneak attack on Israel only five years earlier in the October War, killing thousands of young Israelis. The hospitality with which Sadat had been received by the people of Israel was a true indication of the depth of Israel's desire for peace, Begin said.[28]

Could it be, therefore, that all the grand pronouncements of the past, the symbolic trips, and the draft agreements could not address these concerns? Could it be that, for a lifetime, the two men really did view each other as enemies, enemies to their most cherished values and dreams? If so, this attitude could not be erased by a third party, even the leader of such a powerful and important ally as the United States, by simply asking the two to be reasonable, to forsake short-term goals for peace, to seek mutual trust and friendship.

Carter's reaction to the two leaders' heated exchange, then, downplayed the significance of the interaction. By trying to get the leaders "on track," by trying to "change the subject," he depreciated the deepest concerns that were being expressed. The effect was to convey the message that recognition of pain and suffering, of concessions made, of humiliations endured—what appears to have mattered *to them*—was not important at Camp David. At Camp David, we are here to discuss *real* political issues, Carter seems to have signaled; once that is done, then the peoples of both sides can come together and understand each other.

Carter's implicit assumption was that the real stuff of international conflict was substantive, not emotional; negotiations were over the issues, not attitudes and perceptions. Just as local politics gets in an engineer's way when building a highway, emotion gets in the way of a leader's attempts to reach agreement. Carter's actions in these early exchanges, therefore, likely reinforced the two leaders' view that Camp David was to be little more than hard bargaining as usual, only condensed in time and space. Just as Kissinger had done, Carter would keep them separate, shuttle back and forth to squeeze out concessions, manipulate information where necessary, and, above all, protect U.S. interests. All the pleas for civility and reasonableness were, from the two leaders' perspective, little better than Kissinger's charm and deceptions. They were all tactics in the same game, the only game the Americans play.

This may be a rather cynical view of how Sadat and Begin saw Carter's role. Even if accurate, the two leaders may not have wanted the game to be played otherwise. After all, it was familiar. Sadat and Begin and, for that matter, Carter, probably entered the Camp David negotiations expecting—and preferring—politics as usual. If Carter had proposed a touchy-feely, let's-all-understand-each-other approach, they would have rebelled.

But maybe the trust building did need to come first. Maybe, to engage fully in a joint problem-solving effort, the two needed to know that their most profound fears—Israel's, of getting pushed into the sea; Egypt's of being humiliated in the Arab world—would be recognized and addressed. Thus, a view of conflict that contrasts with Carter's technical approach is one that considers psychological factors like mutual recognition of fears and suffering a *precondition* to settlement. Diagnosis of these factors is necessary before substantive issues can be adequately addressed.[29] Thus, when a third party stresses "issues" and discounts real concerns and needs, movement toward effective negotiations will only be hindered. In something of an irony for Carter, problem solving will be *more* difficult for the mediator to engender, not easier.

This line of reasoning suggests that a mediator's task is not to discourage emotive exchanges but to *use* them; that if a mediator wants to engage in a truly problem-solving process, certain preconditions must be met. Herbert Kelman argues that a third party can use direct, face-to-face interactions of this sort as raw material for enhancing the disputants' understanding of the dynamics of the larger conflict:

> There is no substitute for direct interaction in producing these new insights and ideas for conflict resolution. Certain kinds of solutions can emerge only from the mutual confrontation of assumptions, concerns, and identities in the course of face-to-face communication. In other words, the parties need each other if creative new ideas are to evolve—ideas for solution that are responsive to each party's fundamental needs and anxieties.[30]

The ideas for solution provide the preconditions for effective political negotiations—that is, negotiations over issues. At Camp David, with a news blackout and only one person privy to much of the interaction, the two leaders found themselves in a position never experienced before. For once, they could say what they had long wanted to say. They could say these things not through the filter of official statements and the press but straight to each other. Moreover, they could see the reactions. They could sense when they hit a raw nerve. In such situations, as Kelman puts it:

> Each party can concretely see the intensity of the other's reactions and the genuine and spontaneous nature of that reaction. Moreover, they can see that it was their own actions that produced this response, without intention on their part to be provocative or even awareness that they were touching on sensitive areas. The third party can use such incidents, which are part of the participants' shared immediate experience, as a springboard for exploring some of the issues and concerns that define the conflict between their societies. Through such exploration, they can gain some insight into the preoccupations of the other side, and the way these are affected by the actions of their own side. . . . These preoccupations . . . play an important role in the relations between the conflicting societies. (p. 110)

In short, the leaders could *interact* in a way far different from that in the usual public forums where communication is directed more at one's constituencies and other third parties than at one's counterparts. Thus, although the two leaders may have simply relished the opportunity to vent a little steam face-to-face and out of the public eye, Carter conceivably could have used the encounter to set the stage for more productive negotiations. As it turned out in the ensuing ten days or so, the negotiations were more akin to pulling teeth than to joint problem solving.

This view of intervention assumes that, to perform this function, Carter merely had to be sensitive to the nuances of the exchange and know how to use it to enhance mutual understanding. He would had to have listened actively and refrained from interrupting except to clarify statements and interpret particular exchanges as reflections of the broader conflict. To some extent, Carter tried to do these things. But he was constrained by at least two important factors: his technical orientation and his position as president of the United States.

His penchant for mastering the facts, searching for the magical formula, and discouraging emotive expression led him to openly discourage the interaction he saw. Eventually, he stopped it altogether. When he intervened, he did so to *correct* misperceptions, not to clarify perceptions, intentions, and reactions. In addition, he took notes constantly. Regardless of his intention, both Sadat and Begin could not ignore the fact that a record was being made and would likely be used at some point.[31] To use the face-to-face encounter productively, Carter would had to have set and enforced productive norms of interaction (emotions and personal expression, yes; diplomatic politeness and personal accusations, no); intervened only to clarify statements and point out the meaning of each other's reactions; and, eventually, moved the discussion from backward-looking justification of positions to forward-looking problem solving. Thus, it seems that Carter could have adopted a different approach to facilitating the direct encounter between Sadat and Begin, an approach that might have led to continued interaction between the leaders, greater understanding of each other's positions, and, possibly, active involvement by both in the creation of an agreement. Instead, Carter cut off the discussion, the two leaders ensconced themselves in their respective cabins only one hundred yards apart, and they never talked to each other again for the remaining ten days until the signing.

Carter could have attempted the approach outlined above, and it might have made a difference. As noted, there are good social psychological reasons why face-to-face encounters with adroit third-party interventions can provide the necessary preconditions for effective negotiations. Nevertheless, his technical, nearly apolitical, approach to the mediating task would appear to have counteracted any such attempt. But there is a more important reason why he would have been hindered while trying to assume such an "interactional" approach. This relates to who he was, not as a moral person committed to peace or as an engineer challenged by a complex problem, but as a powerful president protecting and advancing U.S. interests.

Jimmy Carter as president of the United States had strong interests in mediating this dispute, and he had substantial resources to bring to bear. He could make agreement very painful or very profitable. These were the facts that all concerned were well aware of. He could try to distance himself, try to establish a moral or personal or technically reasonable overlay on the dispute. But the fact was that Begin and Sadat were there to bargain, not just between themselves, but with the United States as well. In fact, for both Israel and Egypt, the most important bargain was indeed with the United States, not with each other. And in this bargain Carter carried all the baggage of the United States, not just his predecessors' tactics but the undeniable carrots and sticks all U.S. presidents have.[32]

Did Carter accept this position? Or did he think that he could escape the mantle of U.S. president for the purpose of peacemaking? Could he address fundamental needs or could he only bargain? Several comments in his memoirs suggest that, at least in the early stages of Camp David, he expected to gain the parties' trust and serve primarily as a "neutral facilitator."

In the debate between Sadat and Begin, Carter stated that they "had almost forgotten that I was there."[33] It was as if, presumably, Sadat and Begin suddenly found themselves alone and could now talk freely. But could they really have discounted Carter's presence? Could they have ignored the fact that he was taking notes? Didn't they think, as Carter discovered later and as Dayan affirmed in his memoirs, that the cabins were bugged? In other words, in the two leaders' minds, this was not a dialogue free of an audience. They knew precisely for whom they were performing. Each knew that if he could demonstrate then and there that he was "right," that he was the aggrieved party, that he was the one making all the sacrifices and concessions, then half the battle of Camp David was over. Granted, the emotions were probably genuine, the needs and concerns expressed real, but they were primarily aimed at Carter, not each other. In this exchange, neither leader intended to convert the other. Each was trying to score points with the one party both had to deal with if a settlement was to be reached—the United States. And Carter was "powerless" to do anything about it. The fact that he would eventually have to bargain with each party (or so it was perceived by both Begin and Sadat, if not Carter) would make an interactional approach by Carter very difficult to carry out.[34]

Carter apparently expected the two sides to trust him enough to reveal their true underlying interests and was disappointed when they, especially the Israelis, did not: "The Israeli delegation was very reluctant to trust us with any revelation of its real ultimate desires or areas of possible compromise."[35] And when he did sense he was getting full revelation, it was only from one, lower official:

> Attorney General Aharon Barak was outstanding, and later became a real hero in the Camp David discussions. . . . His frankness was encouraging because it indicated that he trusted me enough to tell me about the Israelis' real concerns. I felt close to both Dayan and Weizman, but neither had been as forthcoming on this issue [of settlements]. (p. 382)

If, indeed, no other Israeli trusted him enough to tell him Israel's true underlying interests, did he really understand the nature of the conflict? Dayan, for one, certainly thought not:

> It was not unpleasant to talk to Carter and Vance even when our views were widely divergent. At no time throughout our stay at Camp David did I doubt their sincerity. But there were times—and that evening [Saturday, September 16, 1978] was one of them—when I felt that neither the President nor the Secretary of State had sufficiently penetrated the core of the complex problems of the Middle East. They did not put themselves in the shoes—or rather the hearts—of either side. They knew what the Israeli and the Arab representatives were saying, but they did not always distinguish between what was being uttered for bargaining purposes and external consumption, and what was the profound expression of the spirit and the yearnings of a nation.[36]

The fact that Carter felt the parties (especially Israel) never revealed their underlying interests and that the parties felt he did not fully understand those interests suggests that, as much as he tried, he was stabbing in the dark. He was tossing out proposals right and left hoping that he might hit on the right formula that would meet their interests. Moreover, his failure to fully understand the parties' true concerns suggests that either his technique was poor or that he was structurally unable to tap the parties' underlying concerns. It may have been a bit of both. But, above all, the protagonists' comments and the inevitable "hard bargaining" that eventually sealed a peace treaty suggest that he was unable to escape his position as leader of a powerful country with strong interests in the region. It was simply very difficult to elicit such revelations when each side was simultaneously in the bargain of its life with the United States.

In addition, each knew that the United States, especially the Jimmy Carter presidency, needed this one. Carter had already spent considerable political capital in the effort, what everyone warned him against doing. And the U.S. presidential election was not far off. To walk away with perfunctory statements about good will and the desire for peace would have devastated the Carter presidency. Most important, the Israelis and Egyptians knew this. They knew that, however sincere his personal wish to bring peace to a troubled land (and some doubted even this), Carter first had to salvage his presidency. Thus, in carrying out the task of a mediator, every request for information, every beseechment to reveal interests, every plea for cooperation, had to be interpreted by each party as, in part, Carter's effort to get agreement—that is, *any* agreement, not necessarily an agreement that protected each side's interests. The result was to limit effective direct interactions and encourage hard bargaining.

In sum, Jimmy Carter was unable to overcome his official position and exploit the benefits of bringing together the two leaders for face-to-face negotiations. His focus on issues and formulas and his denigration of emotions and, by association, the very real concerns and needs of the two leaders, not only impeded any use of the exchange but signaled the true nature of the ensuing negotiations—hard bargaining as usual. It would be fundamentally no different from what the United States had done in the past: send envoys to the Middle East, invite heads of state to Washington, and plead for changes in positions. When a mission did not succeed, the United States would cook up a new approach, a new formula, or a new set of carrots and sticks to push the parties toward agreement. In short, whether Carter intended it or not, and his memoirs and other accounts suggest that, initially, he did not, the Camp David process was nothing new, especially as the leaders of Israel and Egypt saw it. The situation— heads of state at a summit deciding grave issues of war and peace—and the procedures—requesting position statements, recording everything— all served to reinforce established patterns of behavior among all the parties.

Getting Agreement: The Accords and the Treaty

If the above is an accurate interpretation of the limitations of Jimmy Carter's intervention, then why was agreement reached at Camp David and a peace treaty eventually signed?[37] The short answer, as suggested above, is that, in the end, Carter used the resources of his office to play the three-way hard-bargaining game. All sides—but especially the United States and Egypt—needed an agreement of some sort and needed it soon. Carter offered both sides billions of dollars in aid and threatened dire consequences for not agreeing. Egypt helped improve the U.S. position in the Arab world, and Israel helped save Carter politically at home. And Egypt regained its territory from Israel.

But was this all? Again focusing on Carter's practice as a mediator, he may have exploited his structural position—that is, his ability to bargain and to offer concrete incentives—but he also structured the negotiations in ways that compelled incremental moves toward agreement. Importantly, he was able to structure the negotiations because of his position as a third party; it was something neither principal party could have done unilaterally. In this respect, two features of his performance stand out: the high costs of walking out that he created by inviting the leaders to Camp David and the conditions he created prior to Camp David.

Once Sadat and Begin arrived at Camp David, it was very difficult for them to leave with nothing. Not only did the world expect great things from this dramatic summit conference, but Carter, despite his administration's attempts to lower expectations, structured the process to increase the costs of walking out. First, at the outset of the Camp David negotiations, Carter stated that agreement was the objective—"I directed our negotiating group to assume as our immediate ambition a written agreement for peace between Egypt and Israel . . . " and that the United States team (himself included) would "stay as long as necessary to explore all the potential agreements."[38] The meaning was clear: not only would the United States commit substantial time and effort but the blame for failure would sit with Sadat and Begin. Thus, when Sadat did try to leave, Carter told him that the "onus for failure would be on him [Sadat]" (p. 392) For good measure, Carter also made explicit what both leaders knew was the implicit threat in all their dealings with the United States: impairment of the bilateral relationship. Carter told Sadat that he predicted "the possible future progress of Egypt's friendships and alliances—[to be] from us to the moderate and then radical Arabs, thence to the Soviet Union"(p. 392). As long as the United States was committed indefinitely to the process, only Sadat or Begin could break it off and only they could be portrayed as the obstacles to peace.

Second, by conducting the negotiations in the United States, the two leaders were physically separated from their respective capitals. In the secluded setting of Camp David, communication back home—and, even more importantly, communication from back home to the leaders—was greatly hindered. By contrast, when the United States mediates by shuttling between the protagonists' capitals, the respective leaders have ample opportunity to delay, to arouse domestic opposition, to tie their own hands. Moreover, on a given shuttle mission, failure occurs when the mediator returns home empty handed.[39] But when the mediation is conducted on the mediator's home turf, there is no going home. The mediator cannot fail as long as the mediator stays put, only the protagonists can. Once again, with a summit meeting like this, the burden is more on the disputing parties than on the intermediary.

Third, the news blackout made it doubly difficult to arouse domestic opposition. With highly controlled meetings among only a few officials, a leak could be traced relatively easily. In addition, the main protagonists could not prepare a graceful exit by first alerting their constituencies through the media and justifying their positions. They had to leave first, be branded the obstacle to peace, *then* try to justify their departures.[40]

If Carter's effectiveness derived in large part from how he structured the process at Camp David, from the fact that once there, the two leaders found it costly to leave, then what he did *before* to the actual negotiations was critical. That is, the two leaders' willingness to come to Camp David was, in part, a function of the alternatives the third party (as well as other third parties and the principal parties' own actions) created. One factor, especially early on, was Geneva.

For Israel, the Geneva Conference was a serious threat. Because it is very difficult to say no to one's primary ally and benefactor, except for matters of survival, Israel would have been hard pressed to reject such a conference if the United States put all the pieces together. Once there, the pressure to relinquish the territories would have been unbearable with the United States and the Soviet Union, not to mention all the Arab states, ganging up. Thus, whether Carter and his aides intended it (and it appears they did not), all their efforts at pushing Geneva served to push Israel to Camp David.

The second factor was Carter's persistence. Most U.S. presidents are too ignorant of Middle East affairs or too unconcerned to invest much effort. Moreover, the expected political gains at home of a success in the Middle East are often outweighed by the political risks. Everyone in the Middle East knows this, not least the Israelis. Thus, when the status quo is preferred or when further inducements are expected, Israel's best policy is to wait out a president. That often does not take long for, as Quandt argues, the window of opportunity, given the U.S. election calendar, is quite short.

Jimmy Carter, early in his presidency, showed many signs of being unlike other U.S. presidents, however. To the surprise and dismay of the

Israelis, it appeared he actually believed what he said about moral imperatives and working tirelessly for peace. And, indeed, he acted on them. The fact that from early in his presidency Carter never let up was probably enough to convince Begin that Carter could not be waited out.[41] Begin would have to go along to get along and, although he could kick and scream about a huge international conference at Geneva, he could not very well resist a small, private, tête-à-tête in the woodlands of Maryland. In fact, his reported "enthusiasm" in accepting the invitation can be viewed as relief—from the Geneva option—as much as eagerness for a small, three-way summit.

A third factor in setting up Camp David was Carter's use of a proposal. In his first meetings with both Rabin and Begin, Carter did not hesitate to lay out his idea of a just settlement. Although he may have been criticized for taking such bold positions (especially in light of the domestic repercussions) and although they may have signaled hard bargaining as usual, they also were just about the only thing that put Begin on the defensive. For example, at Camp David on the issue of dismantling the settlements in the Sinai, Begin repeatedly pleaded with Carter, "'Mr. President, do not put this in a proposal to us.'"[42] When Carter asked him if he objected to the United States producing a proposal at all, he said he indeed did object. He explained that a U.S. proposal "would become the focal point of dissension and disagreement after we adjourned" (p. 367). Thus, it seems Begin felt that a proposal from the United States would cause him trouble if not force him to respond and to act in some fashion. Begin's objective, it appeared throughout the entire process, was to secure Egypt's recognition, return the Sinai, and maximize U.S. aid, all with minimal concessions on all other issues. Every time Carter came up with another proposal, it was more difficult to achieve this objective. Yes, a U.S. proposal did focus attention, especially in the full glare of the public spotlight. In a secluded private setting, Begin may have reasoned, he would at least have a chance of mitigating the impact of such proposals. Once again, Carter, however unwittingly, made Camp David—that is, going to Camp David, not necessarily what eventually happened—look good compared to the alternatives.

CONCLUSION

Much of Carter's impact on the disputants and their interaction can be inferred from the protagonists' comments and reactions. And much of that, it seems, was not planned. Carter wanted problem solving and resolution of the fundamental nature of the conflict but, when he brought the two together, his actions discouraged the necessary kind of interaction. He wanted a comprehensive settlement involving all parties but, largely as a result of his efforts to convene the multilateral conference, he had to settle for a separate peace between Israel and Egypt.

Was Jimmy Carter effective as a mediator? Certainly. He committed great resources to his peacemaking effort. But the determining factors were not so much his mastery over the issues or the discovery of the best blueprint. Rather, success came because, characteristically for a U.S. president, he bargained with all available incentives and, uncharacteristically for a U.S. president, he persisted.

This chapter provides a partial test of several propositions in part 1. In addition, the Camp David case, like those to follow, demonstrates that a stylized portrayal of mediation misses much of the nuance of mediator-disputant interaction. Five points stand out.

One, with respect to the entry-timing question, rarely does a conflict present the mediator with stark either-or decisions like enter now or enter later. When the mediating party has an ongoing relationship, reconfiguring the bargain is an ongoing affair. In this case, the mediator-disputant bargain began well before Camp David and continued well after. Carter's "prenegotiation"—staking out a moral and political position on the Middle East—began in the election campaign and culminated in what was effectively a threat to convene the Geneva conference. The "postnegotiation," that which sealed the three-way agreement, occurred well after Camp David as both parties squeezed more and more out of the United States.

Two, proposals, as discussed in chapter 3, are a mediator's stock in trade. Camp David suggests that not only do proposals build momentum by creating focal points, they can also be used to threaten a recalcitrant party, in this case, Israel. When the mediator is also that party's chief benefactor, no proposal can be ignored, as Begin's pleas indicated. Thus, when a disputant's primary tactic in a mediated negotiation is to stall, to avoid commitments, to limit the scope of the negotiations, this case suggests that proposals can promote movement by themselves becoming part of the strategic interaction between disputant and mediator.

Three, this case suggests that, as argued deductively in chapter 5, mutual perceptions of mediator bias is possible, maybe common, among disputants. When both parties operate under conflictual norms and discount the gestures of even friendly governments, each can perceive the third party in alliance with the other.

Four, the structural approach of part 1 implicitly assumes that the bargain among mediator and disputants is perceived by all parties in the same way. This case demonstrates the contrary. Not only did Carter and Begin bring different approaches to resolving conflict, they perceived the conflict in fundamentally different terms. Moreover, this case suggests that different perceptions can lead to different and, as here, conflicting strategies. Much of what happened between the United States and Israel can be explained in terms of leaders playing two different games. These differences may have resulted in lost opportunities whether to achieve a more comprehensive agreement or to achieve the limited agreement at less cost to the United States.

Five, the political psychology of mediation and conflict resolution generally must incorporate more than notions of perception and misperception. In chapter 2, I used the concepts of cognitive bias and conflictual norms to develop the principal-neutral mediator distinction. This case amplifies that discussion by illustrating the importance of mutual recognition of sacrifice and fears and how, in face-to-face interactions, the mediator might use those interactions to create the preconditions for effective problem solving.

Chapter Seven

PORTSMOUTH: THEODORE ROOSEVELT MEDIATES BETWEEN RUSSIA AND JAPAN, 1904–1905

BY THE TURN of the century, Japan was nearing the status of a full-fledged power in a system of competing empires. It had discarded the shogunate, opened itself to the Western world, and defeated China to take control of Korea. Russia, meanwhile, had acquired new territory in the Pacific and in China. Expanding from opposite directions into mainland Asia, conflict between the two imperial powers thus seemed inevitable. When diplomatic negotiations failed to settle their competing claims, Japan attacked Russian forces at Port Arthur on the Chinese mainland in February 1904. Initially, Japan had limited war aims and sought an early termination. But as one military success followed another, both the leaders and the public in Japan came to believe that the more decisive the victory, the greater the advantages it could obtain in a settlement. In fact, as the war progressed unexpectedly well for Japan, more and more Japanese advocated an expansion of the war to subdue Russia completely. In this climate of war fever, most Japanese in mid-1905 expected a Russian request for peace to be all but inevitable (especially after the destruction of the Russian Baltic fleet in May 1905). They were shocked, therefore, when, on June 12, 1905, the Japanese leadership, the *genro*, accepted, an offer for mediation from the president of the United States, Theodore Roosevelt.[1] What they did not know was that, after sixteen months of one of history's costliest wars, Japan had nearly exhausted itself. The Japanese public also did not know that from the earliest days of the war the leadership—especially the *genro*, the senior members of the oligarchy that ruled Japan— was preparing the way for negotiations with the good offices of a third party.

Shocked as they were to be deprived of ever-greater fruits of victory, many Japanese concluded that Roosevelt intervened only at Russia's request and, because Roosevelt was known to be pro-Japanese, only after Russia had offered favorable terms of peace. As they were to discover, Roosevelt's intervention was not that simple, nor was his bias so clearly pro-Japan. Moreover, the peace talks conducted in Portsmouth, New Hampshire, under Roosevelt's auspices resulted in peace terms far worse for Japan than most Japanese ever expected.

This case occured at a time when global communications amounted to steamship and telex and when third parties were, at best, meddlers. More often, third parties deprived or robbed victors of their fruits of military victory. But here a principal mediator intervened not to gain the spoils of others' battles nor, as at Camp David seventy-five years later, to promote problem solving or even to trade resources. Rather, here intervention was limited. Unlike Jimmy Carter's mediation, direct interactions with and side payments to the belligerents were of minor significance. Here one sees the difficulties of gaining entry, of role bargaining, and of building subtle forms of influence. In particular, one sees how adroit interventions during bilateral negotiations can encourage movement. The art of proposal making is thus prominent in this case. The impact of the intervention, although not determinative of the outcome, was probably critical to hastening its conclusion. This substantiates a central proposition of part 1, namely, that although intermediary interventions may not be determining factors, they can tip the balance from confrontation to cooperation.

THE CASE

Allies on both sides of the Russo-Japanese conflict—France allied with Russia, Great Britain with Japan—mostly supported the war and did not press for an early conclusion. The United States, although not an ally, was a major financier of Japan's war effort. But by late 1904, President Roosevelt concluded that Japan had achieved its objectives and that Russia should accept peace terms. After Russian forces were driven out of Liaoyang in August 1904, Roosevelt formally urged Czar Nicholas II to make peace. But the czar, known for his sense of divinely inspired nationalism, refused to consider terms of peace. Instead, he sent the Russian Baltic fleet to the Pacific. In an apparent attempt to convince the Russians that he was not pro-Japanese, Roosevelt used informal channels in February 1905 to inform the Russian ambassador to the United States that if Russia felt it could maintain its presence in Manchuria and if it thought the Baltic fleet had a chance of success, it was all right with him to continue the war. Otherwise, Roosevelt said, Russia should seek a peace immediately. The Russian ambassador informed Roosevelt that he had standing instructions to discourage all ideas of peace or mediation. Roosevelt nevertheless tried to influence Russia through its European ally, France. The French foreign minister replied that, although he favored an end to the war, Roosevelt should urge Japan to take the initiative and to offer moderate peace terms.

In Japan, meanwhile, the leaders were looking for a way to bring the war to an end. For military and financial reasons, they knew they could neither conquer Russia nor prolong the war. So the problem was how to get the enemy to the peace table. As early as August 1904, Prime Minister

Katsura Taro drafted a preliminary list of peace terms. These were very similar to the official instructions the Japanese peace delegates would take to the Portsmouth Peace Conference eleven months later. Foreign Minister Komura Jutaro, who would become Japan's chief delegate to the Portsmouth conference, also drew up a list. Taking a hard-line, nationalist stance, Komura put a war indemnity at the top of his list. Differences within the Japanese leadership over the indemnity question were destined to be a major stumbling block in the coming negotiations.

The Japanese leaders did agree that peace negotiations should be limited to the two belligerents. They especially did not want a congress of powers writing the treaty. When Japan fought China in 1894 to end China's control of Korea, Czar Nicholas II had persuaded France and Germany to join Russia in giving Japan "friendly advice" not to take Port Arthur from China in the peace settlement. Japan agreed, but a sense of resentment and humiliation over the "triple intervention" lingered. It was the kind of concession the Japanese were not about to repeat. Although wary of third parties, the Japanese at the same time needed the assistance of one or more powers to get Russia to the table. For this, the United States was the most likely candidate. France was Russia's ally, and Japan disliked Germany because of its role in the triple intervention and because of the kaiser's yellow peril rhetoric. As an ally of Japan and a long-time imperial rival to Russia, Britain could do little to influence Russia. Moreover, despite their military alliance, relations between Britain and Japan were cool. The United States had much better relations with Japan, especially under the Roosevelt presidency. In addition, they knew Roosevelt was eager to try his hand at international diplomacy.

The United States was officially neutral throughout the war, but in private conversations Roosevelt expressed definite pro-Japanese views. In a letter to his son, for example, he wrote, "between ourselves—for you must not breathe it to anybody—I was thoroughly well pleased with the Japanese victory [at Port Arthur], for Japan is playing our game."[2] In June 1904, he told Japanese officials in Washington that, although the time was not yet right, he would be willing to perform good offices for Japan. Furthermore, he would exercise his influence to afford Japan the full fruits of its victory. Those fruits, Roosevelt indicated, included Korea. In addition, Roosevelt obtained assurances from the German ambassador that Germany would not interfere to deny Japan its legitimate rewards.

Although Roosevelt was clearly pro-Japanese, he did not want Russian power destroyed in East Asia. In fact, he most wanted the war concluded and a balance of power established in the region. In October 1904, he told the French ambassador, "From my point of view, the best [outcome] would be that the Russians and the Japanese should remain face to face balancing each other, both weakened" (p. 17). This would best serve

America's interests in gaining access to China and, Roosevelt argued, best meet Japan's long-term interests.

In January 1905, after Japan took Port Arthur, Roosevelt told a top Japanese official that, in a peace agreement, Japan should get Port Arthur, Korea should be put under Japan's influence, and Manchuria should be returned to China as a neutral zone under the guarantee of all powers. Moreover, Roosevelt argued that if Russia was not driven out of Manchuria by military force, it must be removed by putting the area under international control.

Roosevelt took a number of steps in early 1905 to prepare a peacemaking role for himself. He worked quietly to line up British support by conducting discussions of a possible three-power alliance with Britain and Japan. He sent a new ambassador to Russia, George von Lengerke Meyer, with terms of a peace settlement and an offer for good offices. He also conveyed to the Japanese leaders through unofficial channels his unequivocal support for Japan's position on Port Arthur and Korea.

Despite these efforts, by February 1905, Roosevelt failed to bring the parties any closer to the peace table. Russia rejected Roosevelt's advice, possibly recalling the embarrassments of the 1878 Berlin Congress where third powers dictated unfavorable settlement terms after Russia's limited victories in the Near East. The Japanese were still reluctant to take the first step, fearing it would be taken as a sign of weakness because it was widely suspected that Japan was near exhaustion militarily and financially.

In March, Japan achieved another major military success although at great cost. The military leaders knew it was time for peace, so the Japanese war minister, without authority from the cabinet, asked the United States ambassador to inform Roosevelt. The ambassador's telegram was ambiguously worded and created considerable confusion in Washington. Roosevelt worried that the United States ambassador had put Roosevelt forward as the peacemaker. Consequently, Roosevelt informed Foreign Minister Komura that he was not offering his services and that if some other agent, possibly France, were available, he hoped it would be chosen. Komura informed Roosevelt that peace could be had only when the Russian Baltic fleet was destroyed and only when Japan could be assured that the inquiry for peace talks came from Russia.

In April, when prospects for peace negotiations seemed remote, Roosevelt met separately with the two nations' ambassadors. He told the Russian ambassador that a quick peace was in the interests of Russia and also in the interest of the United States, which would regret the exclusion of Russia from the Far East. The ambassador replied that paying an indemnity or ceding territory was out of the question. Besides, he said, Japan could be worn down financially. Roosevelt told the Japanese ambassador that, within a year, Japan might find itself victorious but seriously weakened. Japan should seek a settlement now and refrain from demanding an indemnity. But the ambassador, reflecting Foreign Minister Komura's unyielding stance, declared that Japan had every right to demand reparations; moreover, it would also demand territory, the cession of Sakhalin Island.

At this time, Czar Nicholas secretly asked the French to consult the Japanese on peace terms. France had earlier turned down Russia's request for additional loans to finance the war. But because Germany was increasingly becoming a threat in Europe, France accepted Russia's request, hoping Russia would extricate itself from its Far Eastern debacle and restore a balance of power in Europe. The mediation effort never got underway, however, as other matters facing France at the time caused the French minister to delay action.

In Japan, meanwhile, the genro joined the military leaders to overrule the hardliners in the foreign ministry. They decided that Japan should seek peace immediately and should not wait for Russia to initiate talks. Contrary to Foreign Minister Komura's absolute demands for an indemnity and the cession of Sakhalin, the genro decided that the only indispensable terms would be Japanese freedom of action in Korea, mutual military evacuation of Manchuria, and transference to Japan of Russia's Port Arthur leasehold. In addition, the genro agreed that the United States should be used as a mediator or, more accurately, for good offices, because Japan preferred direct negotiations, accepting help only to get the peace conference underway. Beyond that, the Japanese leaders expected Roosevelt to use no more than friendly influence in an informal way, paralleling, but not replacing, direct negotiations. Soon thereafter, the Japanese leaders officially approved peace terms.

Foreign Minister Komura, thus rebuffed on the terms for making peace, contacted Roosevelt but avoided making a direct request for mediation, hoping Roosevelt would take the initiative himself. In his reply, Roosevelt agreed that negotiations should be conducted directly between the belligerents but did not mention the possibility of U.S. good offices. He added that "it being of course understood that Japan is adhering to her position of maintaining the open door to Manchuria and of restoring it to China" (p. 33). To this, Komura agreed and then continued to send oblique messages, finally making an outright request for Roosevelt's assistance in bringing the two sides together. He did not, however, convey to Roosevelt Japan's peace terms.

Despite Japan's initiative, Roosevelt saw little prospect for convening peace talks soon. He thought the Japanese leaders would be excessive in their demands and he knew the Russian czar was intransigent. Moreover, Russia's Baltic fleet was due soon in Japanese waters. Further moves to end the war would have to await the outcome of that naval battle.

The czar's stubborn hope of reversing the tide against Japan's war machine was dashed in late May when the Russian Baltic fleet suffered a disastrous defeat. The Russian populace was shocked by the loss of virtually the entire fleet and with it some of Russia's best young leaders. Some of the czar's advisers urged peace talks immediately. They concluded that mediation was the only way to get them started and that President Roosevelt was the most disinterested of the chiefs of state. In spite of all this, the czar clung to the hope of one major military success before accepting peace talks.

Meanwhile, on June 1, Japan formally requested Roosevelt's intervention, carefully wording the secret communication to avoid appearing concessionary. Japan asked the president "directly and entirely of his own motion and initiative to invite the two belligerents to come together for the purpose of direct negotiations" (p. 39). Roosevelt quickly agreed but cautioned Japan against pressing the indemnity issue. He believed that if Japan did not include reparations in their demands and accepted only the partition of Sakhalin Island, Russia would agree. This, as it turned out, was exactly what happened several months later. In the meantime, however, Roosevelt had his work cut out for him to persuade the czar to agree to talks and then to set up the conference.

Roosevelt called in the Russian ambassador and argued that there was no prospect of further Russian resistance. Continuation of the war would only lead to increased Japanese demands, and Japan would become a growing danger to all the other powers. Roosevelt said it was not important that he serve as the intermediary, but if the pride of the belligerents prevented them from making the first step, he would undertake to convoke them simultaneously to open negotiations and then leave them to themselves to work out the peace terms. He did not reveal that he already had Japan's consent. He did say, however, that the Russians should pay reparations and give up territory. The United States request was conveyed in a telegram to the czar:

> President believes it would be better for the representatives of the two Powers to discuss the whole peace question themselves rather than for any outside Power to do more than endeavor to arrange the meeting—that is, to ask both Powers whether they will not consent to meet. After the meeting has been held it will be time enough, if need be, to discuss suggestions as to the terms from any outside friend of either party. (p. 42)

Roosevelt added that the meeting should be without intermediaries and should take place somewhere in China. Roosevelt revealed privately that he really hoped they would choose Washington for the negotiations because "then one could without a doubt make some useful suggestions" (p. 42).

The czar responded by saying that Russia would not seek peace or mediation, but it did ask Roosevelt to use his influence to find out the Japanese demands and help moderate them. Then, shortly after Nicholas sent this message and after conferring further with his aides, he agreed to seek a settlement. He reported to the United States ambassador,

> If it will be absolutely secret as to my decision, should Japan decline, or until she gives consent, I will consent to your President's plan that we (Russia and Japan) have a meeting without intermediaries, in order to see if we can make peace. (p. 45)

The czar said he accepted the United States ambassador's assurance that Roosevelt was making the proposal for peace talks with the highest motives and had no ulterior motives. He also asked the ambassador to tell the president that he hoped the old friendship between their countries would be renewed.

On June 8, 1905, Roosevelt sent an official invitation to the two nations to open peace talks. Included in his proposal was an offer to help them find a time and place for the conference, a seemingly simple task but one that proved exasperating for Roosevelt. Getting agreement on a site was especially difficult. Russia preferred Paris but would accept Washington, D.C. Japan proposed Chefoo, a Chinese port city, but would also accept Washington. Roosevelt suggested The Hague but the Japanese would not go to any site in Europe. Roosevelt decided on Washington but Russia in the meantime proposed The Hague. Roosevelt insisted on Washington and eventually the czar concurred. Because the conference was to open soon (in mid-August) and Washington was unbearable in the summer, Roosevelt looked for a cooler location. Newport or Manchester were attractive but swamped with tourists, so Roosevelt finally settled on the Portsmouth Navy Yard on an island near Portsmouth, New Hampshire. The navy yard, Roosevelt pointed out, had guarded entrances so news reporters and others could be kept away from the proceedings. Both countries accepted the suggestion.

As Roosevelt prepared for the conference, he lobbied both sides through letters, emissaries, and personal contacts to be reasonable in their demands. He warned Russia that its situation was hopeless and that if it persisted in the fighting it would lose all of Eastern Siberia. He urged the Russians to pay an indemnity and to surrender Sakhalin Island. He emphasized that he did not want Russia driven out of Asia and the Pacific Coast. He warned the Japanese that their demand for an indemnity could cause a breakdown of the talks.

The entire effort—pleading for moderation, getting agreement on dates, and appointing suitable negotiators—tried Roosevelt's patience. In a personal letter, Roosevelt expressed his exasperation, especially with the Russians: "I have been growing nearly mad in the effort to get Russia and Japan together. Japan has a right to ask a good deal and I do not think that her demands are excessive; but Russia is so soddenly stupid and the Government is such an amorphous affair that they really do not know *what* they want" (p. 57).

The Japanese appointed Foreign Minster Komura as chief delegate. Roosevelt was disappointed in the choice because he had hoped for a more conciliatory official such as a member of the genro. But one candidate from the genro explained that, having favored a policy of accommodation with Russia and opposed the war, those who had taken Japan into war should take responsibility for making peace. Komura was one such person.

The Japanese delegation left Yokohama July 8 apprehensive about finding peace terms that would ensure an honorable return. Their instructions listed three "absolutely indispensable demands": (1) Japanese freedom of action in Korea; (2) mutual withdrawal of military forces from Manchuria; and (3) transfer to Japan of the Port Arthur leasehold and the Port Arthur-Harbin railway. "Relatively important" items included the reimbursement of war expenses, the cession of Sakhalin, the surrender of Russian warships in neutral ports, and ensured fishing rights along the coast. Because these were not absolutely indispensable, Komura was to secure them only as circumstances permitted. "Additional demands"—the limitation of Russian naval strength in the Far East and the demilitarization of Vladivostock—were added for bargaining purposes.

Finally, the Japanese leadership, concerned about Komura's hardline views, told him, "If you should face the unfortunate possibility of the termination of negotiations, you are instructed to report the situation to your home government by telegram and to take appropriate measures only after you have received instructions in response to your report" (p. 59).

Komura, nevertheless, felt that, after so many victories, it was imperative he come home with major gains. Among these, he felt, were reparations and the cession of Sakhalin.

Czar Nicholas had a difficult time choosing a delegation as one nominee after another declined. Finally, he settled on Sergei Witte, a distinguished government official who had served as finance minister and had engineered much of Russia's industrialization in the late nineteenth century. He was, nevertheless, a man Nicholas personally disdained. Roosevelt welcomed the choice because Witte was also known for his opposition to the war. The Russian delegation's instructions seem to have anticipated Japanese demands. Among the absolutely unacceptable demands would be (1) cession of Russian territory; (2) payment of reparations; (3) disarmament of Vladivostok; (4) restriction of Russia's naval power on the Pacific;

and (5) surrender of the railway line to Vladivostok. Russia would recognize Japan's dominant position regarding Korea, but Korea would have to be independent. The delegation was instructed to maintain the best possible relations with the Japanese and not to antagonize them. The delegation was told to stay in constant communication by telegraph with the ministry.

The Japanese delegation arrived first in New York City in late July. Komura went directly to meet with Roosevelt in his home in the town of Oyster Bay on Long Island. Komura gave Roosevelt a list, minus the rankings, of Japan's peace demands. Roosevelt advised him not to demand the disarmament of Vladivostok or the surrender of Russian warships. What worried him most, however, was the indemnity question. He would push the Russians to make some kind of "reimbursement," but Roosevelt feared the talks would fail if the Japanese were intransigent on this matter.

The Russian delegation arrived in New York one week after the Japanese. Witte saw Roosevelt in Oyster Bay and told him that Russia would not be robbed of its honor. He emphasized that Russia was not defeated and that it would not pay any contributions. He added: "If the Japanese do not come around to our point of view, then we will conduct a defensive war to the last extreme and we will see who will last the longest" (p. 74).

On the morning of August 5, Roosevelt hosted the two delegations on the presidential yacht, his only involvement in the opening ceremonies. Roosevelt used the occasion to meet again with the Japanese and to report on his discouraging meeting with Witte.

The delegations took separate ships to Portsmouth, arriving on Tuesday, August 8, amid local celebrations in the city of Portsmouth and at the naval yard. The two delegations stayed in the Wentworth, a large hotel overlooking the water. Roosevelt had encouraged an informal atmosphere in Oyster Bay, but Witte expected to be treated like royalty here and regularly expressed his dissatisfaction with the accommodations. At first, both delegations ate in the same dining room, but the Russians later arranged to be served in a separate room. Reporters also stayed in the Wentworth and hounded the delegates every time they left their rooms. The Japanese showed little concern about the accommodations.

Roosevelt, remaining in Oyster Bay, met again with Japan's special emissary to the United States, Kaneko Kentaro, the day before the delegates arrived in Portsmouth. Roosevelt stressed to Kaneko the importance of not pushing the indemnity issue too far. He advised Japan to talk first of payment for the care of Russian prisoners and then, without mentioning an amount, seek acceptance in principle of payment for war expenses. Roosevelt also proposed that, although he would not be present for the negotiations, if they reached a deadlock, he should be informed immediately. In such case, the chief delegate, Komura, should attempt to drag out the discussions for at least 48 hours during which Roosevelt would send appeals to the major powers and attempt to mediate a compromise.

On their first day in Portsmouth, Witte took the initiative and arranged with the Japanese to meet the following morning to discuss conference procedures. In that meeting, they agreed on language, participation, and scheduling. They also agreed to keep all discussions secret except for joint statements. As it turned out, Witte leaked information freely to the press throughout the negotiations.

The formal conference sessions began August 10. The Japanese presented in writing their demands in a list of ten articles. The Russians met privately to develop counterproposals for each article. They decided to reject four of the articles outright—cession of Sakhalin, surrender of interned ships, limitation of Russian naval power in the Pacific, and payment of an indemnity. In Witte's view, an indemnity was paid only by a conquered country—which Russia was not—and only when the enemy could not be forced out of the defeated country's territory. At the time, Japan was occupying no part of Russia. In place of those demands, Witte suggested to his delegation that Russia propose the formation of a Russo-Japanese military alliance. The idea was soundly rejected by his team.[3]

When the formal response to Japan's demands was ready, Witte cabled it to St. Petersburg and, without awaiting a reply, delivered a translated version to the Japanese two days later. The four controversial items—interned ships, Russian naval power, and, especially, Sakhalin and indemnity—would prove to be the main points of difficulty in the coming days. None were "absolutely indispensable" to the Japanese although three were "relatively important." As such, success would seemed to have been all but certain except that Komura, in the succeeding days, was determined to treat the indemnity and Sakhalin issues as "absolutely indispensable." And, when the negotiations stalled after achieving agreement on other issues, St. Petersburg showed a renewed interest in gaining at least one military victory before concluding peace talks.

Indemnity was taken up on the ninth day of negotiations, Thursday, August 17. Each country came to the issue with its own historical and financial rationales. Japan knew that in every major conflict in East Asia during the past century, the defeated nation paid an indemnity. With a string of military victories, Japan's leaders and the public as a whole fully expected Russia to pay reparations. Moreover, national indebtedness was putting a severe strain on Japan's economy and its ability to carry out postwar reconstruction. Russia had never paid an indemnity and would never do so when Japanese forces were thousands of miles away from its capital. Russia, too, had its financial problems because it had financed the war entirely through foreign loans. It would have to borrow even more to pay reparations. National honor, the Russians repeatedly argued, was the real issue.

Not surprisingly, what had been calm and proper negotiations now turned acrimonious with the reparations issue on the table. At first, Witte would not even discuss the issue stating that Russia would never pay reparations. Japan's proposal to seek another formula for payments was, thus, superfluous. He stated defiantly that Russia was not defeated, but Komura contended that Japan was the victor. The debate continued for more than three hours as the two exchanged accusations and threatened to continue the war. They soon realized that they could agree only not to agree on this issue. Other issues were discussed in the afternoon session, and some agreement was reached. At the end of the day, Witte suggested that they conclude the conference and set Monday, August 21, as the final day. With the indemnity question unresolved, this suggestion was clearly a threat to break up the conference without a treaty. Komura, not to appear desperate for a settlement, agreed to the date.

Witte sent telegrams to St. Petersburg describing the impending failure of the conference. He noted that, although Roosevelt would not want to reconvene a conference after such a failure, it was important that a second conference be held, yet not at Russia's initiative. The two issues blocking agreement were Sakhalin and reparations. He urged his leaders to reconsider these carefully because the continuation of the war would bring the greatest calamity for Russia.

Komura likewise telegraphed home messages of impending failure. He said he did not expect Witte to concede on Sakhalin or reparations. His strategy, then, would be to withdraw his demands for interned warships and limitation of Russian naval power and simultaneously call on Roosevelt for conciliation and mediation. He reminded Prime Minister Katsura that Roosevelt had told him that, in case of ruptured negotiations, Roosevelt wished to take the last measure himself. Komura instructed Kaneko in New York City to see Roosevelt in Oyster Bay and seek his help immediately. Kaneko met Roosevelt the next day, Friday, August 18, and Roosevelt agreed to act. But before contacting the czar, Roosevelt first wanted Witte to send a representative so there would be no appearance of bypassing Witte.

Unknown to Roosevelt and Kaneko, Komura meanwhile went forward in Portsmouth with his offer to withdraw his demands for interned warships and limited Russian naval power if the Russians would cede Sakhalin and consider reparations. In response, Witte asked for a private meeting with Komura without assistants and Komura agreed. Witte explained that he had rigid instructions especially regarding Sakhalin and reparations. Venturing a compromise, he asked Komura if he would consider dividing Sakhalin. Komura said it was possible but he still needed some kind of payment, say for the northern half of the island. The figure would be 1.2 billion yen, exactly what Japan had calculated for reimbursement of war expenses. Witte knew the czar would never accept such a thinly disguised indemnity but agreed to include the 1.2 billion figure in the compromise plan he would refer to St. Petersburg. Progress was made on other issues that day. They ended the day by agreeing that the Monday, August 21, meeting should be postponed a day and possibly longer if instructions did not arrive in time.

On Saturday, August 19, Roosevelt met with Witte's second, Roman Romanovich Rosen, who listened to Roosevelt's compromise plan but did not reveal the plan negotiated the day before in Portsmouth. Under Roosevelt's proposal, Russia would cede all of Sakhalin, and the reparations question would be submitted to nonbinding arbitration. Rosen vehemently argued against the plan but did agree to take it back to Portsmouth along with the message that Roosevelt wanted his suggestions regarded as coming from him as a private person rather than as a formal proposal from the U.S. president.

Meanwhile, the czar was unmoved by the compromise plan offered by Witte and Komura: "In essence the Japanese are rearranging their demands. The relinquishment of half of Sakhalin and the payment of a huge sum for the northern half—this does not at all change my basic view, 'not one piece of land, not one ruble of contributions or replacement of military expenditures,' which means that the Japanese demands are unacceptable."[4] In the same message, Witte was told he would receive his final instructions in a day for ending the conference. Witte telegraphed back to St. Petersburg that he thought world opinion would recognize Russia as right in rejecting reparations, but it would not stand on Russia's side on the question of Sakhalin. If Russia wanted to make sure that the guilt for the failure of the conference was Japan's, Russia should not reject demands about both Sakhalin and military expenditures. He also stated that in giving a final answer to the Japanese, it was absolutely necessary to take into account the opinion of President Roosevelt.

Roosevelt prepared another message for the United States ambassador to Russia, George von Lengerke Meyer, to deliver to Czar Nicholas. As before, Roosevelt warned of the danger of continuing the war and predicted that Russia would lose its eastern provinces. He proposed that northern Sakhalin be returned to Russia and the amount of payment be negotiated later. He sent copies of the telegram to Paris and Berlin and promised the two governments that he would advise the Japanese to conclude the peace no matter how little money they obtained. He also sent a copy to Witte who forwarded it immediately to St. Petersburg.

Roosevelt then wrote to Kaneko saying he did not think the sum of money Japan was seeking should be asked or could be obtained. He warned that if Japan continued the war for an indemnity, there would be a considerable shifting of public opinion against it. In a second letter he said: "It is Japan's interest now to close the war. She has won the control of Korea and Manchuria; she has doubled her own fleet in destroying that of Russia; she has Port Arthur, Dalny, the Manchurian railroad, she has Sakhalin" (p. 137).

Finally, he said, Japan had an ethical obligation to the world at this crisis. Upon receiving this message, Komura responded by saying that there was some room for reduction in the money demand, something he had been recently authorized to do by the Japanese government. Komura never let on that, according to his government's instructions, reparations were not absolutely indispensable.

Roosevelt meanwhile continued to work the major powers for support. France's prime minister concluded that he could no longer do nothing and see the conference fail. He thus decided to support Roosevelt's initiatives and sent word to St. Petersburg concurring with all the elements of Roosevelt's proposed agreement. Russia, said the prime minister, should take the U.S. president's advice very seriously. The German kaiser also lent Roosevelt his support. He endorsed Roosevelt's proposals and told Russia that they would lead to an honorable peace. The British were not so forthcoming, however. This aloofness was apparently owing in part to their disdain for Roosevelt and in part to their peculiarly distant relationship with the Japanese despite the Anglo-Japanese Alliance.

U.S. Ambassador Meyer was given an audience with the czar after the czar received the contents of the president's telegram from Witte. In their two-hour meeting, the czar stated categorically that he would cede no territory and pay no money. Meyer argued that Sakhalin was not Russian territory in the same sense as territory on the mainland, for Russia had held undisputed title only since 1875 when it concluded a treaty with Japan. After this and further discussion, the czar seemed to relent a bit. He assented to the cession of the southern half of the island. Ambassador Meyer then pushed him on payments, but Nicholas would only agree to pay for the costs of maintaining prisoners, not a sum that could be interpreted as an indemnity.

Roosevelt's intervention into the stalled negotiations thus paid off. Not only did the czar concede on territory, but an immediate collapse of negotiations was temporarily averted. Moreover, Witte, with orders to return to Russia, later used Roosevelt's move to continue the negotiations.

Meanwhile, the delegates met at the naval yard Wednesday, August 23, for their last scheduled session of what was expected to be a failed conference. Witte and Komura first met informally to discuss the compromise plan of August 18. Witte conveyed the bad news he had from St. Petersburg rejecting the plan but proposed extending the conference a bit longer, apparently to await Roosevelt's appeal to the czar. They both wanted to avoid a collapse and so agreed to wait until Saturday, August 26, when the report from St. Petersburg was expected. In the meantime, at the formal session, Witte persuaded Komura to agree to the statement that, even if Russia were to cede Sakhalin or to make some other arrangement, Japan could not agree to a plan that excluded reimbursement of war expenses. Witte thus succeeded in placing Japan in the position of continuing the fighting merely for money.

Roosevelt again sent letters to Witte and to the czar appealing for the Russians to pay for the return of Sakhalin. He predicted that if Russia continued the war, it would likely lose all of eastern Siberia. Witte rejected the proposal, and the czar responded by simply repeating his earlier position. The Japanese government replied that it would act on the president's advice and consented to make further concessions on the amount of compensation. The Russian delegates were becoming irritated with Roosevelt's unrelenting "interference" even though Witte had used the interventions to his advantage in avoiding a breakup of the conference.

The final session was now set for Saturday, August 26. Komura had resolved to seek a further delay, but the Russians had paid their hotel bill and were preparing to leave on Sunday. Komura again met with Witte in private. Witte informed him that his government had rejected the compromise plan but that Sakhalin could be divided without payments. Witte then said that he had come to this meeting to end the negotiations, that no more concessions were possible. In Russia, opposition was building to the concessions already made, and the military was prepared to resume fighting. Komura agreed that a solution was not to be found. Because Komura was awaiting further instructions, he asked that they adjourn on Monday, August 28, to which Witte agreed.

That same Saturday, Witte received another telegram from St. Petersburg instructing him to end the negotiations. President Roosevelt should not be insulted but Russia's honor and welfare were far more important, he was told. Komura sent word to Tokyo of Russia's intransigence on the two remaining issues but omitted Witte's offer to cede half of Sakhalin. For Japan to back down on these issues would damage Japan's honor, he asserted, so he was calling off the negotiations. The only hope he had was in his plan to wait in New York after leaving Portsmouth on the chance that the Russians might change their position. The Japanese prime minister immediately cabled back reminding Komura that he was supposed to take his final instructions from the imperial government. He was told to postpone the final meeting one more day so as to get those instructions.

Meanwhile, Roosevelt was despondent over the failure of the negotiations and his efforts. He wrote to a friend: "Just at the moment I am disheartened over what had gone on at Portsmouth. The Russians have taken an impossible position. . . . I think the Japanese want too much money, but this I believe could be settled. The trouble is with the Russians" (p. 152). Apparently, Roosevelt was unaware how close the two sides actually were, let alone how Komura apparently deceived his government on the Sakhalin issue.

Komura's instructions arrived from Tokyo that Monday. He was told to first withdraw the demand for reimbursement. If Russia continued to demand Sakhalin, that too would be abandoned after secretly getting Roosevelt to request Japan to withdraw the territorial demand. If Roosevelt refused, Komura himself was to withdraw the demand. He and the other Japanese delegates were profoundly shaken. They had left Tokyo seven weeks ago fully expecting to realize the great "fruits of victory" they felt Japan rightfully deserved. To return home with little more than a peace agreement, after all of Japan's victories and sacrifices, would be close to treasonous. And yet now they were being instructed to give up everything if necessary.

Late Monday, Witte received word from St. Petersburg. The czar was clear: "Send Witte my order to end discussion tomorrow in any case. I prefer to continue the war than to await a gracious concession on the part of Japan" (p. 158). Although it was clear the delegation was being ordered home, Witte nevertheless decided to make one last pitch for a peace treaty. He would offer to cede the southern half of Sakhalin but no more. He sent a cable to St. Petersburg to this effect. Witte had some basis for believing this offer would secure an agreement because he had heard from journalists that Tokyo had told Komura to drop the remaining demands.

The final meeting was again delayed, this time until Tuesday morning, August 29. Witte met privately with Komura. Three-quarters of an hour later, Witte emerged to announce, "Well, friends, peace. They agreed to everything" (p. 159).

Witte immediately sent a telegraph to the czar. He also sent one to Roosevelt, "To you History will award the glory of having taken the generous initiative in bringing about the Conference, whose labors will now probably result in establishing a peace honorable to both sides" (p. 161).

Celebrations began at Hotel Wentworth at lunch and then continued that evening in Portsmouth. The Japanese did not attend. Kaneko did write to Roosevelt: "Your advice was very powerful and convincing, by which the peace of Asia was secured. . . . Both Russia and Japan owe to you this happy conclusion, and your name shall be remembered with the peace and prosperity of Asia" (p. 163).

Czar Nicholas was stunned by the agreement. He sent a telegram to Witte saying only, "Do not sign the conditions of peace as long as the size of the payment for the maintenance of war prisoners is not established" (p.

165). Only later, after congratulatory messages from around the world poured into St. Petersburg, did the czar accept the outcome. By the time Witte got back to St. Petersburg after his celebratory tours of the United States and Europe, the czar welcomed him home and honored him with the title of count. The Russian press was nevertheless critical, viewing the terms as unworthy of the accomplishments of the Russian army. Overall, however, the Russians, especially those outside St. Petersburg, rejoiced at the news of peace. In Japan, it was a different story.

The Japanese newspapers were openly hostile: "Weak diplomacy," "betrayal," and "defeat" were terms commonly seen. In Tokyo, three days of rioting followed the news of the agreement. The Japanese delegates, upon their arrival, had to be sneaked into Tokyo to avoid the mobs. The government formally ratified the treaty without public discussion.

Elsewhere around the world, the reaction was mostly positive. France's prime minister spoke of the grandeur of the result that President Roosevelt had attained and the French president declared that "the French Republic is proud of the part played by her American sister in this historic event" (p. 169). The German kaiser praised the agreement and, of Roosevelt, said, "Shining in the history of our times will be the record of President Roosevelt's services, whereby the conclusion of peace was made possible" (p. 170). British officials were shocked that their ally, Japan, had backed down. They blamed Roosevelt in part for it. The British foreign minister wrote, "I think myself that the American financiers got at the Japanese plenipotentiaries and said they would not lend any more money for war purposes" (p. 171). Talk of a move by Roosevelt to threaten a financial boycott of future Japanese loans also surfaced.[5] Eventually, the British acknowledged the need for peace and praised Roosevelt for his contribution. At home, Roosevelt was widely praised: "Theodore Roosevelt stands unchallenged as the world's first citizen"; and "He has sheathed the swords of a million men."[6] Shortly after, he was awarded the Nobel Peace Prize.

ANALYSIS OF ROOSEVELT'S INTERVENTION

Why did world leaders and belligerents alike heap praise on Roosevelt? Why the Nobel Peace Prize? Was his advice really so "powerful and convincing" as to secure peace? Or was he, in the final analysis, little more than a good host? A careful look at the nature of the conflict and his role suggests the answer lies somewhere in-between these extremes. Where realists would discount his impact altogether, pointing instead to the power relationship between the belligerents, Roosevelt did influence the outcome of the Russo-Japanese conflict. And where statesmen and headline writers prefer to see a great personality in every peacemaking success, Roosevelt's effect was not to end the war. To understand what impact he did have, it is first necessary to interpret his behavior as a third party. This can be done in terms of his major decision problems: party acceptance and entry timing; his search for an appropriate role; and his attempts to build intermediary influence.

Entry and Acceptance

As the Russo-Japanese war proceeded without an obvious end and Roosevelt deemed a U.S. role advantageous, he faced two conflicting decision problems as a potential intermediary. The first was to gain entry—and thus gain the parties' acceptance; the second was to effect an outcome that met his and his country's interests.

To gain the parties' acceptance, Roosevelt first had to convince them that a third party would be useful and that he was the best candidate. Because both sides were concerned they would appear weak if they initiated talks, the obvious solution was to allow a third party to take the first step. But recent history made both sides wary of a major power or a concert of powers that would impose a settlement. Consequently, Roosevelt took pains to assure both sides that he had little interest in "mediating" in the traditional sense but simply wanted to help get things started; that is, he would provide so-called good offices. Once they agreed to talk, he reinforced his limited role by staying physically removed from the negotiations. To this point, then, he assumed a highly restricted facilitating role, acting as little more than a conference chairman, booking rooms and providing tables.

Roosevelt's second decision problem was to increase the likelihood that the parties would settle and would do so on terms favorable to him and to U.S. interests. His personal motive was to establish a reputation as a world statesman. His national motive was to ensure a balance of power in Asia and an open door to China. His balancing act, then, was to remain a mere convener yet urge an agreement favorable to himself. Thus, although he had to convince each side it would do well, he also had to encourage both sides to moderate their demands and expectations. The inevitable result, especially as negotiations began to falter, was for Roosevelt to take a more active role.

As Roosevelt began to tip the balance from convener to active intermediary, he incurred risks. One risk was to the U.S.'s fledgling role as a major player in the established system of powers. Britain already resented his efforts, and the other powers were only reluctant supporters. A second risk was that he would alienate one or both of the disputants and thus exacerbate tensions and give them a pretense for ending negotiations. Roosevelt balanced these competing aims by moving slowly at first, insinuating himself into the process as it developed and as circumstances permitted.

Entry and gaining acceptance, thus, are not as clear-cut in practice as that portrayed in chapters 4 and 5. Both decision problems make for a delicate balancing act. They do, nevertheless, partially determine the mode and extent of influence the mediator has once in the dispute.

Modes of Influence

Roosevelt's decision problems provide the context for understanding his impact on the dispute. As with any attempt to explain an event involving a complex set of factors, it is impossible to calculate the precise importance of one factor. Here, the disputants' balance of forces, domestic politics, and internal decision-making processes were certainly the major factors determining the end of the war. But when and how the war would end can be attributed in large part to Roosevelt's intervention and the movement it precipitated. The war could easily have dragged on at great cost to both sides. What, then, were Roosevelt's bases of influence, and how did these affect the dispute?

In his capacity as intermediary, Roosevelt was a principal mediator.[7] As president of a rising power in a time of rapidly shifting alliances, Roosevelt conducted implicit bargains with the parties. From them he wanted improved relations, especially with Japan, and access to China. From the international community, he wanted admission to the league of world powers. The United States was already an economic power, but it did not have the stature of a major political and diplomatic player. To get a peace treaty signed that ended one of history's costliest wars would have contributed substantially to achieving that stature. In short, Roosevelt was bargaining with Japan and Russia to meet several important but indirect interests: improved relations with each, access to a major market, and a diplomatic success. To achieve the diplomatic success, he only had to get an end to the war; the specific terms were not important as long as the United States got access to China, a virtual certainty if a peace was negotiated rather than a victory won on the battlefield.

On the other side of the bargain, Japan looked to the United States for financial and, it seemed, moral support. The Europeans still looked condescendingly upon the Japanese. Many of the discriminatory treaties of the Tokugawa period were still in place and the great powers balked at renegotiating them, the effect being to deny Japan the status of a world power. Despite Japan's alliance with Britain, the United States was the one power that could—or would—give Japan international standing. Consequently, the United States could trade upon Japan's need for legitimacy and financing (whether for the war or for reconstruction) to squeeze concessions from the Japanese.

Russia was less dependent on the United States but increasingly desperate for a way out of its Far East debacle. Germany's threat to the European system and Russia's repeated military setbacks and serious domestic unrest all made peace imperative. Russia also appeared to want improved relations with the United States although its immediate concern was to get pressure applied on the Japanese to moderate their demands in peace talks. The United States presumably could do so through financial means because it was a major financier of the war.

On the whole, the bargaining relationship between the United States and each of the protagonists was not a strong one. The mutual dependencies were not, for example, on the order of those between the United States and Israel and the United States and Egypt seventy-five years later. Nevertheless, the important point is that, however limited Roosevelt's bargaining power, his relationship was, nevertheless, fundamentally a bargaining one. He could neither claim to be disinterested nor insignificant in the calculations of the great powers. In a time of rapidly shifting alliances, the United States, as a rising power, had to be factored into everyone's balancing equation.

Although Roosevelt was implicitly bargaining throughout his intervention, he was, nevertheless, an actor "in between." He was negotiating for nothing but a bilateral agreement between Japan and Russia, albeit one that met U.S. interests. The specifics of his practice as an intermediary—entry timing, procedural initiatives, and multilateral diplomacy—reveal how he used his position to build his bargaining influence in the dispute.

The timing of Roosevelt's entry enhanced his influence once talks began. Early in the conflict, he downplayed any mediating role, emphasizing the need for talks. He launched an all-out effort to gain acceptance only after the decisive naval battle. It is not clear, however, if delaying entry was a deliberate strategy to increase his mediating influence once in the dispute or an acceptance of his relative impotence in the parties' military calculations or a reflection of his hesitancy owing to the risks of involvement. Whether deliberate or not, when the two sides agreed, both were on the verge of financial collapse if not military exhaustion. The talks began, therefore, with both sides facing very unpalatable alternatives to a negotiated agreement. Given these alternatives, Roosevelt had to say very little to impress each side with the value of keeping the negotiations going at Portsmouth. Moreover, Roosevelt helped worsen Russia's alternative by lining up France, Russia's major financier, against the war and in support of his proposals. He may even have implied a cutoff of U.S. aid to Japan to worsen Japan's alternative. Of course, France's primary concern was the balance of power in Europe, but Roosevelt can at least be credited with spurring France to act at a crucial moment, when earlier in the conflict it was reluctant to do anything. In sum, consistent with the entry-timing argument of chapter 4, Roosevelt enhanced his bargaining leverage vis-à-vis each disputant by waiting until their alternatives to a negotiated agreement were poor. He then gained even more leverage by worsening those alternatives once involved.

A second example of influence building in his practice was the procedural measures he initiated. As an intermediary, Roosevelt did the little things neither of the two belligerents could do on their own. He initiated the talks (although Japan secretly requested him to do so) thus alleviating each side's fear of appearing weak. He designated a site (after receiving their preferences) and helped set the dates. Given their sensitivity to outside interference and their fears of appearing too eager to seek peace, any of these seemingly minor procedural issues could have thwarted the peace talks if attempted directly by the belligerents. At a minimum, then, Roosevelt made a difference by resolving these issues himself. Moreover, once the site was chosen and the two delegations made their journeys, face-saving was no longer an issue; the two sides could agree readily themselves on the remaining procedural issues. Of course, in handling procedural matters, Roosevelt also gained access and a modicum of control. It was no accident that the United States became the host country and Portsmouth, only one day's journey from Oyster Bay, the negotiating site. Thus, the mediator's proposals not only created focal points for interim and conditional agreements as discussed in chapter 3, they afforded the mediator a bit more leverage.

A third example of Roosevelt's influence building was his persistent lobbying of the leaders and their representatives. Unlike France and the other powers that interceded irregularly and mostly only at the last minute, Roosevelt continuously sent messages to the belligerents from early in the conflict until the very end. For sure, most of these neither compelled nor swayed a decision, the possible exception being his message to the czar with Ambassador Meyer's follow-up resulting in the concession on Sakhalin. What was most important, rather, was that the flurry of messages continued so that at the right moment one negotiator could seize upon them as the necessary excuse to prolong negotiations. In the final days of Portsmouth, when the obduracy of the czar and the machinations of Komura could easily have led to the resumption of war, Witte used Roosevelt's "interference" to avert his superior's orders. Witte's plea to accept Roosevelt's position was credible back home because the source was credible as an actor (in part, no doubt, because the Russians had already committed themselves to conducting negotiations under Roosevelt's auspices) *and* as a nonbelligerent. In short, at this point in the negotiations, only a player both involved and removed, a player active but only acting in between, could serve the necessary scapegoat function. It would have been pointless to cite international law or some vague notion of "world opinion." Roosevelt's position gave Witte the concreteness and immediacy to make the Russian leadership defer, at least temporarily, to Roosevelt and hence to the continuation of the negotiations.

In sum, these three examples of Roosevelt's practice illustrate the subtlety of his influence. His legitimacy as a bargaining agent was based on his position as leader of a rising power. Although Roosevelt implicitly used this position in all his dealings, he also used his position in the middle to do what no other actor could do. Did he, then, make a difference? Reasonable counterfactual arguments suggest he did but not in the sense of determining war or no war; larger forces determined whether the war would end. What Roosevelt did was hasten its conclusion and help ensure that it would not resume.

Reducing the Duration of the Conflict

Common wisdom has it that nations seek peace when one side is vanquished or both are exhausted. Leaders choose negotiation when they cannot prevail unilaterally. The implication is that, until they decide to negotiate—that is, until they make an official, usually public, declaration—they are not prepared to negotiate. Underlying this view is the assumption of rational decision making: actors seek to prevail until the expected benefits no longer exceed the expected costs. When the costs do exceed the benefits, they "decide"; that is, they declare their willingness to negotiate. The evidence for such a calculation is simple: had they wanted to negotiate earlier, they would have done so; the costs must not have been high enough. The reasoning, of course, is circular.

What a detailed examination of a case like Portsmouth reveals is that leaders often seek alternative means of resolving disputes well before they "decide," that is, well before the world or, for that matter, one's opponent, is aware of it. In the Portsmouth case, the Japanese prepared for mediation almost at the same time they began hostilities. Even Czar Nicholas, known for his unyielding pursuance of national greatness and his desire for at least one military success against Japan, approached the French to intercede with the Japanese, and this nearly three months before he agreed to Portsmouth. In short, leaders seek alternatives to force well before their efforts are generally known. Only the scrupulous historian, an occasional investigative journalist, and selected intermediaries may know of such efforts, however.

This insight into a leader's decision making, one not likely to result from the stylized argumentation of part 1, has an important implication for intermediary intervention and peacemaking generally. An intermediary may not change a leader's military and economic calculations or the point when the leader begins to explore alternatives (although some intermediaries may do even this). But once the disputant's exploration begins (realistically, it may occur throughout a conflict as the Japanese example shows), the intermediary can accelerate the peacemaking process. By the very suggestion of employing an intermediary, the disputants are presented with a real alternative to force. In times of high stress when decision makers tend to narrow options or to latch onto their first course of action (say, hostilities), a suggestion of this sort can be significant. An offer of intermediary intervention thus facilitates the leader's transition from the exploration phase—Are there alternatives? Are they favorable to my interests? Is at least one better than prolongation of the conflict? Is one better than the others?—to the official decision phase.

In the Portsmouth case, had Roosevelt not made himself available, the conflict could easily have dragged on. Significant elements in both Japan and Russia seemed to have put loss of face and national honor above the continued loss of life, financial ruin, and, possibly, domestic turmoil (especially in Russia). Neither side would initiate talks and neither would accept the imposition of a conference of powers. France may have eventually stepped in as an intermediary, maybe even Britain. The difference Roosevelt made, though, was to step in relatively early to exploit and encourage the forces of moderation and peacemaking on both sides. He did this in at least three ways.

First, he gave comfort to those elements favoring an end to the war. In both Japan and Russia, moderates could cite the opinion (and, possibly, the implied threats) of the leader of a friendly and powerful actor. Second, the intervention enabled the moderates to form alternative channels of communication with the negotiators. For example, were it not for Roosevelt and Japan's special emissary in New York, the Japanese prime minister would have had to rely entirely on Komura and the Foreign Ministry for information on developments. Given Komura's hardline orientation and his deviousness, the outcome could have been far different had he pursued the indemnity question.

Third, Roosevelt reinforced those who knew best when Japan had spent itself militarily. Japanese military leaders, not the foreign ministry officials, were some of the earliest advocates of ending the war and the first to make overtures to Roosevelt. This was because they, not the diplomats nor the public, could best assess the strategic reality of having reached the point where victory turns to defeat as Japan pushed Russia farther toward its borders.[8] An intermediary intervention can serve even a victor's self-interest by arresting its victories in advance of this reversal point. In all three ways, Roosevelt's intervention was effective not because it reversed the forces of power but because it interceded to augment decision-making processes already underway.[9]

CONCLUSION

A detailed examination of a case like Portsmouth reveals that an intermediary's behavior can be understood in part by the peculiar requirements of gaining party acceptance, timing one's entry, and building influence as discussed in part 1. It also shows that an intermediary's role can evolve considerably as the intervention proceeds. For Roosevelt, this evolution was, in part, deliberate; he entered cautiously, downplaying his involvement and demonstrating his distance (even physically) from the belligerents' negotiations. But once his proposal for talks and for a site were accepted, he stepped up his activity. It is conceivable that if either Witte or the Japanese leadership was not so forthcoming at the last minute, Roosevelt would have traveled to Portsmouth himself or invited the chief delegates to his home. On the other hand, if the negotiations had not stalled and had not appeared to be on the verge of collapse, Roosevelt might have done little more than offer encouragement.

Thus, Roosevelt's activity and the way the role evolved were in part determined by the course of the negotiations themselves. He could not substantially affect the negotiations—the primary factors being the belligerents' balance of power and their domestic conditions. But he could do what the belligerents could not do by themselves—initiate talks, propose a site, and provide legitimacy or pretenses for conciliatory moves. And he could affect the individual negotiators' interactions with their home governments and their internal deliberations. In fact, as a general proposition, one not developed in part 1, it may be that an intermediary's primary impact depends less on what happens at the negotiating table and more on what happens vis-à-vis each party's internal bargain.

Four additional general points deriving from this case study build on the propositions of part 1. One, in chapter 2 I hypothesized that intermediaries deliberately limit their involvement and even their capabilities so as to assume, or reinforce, the role of a neutral mediator. Here, we see self-limitation for another purpose, that is, to get in, to get a piece of the action. This was necessary in part because of the two parties' historical experiences but is probably generally true any time disputants fear meddling in their sovereign affairs.

Two, an intermediary's proposal, in addition to its use in creating a focal point as discussed in chapter 3 or in threatening a disputant as in Camp David, can be seized at opportune moments by disputants to delay, to override superiors, or to sway constituencies. An intermediary's proposals, therefore, may be significant less for their substantive contribution than for their scapegoating function. A negotiator can cite international law or "world opinion," but when negotiations are at a critical stage, the immediacy and concreteness of a proposal from a credible party who is involved in, but not party to, the dispute is likely to be more effective.

Three, this case suggests that leaders seek alternatives to force (even while continuing to use force) well before such efforts are generally known. If anything, these efforts are known only to insiders, the occasional investigative journalist, selected intermediaries, and the scrupulous historian. Analyses and policies that discount the possibility of a search for alternatives prior to its public expression miss an important element of conflict and its potential for resolution. Intermediaries in particular must recognize that what they hear over the airwaves—messages designed to intimidate adversaries and assure constituencies—are not necessarily reflecting underlying flexibility. An intermediary's persistence in the face of apparently low odds can work, as seen here and in the Camp David case, because little-known opportunities arise and are exploited by adroit interventions.

Finally, this and the Camp David case suggest that even a principal mediator is not a major determinant of a conflict outcome. In the Middle East, the 1973 war and Sadat's trip to Jerusalem were the key factors. In the Russo-Japanese conflict, mutual exhaustion was the major factor. The mediators in each case, however, were instrumental in hastening the conclusion of those agreements, not through exercising "power" alone but, especially at Portsmouth, by employing subtle forms of influence. Thus, although it is tempting to conclude that intermediaries, especially principal mediators, are major determinants of a conflict outcome, in these two cases it does appear that they were, in fact, more like tipping agents, as discussed in chapter 3. The Portsmouth case raises the additional feature of intermediary intervention, however, that such tipping can be critical to getting agreement sooner rather than later.

PART THREE

Intermediary Intervention in Practice: Neutral Mediators

Chapter Eight

VATICAN: POPE JOHN PAUL II MEDIATES
BETWEEN ARGENTINA AND
CHILE, 1978–1984

SOME DISPUTES—especially minor ones like many territorial disputes—seem to simmer for years, even decades, with little action and little reason to settle them. They can linger harmlessly or, owing to a shift in the balance of power or to domestic turmoil, they can become pretexts for belligerence. When a belligerent path is chosen, a direct solution is often difficult to achieve, and third parties are useful in promoting a settlement. In a century-long dispute over a few islands at the tip of South America, Argentina and Chile narrowly averted war by turning to a mediator, the Vatican. The road to settlement was long and uncertain and, as will be seen in the following case and analysis, events could easily have overturned the Vatican's efforts. The important question is how, in its capacity as a relatively "neutral mediator,"[1] the Vatican capitalized on its limited opportunities to shift the parties from a belligerent to a problem-solving path. As will be seen, at many points, the Vatican was successful only in keeping the parties at bay, not at pushing a settlement. In the end, that proved quite enough once domestic factors, especially those in Argentina, changed.

THE CASE

When Spain divided the southern cone of South America into two countries, the task was simple: it traced a line from north to south along the tips of the highest Andean peaks that apportioned everything east of the line to Argentina and everything west to Chile. At that time, it mattered little that in the southernmost region the mountain peaks are not neatly arranged in a north-south pattern. An 1881 boundary treaty appeared to correct the problem, but the eastern mouth of one passage, the Beagle Channel, was left ambiguous. Chile, not surprisingly, claimed an easternmost interpretation of the channel's mouth whereas Argentina claimed a westernmost. The difference? Three barren little islands occupied mostly by sheep.

As a result of this ambiguity, the southern tip of the continent was the site of sporadic incidents between Argentina and Chile throughout the first half of the twentieth century. By the 1960s, it had become clear to both sides that the issue of the boundary—apportioning land—and the associated maritime delimitation—setting jurisdiction over waters—had to be settled so the two countries could turn their attention to questions of regional economic integration. For example, Argentina had long dreamed of transporting its vast agricultural products in the interior directly across the Andes and out Chilean ports to its Pacific destinations. Similarly, Chile had long wanted grazing rights in times of drought on Argentina's vast but unused plains. Such arrangements were hampered by the dispute over the Beagle Channel islands.

Consistent with a 1902 treaty, the two countries decided in 1971 to submit the matter to arbitration. A panel of jurists from the International Court at The Hague agreed to hear the case. Although Argentine President General Alejandro Lanusse, expected to get navigational rights and one or two islands, for him, the real issue "was to finish with the problem" and get on with matters of regional integration.[2]

On May 2, 1976, five years after its submission, the arbitration court handed down its award, the *Laudo*.[3] As both sides had expected, Argentina retained navigational rights to its naval base in the channel, and Chile was awarded the three islands. The panel also determined that they Laudo should be executed within a period of nine months.[4]

But, between 1971, when the issue was submitted to arbitration, and 1977, when the Laudo was delivered, things had changed, particularly in Argentina. Deteriorating economic and social conditions led to a military coup by General Jorge Videla. The new government determined that the Laudo was unacceptable because it would allow Chile to project its maritime jurisdiction into the Atlantic. And then, according to one Argentine participant, "during [informal] negotiations, Argentina's hunger began to grow."[5] That is, it wanted islands. It needed islands to preserve its long-held "bioceanico" principle: Argentina in the Atlantic, Chile in the Pacific. Without some base in islands, whether in the channel or to the south, Argentina could not prevent Chile from claiming part of the Atlantic. The Argentine foreign minister expressed the mood of the government regarding the Laudo: "No commitment obliges a country to comply with that which affects its vital interests or that which damages rights of sovereignty."[6]

Throughout these informal negotiations, Chile would only discuss maritime delimitation, not islands and channel navigation, issues that were covered—and, Chile felt, settled—in the Laudo. But Argentina wanted to negotiate over all issues to achieve a comprehensive and definitive solution to the entire question of boundaries in the southern region. And it wanted what it often referred to as a "politically valid" and durable settlement, not a judicial decision that could be easily rejected in the future by either side as conditions changed.[7] General Osiris Villegas, one of Argentina's chief negotiators at the time, expressed Argentina's view this way in a 1982 book:

> The [process] must result in drawing a boundary that is honorable for Argentina, respects its legitimate rights to territorial integrity and protects its permanent interests in the southern region. *This is the political objective and not peace.*
>
> To give priority to the preservation of the peace over the national interests, would be a sign of weakness. Universal experience shows that the countries that demonstrate weakness in the conduct of their external affairs, do not achieve good results. Weakness brings disregard from an adversary and provokes contempt and systematic aggression.
>
> To get a solution that satisfies the national interest, there are only two ways: the political solution that protects our rights or the occupation of the islands in dispute, as an act of sovereignty.[8] (Villegas's italics)

As the nine-month review and implementation period stipulated in the Laudo came to a close, it was clear that informal negotiations would not succeed. In an attempt to break the impasse, the two presidents, Videla of Argentina and Augusto Pinochet of Chile, met on January 19, 1978. But they could only agree to meet a second time, the date tentatively set for January 26.

On January 25, to the astonishment of the Chileans and outside observers, Argentine Foreign Minister Oscar Montes announced that "the decision and Her Britannic Majesty's Award . . . are null and void . . . and the Government of the Argentine Republic . . . does not consider itself bound to implement it."[9] Argentina cited the arbitration court's distortion of Argentina's arguments and asserted that the court exceeded the scope of the dispute as submitted, exhibited contradictions in reasoning, made faulty interpretations as well as geographical and historical errors, and committed systematic one-sidedness favoring Chile. The commander of Argentine naval operations summed up the Argentine military's view: "Argentina will not allow co-ownership in the South Atlantic. . . . As commander of naval operations, I can assure everyone that all the components of naval power are ready to assume the role that is given them in their area of responsibility. The Argentine armed forces are not pacifists, but pacific. We are aggressive, but not aggressors."[10]

Chile was shocked. Chile's air force commander said he was outraged and that "it is inconceivable that such a matter could go on in the twentieth century."[11]

Argentina pressed Chile to resume talks and, although reluctant, President Pinochet did name a military commission to meet with the Argentines. These meetings eventually led to a procedure for initiating a new round of negotiations. On February 20, 1978, the two presidents met in Puerto Montt in southern Chile and agreed on a formal, three-stage negotiation process.[12] The first stage, establishing procedures, was completed in May. In the second stage, for which six months were allotted, progress was made on some of the "integration" issues. But the most fundamental questions—islands and maritime delimitation—could not be resolved. Private meetings between the two delegation heads, an attempt to combine the question of islands with that of waters, a proposal to create a "common zone," and an offer to include questions about the Straits of Magellan all failed to get movement. A Chilean advisor later explained why all these ideas ultimately proved fruitless: "Argentina tried to get some islands and we were not in a position to give them any one of them. Not the smallest one. We could be flexible on the fixing of limits on the sea and we told them that, very often. . . . We could look for further solutions working together on certain aspects, economical and other, but nothing which is not in our [interests]."[13]

With negotiations deadlocked and the six-month period prescribed in the Act of Puerto Montt scheduled to end in October, President Videla appeared increasingly flexible and was willing to consider those suggestions proposed by his Foreign Ministry and its negotiating delegation. But his was not the only voice in the Argentine leadership. For example, in August, the army's commander in chief, General Roberto Eduardo Viola, stated that "Sovereignty is not to be negotiated."[14] And navy commander, Admiral Emilio Massera, reacting in part to discussions of bringing in a third party, declared that "Our homeland cannot be amputated. . . . Argentina is not disposed to permit third parties to judge and decide about what is ours."[15] A month later, he added that "When . . . we are in a conflict, we are going to fight until . . . victory . . . or . . . death."[16]

Across the Andes, the position of Augusto Pinochet, Chile's commander in chief of the armed forces and president of the Republic, in that order, remained clear, coherent and unchanging. A member of the Chilean delegation summed up the Chilean position by explaining that to give up one island "was impossible for us because it is not [a matter of just] an island, . . . but it is the principle, the principle of the treaty. We have the treaty and we can't [violate] the treaty. . . . I would say that the principle interest was and is that treaties have to be complied with. . . . It's not only the legal principle but it is a political principle. So, therefore, it's the basis for international policy."[17]

As these second stage negotiations proceeded—and faltered—both countries moved on other fronts. Argentina put economic pressure on Chile, delaying trucks at the border, closing some border passes, impeding shipments to Chile from Brazil, and charging trucks as much as $1000 for "escorts."[18] Argentina also expelled a number of Chilean citizens, including migrant workers.

For some of Argentina's leaders, economic measures and tough talk were not enough. They had another idea. The Argentine foreign minister, Oscar Montes, recalled that as negotiations were showing little progress, and no solution was in sight,

> We began to think of occupying the islands. For me, it did not mean war, however much many in Argentina felt that the occupation of some of the islands did mean war.
>
> This is my personal opinion that was not shared by many people [including some] in the Junta, in the Government.[19]

The idea of occupying the islands was aimed only at compelling Chile to negotiate. Both Argentine and Chilean sources indicated that the idea was no secret to Chile at the time.

But the military was playing with more than just words. In June, the Argentine army and air force conducted maneuvers and engaged in war games in the southern region. In September, numerous cities in the interior of Argentina conducted air raid and blackout drills. On October 12, 1978, one-half million Argentine military reservists were called up. Blackout drills were continued into October in various cities. In Buenos Aires, for example, a blackout drill on October 24 at 10:00 P.M. was complete with sirens and alarms. It was reported to be a complete success except for the Chilean embassy.[20] Reports also circulated that schools were being readied for the stationing of troops; railroad yards were being prepared for the transport of military equipment; red crosses were being painted on hospitals, and casket production had been stepped up. In addition, throughout the crisis in 1978, Argentina built up its stock of armaments. For example, Argentina bought twenty-six Dagger fighter jets from Israel and seventeen new tanks from Austria.[21]

For its part, Chile was taking its share of military precautions as well. Foreign Minister Hernan Cubillos explained: "During that whole year, we reinforced all our military divisions at specific points along our front. . . . We kept a very strong division in the North, in December, in . . . any pass of the 'cordillera' [mountain range] where attacks could happen. In spite of the fact that Chile would attack on the south, we didn't move those divisions south. We kept them at a place [where] we knew they would attack. I think they were very impressed that we didn't move one single military man from the North to the South."[22]

In the waning days of October, the date of November 2 came to be referred to as "D-Day." If an agreement could not be reached, it would be the first day that the two countries would lack a jointly agreed means for resolving the Beagle Channel dispute. And both sides knew that with bellicosity in the air, the slightest misstep could lead to the most serious consequences.

Despite several last-ditch efforts, negotiations indeed collapsed the end of October. Both countries immediately began a total mobilization of armed forces. Troops converged on the border, and the two navies began moving south.

November 1978 thus became a month of extreme uncertainty and tension. Both countries maneuvered at home and abroad to garner support for their respective positions while seeking a way out of the crisis.

Soon after the collapse of the negotiations, Chile's Foreign Minister Cubillos sent an official diplomatic note to the newly appointed Argentine foreign minister, air force Brigadier Carlos Washington Pastor (brother-in-law of President Videla) proposing that the dispute be submitted to the International Court as provided for in the 1972 treaty.[23] The unofficial but unmistakable response was that if Chile were to go to the court, Argentina would consider it a casus belli.

Part of Chile's international strategy was to solicit the support of the Vatican.[24] Earlier, in mid-1978, Chile's foreign minister, Hernan Cubillos, had seen Pope John Paul I at his inauguration. As a result of that meeting, the pope issued a letter to a regional bishop's conference in South America encouraging the local churches to use their influence to achieve a peaceful solution to the conflict. By the time the negotiations collapsed, a new pope had been inaugurated and Cubillos arranged an audience with him, John Paul II.[25] The pope had been in office only five days but, by the time Cubillos arrived, he had been briefed on the dispute and had personally reviewed various maps and documents. In that meeting, Cubillos encouraged the pope to do something, maybe send an emissary. At this point, there was no talk of mediation.

In Santiago in November, the Chilean Foreign Ministry formed a special working group to handle the delicate and increasingly dangerous situation. The group considered appealing to outside parties such as the Organization of American States, the United Nations, and other powers, as well as the possibility of unilaterally resorting to the International Court. But not until early December did anyone consider requesting a mediator. Many in the group preferred a judicial solution but, given that negotiations had collapsed, armed conflict was looking increasingly likely, and Argentina viewed a unilateral application to the International Court a casus belli, mediation appeared to be the best choice. The question was who would be requested and whether Argentina would agree.

Hernan Cubillos described Chile's reasoning regarding the choice of a mediator:

It had to be a country powerful enough so that the suggestions it would make as mediator had power behind them. . . . And when we talk of power, I'm talking about influence, moral power, political power, economic power. It is obvious that a suggestion from a country with those attributes is more powerful than from a little island nation in the Caribbean that you can get away with saying, to hell with your suggestions. I don't think it would have excluded Switzerland because, by the fact of its neutrality, it has been accepted as a meeting place for many kinds of things.

We were looking for a country where legal tradition and legality were important and understood more or less the way we understand it. And as we had a very strong legal case and an award in our favor [the Laudo], we felt that we had to have a country that was willing to understand the importance of that settlement and one that respected international law.

So basically, those were the types of countries we were looking for—[powerful enough to] impose a suggestion so that you couldn't get away easily. . . . We also understood that things having reached the point at which they were, it would be difficult to start a war if a country with those characteristics had said something. It would have made it very difficult for the Argentineans to go to war after the arbitration award and after the suggestion from a country with those characteristics.

We were so sure that a ruling would be in our favor, that we were not afraid of what would come out of the suggestion. We were more looking for that suggestion to be acceptable and be seen by the world at large and, of course, [for] Argentina, as something which they couldn't get away [from].[26]

With these criteria in mind, the special working group came up with a list of five countries. At the top of the list was the Vatican and Pope John Paul II. Chile sent a diplomatic note to Argentina, first suggesting that they submit the problem to the International Court, and then, if that was not acceptable, that the two countries seek the mediation of a friendly nation. The Argentine foreign minister, Pastor, accepted the idea of mediation and the two ministers decided to meet personally in Buenos Aires December 12 to select the mediator.

To this point, Argentina had made few overtures to the outside world for support or assistance (other than procuring military supplies). Only at the last minute did it send missions to the Organization of American States and the United Nations Security Council. The possibility of mediation, nevertheless, was discussed throughout the Argentine government, media, and church. A variety of possible mediators were considered including the king of Spain, the United Nations, the queen of England, UN Secretary General Kurt Waldheim, Henry Kissinger, and the pope. The Argentine ambassador to the United States qualified the official discussions, however, by saying that only a "friendly government" would be considered, not an individual.[27] In addition, by one report, the mediator would have to be completely neutral, from outside Latin America, and would only be asked to consider those issues the two countries agreed to submit to mediation.[28]

While mediation was discussed in Argentina, it was by no means seen by everyone as the best way to resolve the problem. Some outrightly opposed papal mediation. In a 1982 book, General Villegas explained the objection: "We find ourselves confronted with safeguarding the national interest not having conducted it in a theater of operations where success is possible, but in the halls of the Vatican, where the results are uncertain. For such matters it is possible that triumph is not produced from justice, reason, or the law, but the fruit or the imposition of the strongest will, which *until now is not ours.*"[29] (Villegas's italics)

Until the end of December, the Vatican was officially silent on the question of papal mediation. Reports in early December made it clear that the Holy See considered that any "eventual mediation would be a delicate task for various reasons" and, as the papal nuncio to Argentina, Pio Laghi, said in Buenos Aires, it is "premature to speak of mediation."[30] On December 11, the pope did cable the presidents of both countries to encourage a peaceful solution. Nevertheless, the Vatican stressed that, without a formal request from the respective governments, the pope could not step in no matter how serious the matter.[31]

Cubillos arrived in Buenos Aires the night of December 11, 1978. He attended a dinner hosted by Videla, Pastor, and several other high-level officials. Among the guests was Papal Nuncio Pio Laghi. Taking Cubillos aside, Pio Laghi explained that he had had long talks with Videla. He trusted Videla and was sure an agreement could be reached. The official meetings began the next morning. Cubillos recalled the events of that day.

> December 12th is a day I will never forget. Things were really hot. The *ambiante* in Buenos Aires was one of war. I was received with proper protocol that corresponds to a foreign minister. Troops and all sorts of things, everything done very carefully. But there was a mob outside our embassy and outside the foreign ministry and I was picketed all along wherever I went as the guy that wanted war. . . .
>
> I started the morning by paying an official visit to President Videla. . . . I was so concerned about the power structure of Argentina that I did something completely on the spur of the moment which I had not planned on doing, but remembering the conversation with Laghi the previous night [and] having seen so many signs that Videla didn't have any power. . . . I said something that really created a shock. . . . I said, Mr. President, . . . I want

to be sure that your minister has the power to reach a decision, I want to be sure he has the same power I have, which I suppose comes from you. . . . I don't want any of our sides to make mistakes. Just as your ambassador in Santiago has tried parallel ways of solving the problem, sidetracking my foreign ministry and has, I think, informed you wrongly about the way we operate in Chile and our chain of command and power and decision making on this issue, I want you to be absolutely sure that everything in Chile is going to be done through me and I have the power to act. So I don't want you to be confused as I don't want to be confused by the information we receive in Chile that you have no power and that you really depend on the Junta and the generals. . . .

Videla said, . . . Mr. Minister, if you were not such a nice person, and we didn't know each other before, and I really would ask you to leave, because that is a very unproper question. And after having said that, he went on for an hour explaining to me the power structure in Argentina, of how in spite of the way it appeared outside, he had more power than any president of any republic that I knew of. . . . Well, the Argentines like to boast, but this was very strong and in a meeting that was supposed to have taken five minutes, took an hour alone and that hour was taken by Videla explaining how powerful he was. So, [he said], go at ease, make the decision, reach an agreement with my foreign minister, and you can sign the accord this evening. . . .

So, we went to the Palacio San Martin. I had taken a group of people with me to write the proper documents, if we reached an agreement. We entered into a meeting alone . . . with Pastor. And we sat down and he opened the conversation by saying, Mr. Minister, . . . so that we don't lose any time, I want to make it clear to you that we have accepted your suggestion of mediation, but for the Argentine Republic, the only mediator possible is his Holiness the Pope. I looked him straight in the face and said, "Agreed. What else?" And he could not continue the conversation.

Now, looking back (because we have analyzed this many times), the Argentines played that card sure that we would not accept the Vatican as mediator. But I think that they made a great mistake there. Why did they think that we would not accept the Vatican? Because relations between the government in Chile with the local church were lousy. But what they didn't understand, . . . we had the [local] church on this matter on our side. And obviously, we would accept the Vatican if it is number one on my list. But it was incredible, I will never forget that minute, he was so taken back that he couldn't continue the conversation. He didn't even pretend to. . . .

I think he wanted to end there and say that it had failed because they did not accept the Vatican. In five minutes I was out of there, and we agreed to ask our delegations to get together and write an agreement, and we agreed to sign it at 4:00 P.M. Then he came back and said, . . . to be double sure that we won't have any problem, I will check with Videla. . . .

So I stayed with my delegation waiting and about an hour later he came beaming, smiling, and said, I have full green light, again. And so, go and write [it up], and let's meet here at four to sign the agreement. And our delegation started writing the document, which was very simple. . . .

Five minutes before I left, around 3:30 P.M., I received a personal call from Pastor who was practically in tears saying, I have been *desautorizado* [disauthorized]. There will be no signing of an agreement, I am not authorized to sign anything. President Videla has been desautorizado by the Junta and no agreement can be made. It was like speaking to somebody who was knocked out; he had no reasons to give, he had no excuses. They had proposed the pope, I had agreed. We had had no bargaining, and he couldn't sign.

There was an official dinner for me that evening set up as part of the program. . . . The only thing he said, "I hope you will still come to my dinner for you." I said I would because I still had hopes that such an incredible event would be sorted out during the evening.

Well, there I called Pio Laghi, the nuncio, and told him the full story. I think that was the first time . . . Pio Laghi had learned that we had agreed on the Pope. . . . He couldn't believe it. . . . Less than twelve hours before, he had told me, you will reach an agreement that will be honored. . . . Pio Laghi immediately went to see Videla and everybody started moving and our ambassador saw a lot of other people and we made it known what had happened.

I know the Junta met all evening, but when Pastor and his delegation arrived at the dinner, Pastor explained to all of us that it had been impossible to reach a decision in the Junta. With tears in his eyes (he was truly crying), he said that this was the most horrible thing that had happened to him in his life, that he was going to resign tomorrow. We had a sort of funeral dinner. It was incredible.[32]

Cubillos returned to Santiago on December 13 and informed President Pinochet, the U.S. ambassador to Chile, George Landau, and the Vatican, via the nuncio in Chile, of the failure to reach agreement. In Buenos Aires, meanwhile, the Junta met in permanent session in the "Condor," headquarters of the Argentine air force. Videla was not invited. Pastor and the head of the Joint Chiefs of Staff shuttled between the Condor and the presidential palace.

As word of the failure to choose a mediator spread from both capitals and war looked imminent, both countries solicited the help of the international community. Chile sent representatives to the United States, the Vatican, China, and the OAS. Argentina sent delegates to Washington, Paris, Bonn, the Vatican, and the United Nations. On December 15, U.S. President Jimmy Carter publicly called upon both Argentina and Chile to cease belligerent acts and resolve the issue peacefully. But as Ambassador

Landau noted in retrospect, "It became evident that the United States had practically no leverage with any of the two military governments which distrusted the Carter administration and found its stand on human rights annoying to say the least."[33]

In Buenos Aires, on December 14, the day after Cubillos left without an agreement on a mediator, Papal Nuncio Pio Laghi visited President Videla at the Casa Rosada [Pink House], the presidential palace.

Laghi had earlier received information from a highly reliable source in the military that Argentina had a pact with Peru's military government with which Argentina had good relations. The pact provided for a simultaneous invasion of Chile. By invading, Peru could have expected to reclaim territory from Chile lost in the 1879 War of the Pacific.[34] And, Laghi reasoned, if Peru joined in the fray, Bolivia could be tempted to join as well. Bolivia had also lost territory in the War of the Pacific but, for Bolivia, one of the poorest countries in Latin America, the loss had relegated the country to the status of a landlocked nation. If these two countries were to join, Laghi and other observers reasoned, neighboring countries might be similarly tempted to enter. Rumors were already spreading that Brazil, long in competition with Argentina for hegemony in the region, would join on the side of Chile.[35] Later, however, Brazil was reported to offer its services as a mediator.[36] In short, Laghi had good reason to expect that fighting in the southern tip of South America could easily spread throughout the region.

In their December 14 meeting, Videla told Laghi that he had given orders to invade the islands. The date would be either December 21 or 22, a week away. Videla explained that he had little choice: if he did not give the orders he would be removed and those with extreme views would take over.

Laghi asked Videla if he realized this meant war. He did. Laghi asked him whether a message from the pope would help. Videla told him it would not, it would be worthless. The invasion was inevitable. Nor would a letter be enough. Then Laghi asked him, if the pope contacted Pinochet and him directly and set up some kind of three-way communication, would that help? Videla: Maybe.

With that, Laghi immediately contacted Rome via cable and secret code as well as the U.S. ambassador and other officials. Despite the lack of U.S. leverage, the United States did play a role at this point. Ambassador Landau, who had followed the dispute closely and had been kept regularly informed of developments by the Chilean Foreign Ministry, provided a conduit of information from South America to the Vatican.[37] From U.S. intelligence monitorings in the southern cone, Landau knew when Argentina's invasion was imminent. On or around December 19, Landau also learned that the pope intended to intervene in some manner but that he would wait until after Christmas. Apparently, the Vatican was convinced that no Catholic country would launch a war during the Christmas season. Landau immediately conveyed the urgency of the situation to the Vatican.

On December 17, Argentina sent top military officials to Santiago to speak with their counterparts but, as before, their efforts proved fruitless.[38] Meanwhile, armed forces of both countries were at a full state of alert. Warships were sailing just hours apart in the Straits of Magellan. In Argentina, December 22 had been finally set as the invasion date. But the weather was unfavorable that day, so the invasion was delayed 24 hours.

Then, at 10:00 A.M., Argentine time, on December 23, Pope John Paul II notified both countries he was sending his personal envoy to both capitals. Military activity on both sides came to a halt. Argentina immediately suspended maneuvers, reopened the borders, and withdrew its naval fleet from the southern region. On Christmas Day, Cardinal Antonio Samoré boarded the only flight out of Rome bound for two Catholic countries in turmoil in South America.

The Vatican described Samoré's mission as strictly information gathering, to offer the Holy See's "good offices" by shuttling back and forth between the countries. Officially, there was no intention to suggest that the pope mediate the dispute. Based on the information available at the time, Samoré determined four specific objectives for his trip: get the two countries to refrain from the use of force; arrange for the military situation to revert to the status quo; resume a dialogue; and find a way toward agreement. To achieve these objectives, Samoré would need access to all concerned on both sides. This, he understood before he left, was promised by both countries. He also knew that to gain their trust and reduce tensions, he would have to show no partiality to either side.[39]

Samoré arrived in Buenos Aires the day after Christmas and was greeted by some two thousand well wishers shouting, "No to war, yes to peace."[40] He first met with Foreign Minister Pastor and then with President Videla. The following day, December 27, Samoré met with the full Junta. He soon learned that although Argentina was interested in the possibility of papal mediation, certain conditions would have to be met. First, any resumption of negotiations would have to be considered a continuation of the political process set up in the Act of Puerto Montt. In this act, the two countries, by Argentina's interpretation, would continue negotiations in the third stage if all matters were not settled in the second stage. Chile's contrasting position had been that, because negotiations had failed, they could not be resumed, and a new forum would be needed. This position, as Argentina saw it, resulted in the stalemate of late 1978 that nearly led to war. Argentina also demanded that the Laudo, the 1977 arbitration award favoring Chile, be considered "irrevocably null." Third, Argentina considered the "bioceanic" principle—Argentina in the Atlantic, Chile in the Pacific—to be an essential basis for any agreement. And, fourth, the scope of the mediation would have to be determined in advance. Although Argentina had all along wanted to submit the matter to mediation, the failure to reach agreement in the December 12 meeting between foreign ministers Pastor and Cubillos was owing to this requirement that a clear delineation of issues be made before the mediation. Chile's demand in the December 12 meeting, that there be no restrictions on the scope of the mediation, was viewed in Argentina as an approach "closer to arbitration than one to mediation."[41]

On December 28, Cardinal Samoré traveled to Santiago. He was greeted at the airport by Foreign Minister Cubillos and went directly to Cubillos' private residence for lunch and preliminary talks. Cubillos described the meeting:

> He was a prince of the church; cardinals are princes of the church. There is a sense of royalty in the way they conduct themselves. They can appear to be very humble, but they have a very clear understanding of their authority, their rank, and all that goes with that. Samoré was even more than that; he was very strong, and he had a sense that he could impose himself on people very easily. . . .
>
> We sat for lunch, and he started testing me. It was one of the toughest meetings I have ever had in my life. We were alone, and he said that we couldn't be inflexible to find solutions to the problem, that we had to give something up—he didn't mention islands, but we had to give something up—that we didn't have a good case, that we had a lousy international public opinion about Chile, [that] we had the world against us, that we had a horrible record of human rights, and that we would find no support in anybody.
>
> This was clearly a surprise. But very rapidly I understood that he was testing me. Then I said that we would not change a comma of what was our position because it was fair, that it was right, that there was an arbitration award, and that I was completely surprised that somebody like him would even suggest that we go against international law. [I said] I am disappointed by your approach. We had a very tough interchange, really.
>
> [He replied that] if you don't do something and give something to them, you are going to have war.
>
> And I said to him, we are not going to change anything. You can't talk about our internal situation as an excuse. Well, I'll tell you, you've got a divided church here in Chile, you've got a lousy church here in Chile. It is very difficult for us to accept the relations with the church. It went on that way.
>
> Samoré answered, saying that, seeing your inflexibility, your rigidity, . . . I am going back to Rome this evening and tell the pope that there is no hope in us doing anything and that my mission has ended in failure.
>
> I am sorry, I said. That is up to you.

Then, [he said,] I would like to take the limousine to the airport.

I called the lieutenant in charge into the dining room, [and told him to] please get the car ready, the cardinal is going back to his place. As the lieutenant left the room, Samoré smiled, touched my arm, and said [he was not serious].

I think he did the same in Argentina, by the way, the same approach. I think he was trying me out, seeing how strong we were, how determined we were, and he found out immediately. Of course, he didn't go back.[42]

From that point on in his visit to Chile, Samoré asked questions and listened. He met with government officials who stressed the legal and historical justification for their position and explained that they could see no reason why they should accede to Argentina's threats. Santiago Benadava, a respected international legal scholar and probably the only non-Catholic Samoré met with (and who later became alternate chief of the delegation in Rome), put forth the argument (as reconstructed by Cubillos):

I am a professor of international law. How can I expect to teach international law to my students in the future if the church doesn't support this? In the arbitration award and the legal case we have, if you can find something wrong with the legal approach or the legality of our case, you should say. But if you act against us, suggest something against us in these things, it would be very difficult for young people in Chile to understand the church in the future.[43]

After these meetings with Foreign Ministry officials, Samoré saw President Pinochet. It soon became apparent to Samoré, according to Cubillos, that Chile had one coherent, unwavering position on the matter, and it did not take long for Samoré to learn what it was. In brief, Chile stood on its legal right to the three islands as established historically and as confirmed in the Laudo. All that remained to be resolved was the maritime delimitation and any other issues such as the boundary determination of the eastern mouth of the Straits of Magellan. Because the Chilean position was so clearly stated and justified and allowed for no compromise, on future visits Samoré had little to discover. Says Cubillos:

Every time he came he would see Pinochet, not because he had anything to tell Pinochet, but [because] he wanted to do exactly the same thing he had done in Argentina and to spend the same time he had spent with Videla as with Pinochet . . . and [similarly] with the Foreign Ministry. We didn't talk about the problem anymore, just talked and did the protocol things.[44]

Throughout his talks, Samoré stressed repeatedly that he was not there to mediate or to arbitrate but to offer his "good offices" in search of a solution:

I speak rather of mission and not of mediation, in a technical sense, because mediation is a juridical term that gives to the mediator, if not authority, at least the possibility of making proposals, not only to listen or to invite the parties. But we are still not in this phase.[45]

Once he acquired the necessary background information, however, Cardinal Samoré was prepared to search for an understanding, encourage a dialogue and, possibly, establish a procedure.

One speaks much of peace, and peace is the work of everyone, it is the fruit of a collaboration of the spirit in everyone. We must ask God Our Father, prince of peace and the Holy Virgin, queen of peace, but also, I would say, one must force it.[46]

On his return trip to Buenos Aires, Samoré went on to say that the papal intervention was something entirely new. It was "not to continue the negotiations in a strict juridical plan nor in a political plan in the sense that it means to dispense with the law, but rather in a new plan, in a higher plan—if you permit a priest to express it like this—spiritual. In this framework, the two nations could face each other, not oppose each other, the two nations could respect the suggestions given them by the Holy Father." Regarding the difficulty of resolving the differences, he said, "Before coming, I already knew that it was a difficult situation. I had been informed completely. Yes, very difficult. But what I found surpassed my understandings and predictions."[47]

On December 30, Samoré announced that, lacking a prompt success, he would alternate between the two countries "for as long as necessary in an attempt of the Holy See to avoid war."[48] "I'm in no hurry," he said.[49]

Cardinal Samoré spent three days in Argentina and then returned on January 2, 1979, for roughly equivalent time in Chile, meeting with Cubillos and Pinochet. It was after these meetings that Samoré began to speak publicly of a trilateral (Argentina, Chile, and the Holy See) meeting in Montevideo. It was becoming increasingly clear that he was seeking an agreement to submit the matter to papal mediation in Rome.

In this process, Cardinal Samoré, after determining the two side's positions, began delivering concrete proposals from each side to the other. According to Cubillos, Chile's proposal was always the same—submit the matter without restrictions to papal mediation. Argentina offered a number of proposals, all of which Chile turned down. On one trip, Samoré actually carried seven different proposals from Argentina. At some point in these exchanges, Samoré began to draft proposals of his own. Early versions were shown either directly to both sides for suggestions and modifications or conveyed through their respective ambassadors. In the end, Cardinal Samoré went through some sixteen drafts before the two sides agreed.

On January 4, Samoré spent two days in Buenos Aires talking extensively with government and church officials. By one account, Samoré encountered considerable evasive talk in these meetings but eventually received the support of the top decision makers. The Junta, after meeting for eight hours on January 5 to discuss the Beagle Channel matter, agreed to submit the dispute to papal mediation.

With both sides in agreement on terms, Cardinal Samoré scheduled for January 8 a signing ceremony between the two foreign ministers in a neutral place, Montevideo, Uruguay. But all was not strictly ceremonious.

On the Argentine side, General Luciano Benjamin Menéndez, commander of the Third Army Corps in Córdoba, the most powerful and often most independent army division in Argentina, was not happy. He had already expressed his view of the Beagle Channel affair and the pope's intervention when Cardinal Samoré first arrived in South America in late December: "Argentina's right over the Atlantic is unyielding" and "all means for safeguarding the dignity of the nation will be employed."[50]

Now that an agreement was about to be signed, Menéndez was threatening action. Rumors spread that he would make a move toward Buenos Aires and overthrow the government of Videla and the Junta. Although that threat never materialized, he did, nevertheless, come to Buenos Aires on January 8 with a contingent of troops dressed in full battle fatigues. His plan, apparently, was physically to stop Foreign Minister Pastor from going to Montevideo. But, by one account, Menéndez arrived just as Pastor's plane was taking off. (By another account, Menéndez actually reached Pastor and demanded that he not go. Pastor told Menéndez that he had orders from Videla and then proceeded to fly to Montevideo.)[51]

When Pastor got to Montevideo, he was greeted with another surprise, this time from Cardinal Samoré. Throughout his shuttling between capitals, Samoré never dealt with the touchy issue of force withdrawals. Both countries had retained ships and troops in the southern region at a level far exceeding that of normal—that is, at levels higher than those before the 1978 build-up. But for Cardinal Samoré to have raised the issue would almost certainly have inflamed the Argentine hard-liners and made an extension of the pope's intervention—that is, mediation—impossible. At the same time, not to have such a withdrawal to the status quo ante would, Samoré reasoned, make mediation in Rome nearly impossible because the slightest military provocation in either country could jeopardize the negotiations in Rome.

Samoré solved this dilemma by preparing a second part to the Act of Montevideo that provided for the renunciation of the use of force and a return to the status quo ante (that is, to the beginning of 1977). But he only presented it to the ministers once they arrived in Montevideo. Because the expressed purpose of the Montevideo meeting was to do only one thing—sign the agreement, not negotiate—they were effectively presented with a fait accompli addendum to the agreement.

Cubillos had no problem with the addition and agreed to sign. Pastor called President Videla and talked for nearly an hour. They decided they could sign but that this particular provision would have to be secret. Both Cubillos and Cardinal Samoré objected and, after further talks, Videla gave the go-ahead. All this presumably was done without consulting the Junta. Pastor returned to Buenos Aires and reportedly delivered the agreement to the Junta explaining that they could accept it or accept his resignation. It was accepted. Once the pope agreed, the Beagle Channel dispute, nearly one century old, would be transferred to the Vatican for negotiations under the auspices of Pope John Paul II.

The Act of Montevideo was carefully crafted to be specific enough to commit the countries to avoid hostilities yet vague enough not to contradict stated positions. For example, the arbitration award of 1977, the Laudo, was not mentioned. From the Argentine view, the Laudo was not only null because of Argentina's renunciation but reference to the Laudo served to intensify feelings and hinder resolution. The act made no reference to the "Beagle Channel," which, from the Argentine view, would have prejudiced the proceedings toward the Laudo. Instead, the act alluded to "all controversial aspects of the problem in the southern zone." This phrasing seemed to meet Argentina's desire to consider all issues in the controversy, including islands. It also met Chile's position, held since Argentina rejected the mediation idea on December 12, 1978, that no restrictions should be placed on the scope of the mediator's effort. At that time, Chile had interpreted Argentina's request for putting strict limits on the issues that could be covered in a mediation as an attempt to continue its efforts to pressure Chile into conceding islands in which the mediator would only endorse those concessions. Although the wording in the Act of Montevideo was vague, Chile did not insist on its previous position held throughout the Puerto Montt negotiations, namely, that Chile would only discuss maritime delimitation and issues outside the Laudo, not the question of islands within the region covered by the Laudo.

The Act specified that the two governments "could inform the Holy See of such objectives of the controversy as the antecedents and criteria that they consider pertinent, especially those they considered in the course of the different negotiations."[52] This wording allowed Argentina to portray the mediation as a continuation of the direct negotiations as Argentina interpreted the 1978 Act of Puerto Montt. The only difference was that the negotiations would be conducted under the moral guidance of the pope. An Argentine author explained the Argentine view of the process this way: "What is important in such an accord is the return to direct bilateral negotiations because, having submitted the question to arbitration of the British Crown, and as this was an unsuccessful attempt, the political necessities of the time demanded the search for an alternative. . . . That, finally, is direct negotiation with the aid of a mediator."[53]

On January 9, 1979, Cardinal Samoré departed for the Vatican with a peace agreement in hand, his shuttle diplomacy a success. What remained was the uncertain process of mediating a dispute that had eluded solution for nearly one century.

When Cardinal Samoré arrived back in Rome, mission accomplished, he had, most importantly, forestalled hostilities between Argentina and Chile and extracted promises from them not to resort to force. In addition, he had established a line of communication between the two nations and arranged to continue that communication at the Vatican in the form of mediated negotiations under the auspices of Pope John Paul II. Cardinal Samoré took this agreement signed by both nations immediately to the pope who, noting the difficulties such an effort would entail, accepted their request for mediation.

With this accomplishment as a fitting and dramatic conclusion to a long and distinguished diplomatic career, Cardinal Samoré was eager to get back to his work as the librarian and archivist of the Holy Roman Church. So he found it a bit unsettling when the Holy Father asked him in April to serve as his personal representative to conduct the Argentina-Chile mediation effort. It was a request he could not refuse. Because everyone expected the mediation to be wrapped up in six months or so, Samoré was assured it would not be a terrible burden. Little did Cardinal Samoré realize that the mediation would take not six months but six years or that halfway through that period his health would fail him. Moreover, he could never have foreseen the long, agonizing hours, days, and months that would be required to bring the two nations to an agreement.

The delegations from the two countries arrived in early May 1979. Argentina began with seven permanent members of whom two were jurists, one military, and four diplomats. Ambassador Guillermo R. Moncayo, a legal counsel to the Foreign Ministry and legal scholar, headed the Argentine delegation. Chile began with two permanent delegates, both diplomats, and later added a third. Enrique Bernstein, a senior diplomat, was chosen to lead the Chilean delegation. In a 1986 interview, then foreign minister, Hernan Cubillos, described his instructions to Bernstein: "I remember telling [Bernstein], 'Your main mission is to go to Rome and win the confidence [of] and [establish] credibility with the Cardinals, especially with Samoré and the pope . . . so that we are believed.' And he did a splendid job. He first of all won the confidence of Samoré. They became friends. [He] trusted him."[54]

The mediation got underway officially on March 4, 1979, in a solemn ceremony in the Vatican with the pope.[55] For the first few months, the mediation team educated itself on the issues and asked for clarification of the parties' positions but made no attempt to find a solution. On September 27, 1979, the pope received both delegations to advance his concept of the spirit and procedures for negotiating a solution.[56] He reminded the two countries of the commitment they had made: "[Your countries] made a solemn undertaking at Montevideo not to have recourse to force in the mutual relations of the two States, to bring about a gradual return to the military situation existing at the beginning of 1977, and to abstain from adopting measures that might upset harmony in any sector." From there, the pope spelled out his view of the role of the mediator. "[Trust] is a necessary premise in order that the mediator may feel more secure in his efforts which are of the very essence of mediation, which does not conclude with decisions, but is unfolded by means of advice. Relying on this trust, the mediator, after having asked God for enlightenment, presents suggestions to the Parties with the purpose of carrying out his work of rapprochement, aimed at safeguarding the fundamental interests of both, the supreme good of peace."[57]

The pope then suggested several "ideas" for procedure. The first step would be to seek "points of convergence between the positions of the two parties." Recognizing that the two countries held widely divergent positions, such points, nevertheless, could be found because the two had negotiated directly in 1978 and had found at least partial agreement on some issues. The second step would be for the two countries to consider the "possibilities . . . to collaborate in a whole series of activities, inside and even outside the southern area. From the development of these activities, unquestionable advantages can be derived for the welfare of both peoples and also—why not?—for other nations. I believe that the discovery and consequent preparation of wide areas of cooperation would create favourable conditions to seek and find the complete solution for the more complicated questions involved in the controversy: a complete and final solution that must be reached."[58]

Last, the pope stressed the need for reestablishing an "atmosphere of mutual trust" and hinted at the need for restraint in using the media. In fact, as the mediation proceeded, the mediation team insisted that public communications be made jointly and through the mediation team to avoid poisoning a positive atmosphere. Because low points in the process were inevitable, the mediators reasoned, to report regularly and independently to the media might give the impression that the mediation was failing, which could encourage either country to resort to other measures.

Although the pope set the tone of the mediation and laid out a general framework—that is, to seek points of convergence, expand the scope of issues, and build trust—the day-to-day procedures were left to be developed by Cardinal Samoré, in consultation with the delegations. Although the Vatican is well known for having a highly professional diplomatic corps, no one in memory had ever conducted a formal mediation process. Consequently, the procedures adopted throughout the mediation effort were developed ad hoc; all participants learned as they went.

The mediation team had determined from the very beginning that the meetings should be held separately.[59] This enabled the delegations to "present their points of view on the concrete problem. We got down to the basics of the problem, to the positions of the two parties and our concern heightened, because we understood the situation in a much clearer way. We spent 4–5 months in separate meetings, in a stage of information [collection] which lasted until September of last year [1979]."[60]

In October, the team instituted a procedure whereby separate meetings would continue to be held but with the intention of preparing for eventual joint meetings.[61] It soon became clear that in this more active phase of the mediation, the first task would be to set an agenda. Each delegation met regularly with the mediation team (still separately) to come up with a list of issues deemed not only important but "opportune." In this case, "opportune" meant an issue on which there was little conflict of interest and that appeared amenable to agreement. The mediation team would review these issues and sometimes ask for revisions in the description of the issue to make it more palatable for the other side.

When the mediation team determined that a given issue was deemed suitable as an agenda item, it would call a joint meeting. The expressed purpose of the joint meeting was to agree on the agenda item as developed in separate meetings but no more. Once such agreement was obtained, the mediation team would ask both delegations to develop a working paper on the issue. These working papers provided the mediation team with the basis for the development of an agenda that was then presented to both sides, again in a joint meeting. Although, overall, joint meetings were rare and most communication was transmitted by the mediation team, several joint meetings were held during this period. These covered such major issues as the concept of a territorial sea and fishing rights.

The understanding throughout this process was that any agreement on agenda items or any change in position would not constitute a commitment or prejudice future stages of the negotiations. Despite such assurances from the mediation team, however, the development of an agenda and the production of working papers resulted in little progress toward getting either party to move from its initial position.

Cardinal Samoré, nevertheless, continued to conduct negotiations. By May 1980, after conducting some two hundred meetings,[62] the mediation team shifted the new focus to the central issues of the dispute—namely, the demarcation of territorial and maritime boundaries.[63]

Despite the mediation team's careful preparations of both the delegations and the public, these central issues proved to be just as intractable to the mediation team as they had been to the two parties. These issues became the source of considerable frustration and discouragement for all involved. Cardinal Samoré, nevertheless, pushed on with separate and, occasionally, joint meetings. He requested more working papers and reminded each side that, in the event the two sides agreed on a given issue, such agreement would not constitute a binding agreement until an overall solution was reached. In addition, he made a practice of asking a series of questions of each party, probing for what would be minimally acceptable, what would be flexible, and what positions could be adjusted.

The cardinal's persistent and patient questioning proved successful in gaining increased flexibility from both sides and was continued throughout the rest of the mediation.[64] In addition, during this latter part of 1980, Cardinal Samoré began to relay one side's position to the other side. Although both sides knew he was doing this, they did not know what he said to the other side nor what was that side's response.

After a year of examining both sides' positions and seeking some ground for compromise and after conducting several hundred meetings, Samoré asked each side to separately draw up what it thought would be a reasonable, comprehensive solution to the dispute. Samoré found the draft solutions disappointing, however. It was clear the two sides were still far apart. So Samoré delivered a series of questions designed to discover where the parties were flexible and where creative solutions could possibly be located. For example, at some point in this year-long process, Samoré had asked Chile whether the Cape Horn meridian could serve at least as an overflight boundary, if not a territorial boundary. In this case, Chile did not agree at first. But after months of persistent questioning by Samoré and his insistence that Chile must give something, Chile did grant that Cape Horn could be used for navigational and overflight delimitation.

With the parties' suggested solutions in mind, Samoré then drew up his own version of a possible solution and delivered it to the parties. Their responses revealed that still there was no room for agreement, and Cardinal Samoré conveyed his assessment to the two parties. Once more, Samoré asked for new positions from both sides in the hope that they could come together. Still, no agreement was in sight.

Throughout this process, all transactions were conducted through the mediation team such that neither side knew what the other side offered, what was one side's response to a proposal, nor what the mediation team discussed with the other side.

With no solution in sight and both sides unwilling to make concessions on the key issues, Cardinal Samoré felt compelled to recommend to the pope that he take one of several options. One option could have been to suspend the mediation, refrain from any further intervention, and leave the two parties to negotiate directly. Another was to suggest that the pope

make a concrete, take-it-or-leave-it proposal to the two parties. A third
option was to recommend that the pope urge both sides to change their
positions such that a formula for agreement could be found. These options
were first conveyed to the parties. As a result, the two parties continued
to submit positions, only this time, Cardinal Samoré would simply reject
them if no movement was evident.

When significant movement was still not forthcoming, it became apparent to everyone that a more direct involvement by the pope was in
order.[65] Two options were initially considered. One, the pope could send
a personal representative to each country's highest authority, or, two, he
could request that Cardinal Samoré speak directly with each delegation's
foreign minister. Both delegations elected to reflect further on the cardinal's proposal. To encourage such reflection, the two delegations had an
audience with the pope in which he explained that their positions were
still far apart. But he also informed them that he would soon develop a
proposal to deliver to both sides. And, so, for the remaining months of
1980, the pope, in consultation with the mediation team, prepared such a
proposal.

On Friday morning, December 12, the pope received the two delegations with their respective foreign ministers to deliver his proposal, *La
Propuesta* (the proposal).[66] He asked the two sides to recall that, in late
1978,

> God, the Father of all, drove me to make a gesture of peace, not an easy one,
> so bold, risky, compromising, but also full of hope.
>
> A similar act is what I now venture to ask . . . of your peoples and, above
> all, of the highest authorities of both countries: for the latter, defenders they
> are of legitimate national interests, I wish the incomparable reward that his-
> tory will remember them also for their courage in staking on peace at a diffi-
> cult moment and for having thus given to the world . . . an example of wis-
> dom and common sense as the principle of government.[67]

The ministers with their respective delegations, then began their review. It was the first time any representative of either country had seen
the proposal in any form. The details of the Propuesta were not made
public at this time but some of their general provisions were openly discussed in Rome. For example, part of the Propuesta called for a "Zone of
Peace" in the southern region. Cardinal Samoré explained that this would
be a zone where offensive weapons would be banned so that "this zone of
peace would reflect over the continental territory of the two nations and,
therefore, constitute the base, the 'trampoline,' for an overall declaration
of peace between the two nations."[68]

In Argentina, specific parts of the Propuesta began to appear in the
press by the end of the year. These accounts revealed that Chile would

have received all the disputed islands between the Beagle Channel and Cape Horn but would only have received limited offshore rights on the Atlantic side of the meridian passing through Cape Horn.[69] In addition, a so-called "Mar de la Paz" (Sea of Peace), a two hundred-mile-wide maritime area would have been established in the contested region.[70]

On January 8, 1981, Chile publicly announced that it had accepted the Propuesta. Argentina, on the other hand, never responded officially to the Propuesta. In March 1981, Argentina did send a message to the pope, expressing its objections to the Propuesta. Still, Argentina neither accepted nor rejected it.[71] For its part, Argentina wished to continue negotiating. Chile, on the other hand, considered the Propuesta final and resisted the mediation team's efforts to find some opening for agreement.

With the status of the Propuesta in limbo and Chile reluctant to resume negotiations, the mediation of the Beagle Channel dispute in Rome was at a standstill in early 1981.[72] Moreover, a series of events back home raised tensions between the two countries and further derailed attempts to revive the negotiations. In a move initiated by Argentina, the border was closed and citizens were harassed and detained. Because the two countries could not negotiate directly, these issues became the subject of negotiations in Rome while discussions on the Beagle Channel were set aside.

A near tragedy in Rome—an assassination attempt on the pope—may have been the key to breaking the impasse, however. When the pope returned from the hospital and was greeted at the Apostolic Palace, only two people spoke with him. One was Cardinal Samoré. By one account, the first thing he asked about was the progress of the mediation, and Cardinal Samoré explained how it got sidetracked. The pope expressed his fervent desire that the two countries overcome their new border dispute and his hope that the mediation would progress and the Beagle Channel dispute be resolved. In a public statement, Cardinal Samoré asked that the pope's wishes be conveyed directly to the respective governments.[73] Soon after this papal request for a "noble gesture," the two countries released their prisoners and reopened the border.

Negotiations on the Beagle Channel, nevertheless, remained stalled throughout the remainder of the year as Argentina sought to delay the process. Then, on January 21, 1982, Argentina announced it was terminating the two countries' 1972 General Treaty on the Judicial Settlement of Disputes. The treaty had a ten-year limit after which it could be renewed or unilaterally terminated. The treaty stipulated that if direct negotiations were unsuccessful, any outstanding differences would be submitted to the International Court at The Hague. If Argentina's denunciation was carried out and if at some time mediation failed, the two countries would be left with no mutually agreed forum for resolving their differences. As provided for in the treaty, Chile had just eleven months to act—that is, to decide whether to unilaterally submit the Beagle dispute to the International Court or to conclude an agreement by some other means. The mediation team, meanwhile, assured both countries that it expected a mediated agreement by the end of the year.

For its part, Chile rejected categorically any suggestion of resuming negotiations. The Propuesta was delivered, Chile had accepted it, and all that remained was for Argentina to do the same. Moreover, Chile felt that if it was actively engaged in negotiations on the topic at hand, that is, the Beagle Channel dispute, the International Court at The Hague would not hear its case.

Movement picked up when Argentina sent as its new ambassador to the Rome negotiations, Ortiz de Rozas, a friend of Chile's chief negotiator, Enrique Bernstein. The two began to meet informally, a rare occurrence up to this point in the Rome negotiations. And, unlike before, the mediation team decided to encourage these private, direct talks, and to take advantage of the personal affinity between the two lead negotiators.

The mediation team made several suggestions to encourage negotiations. The first was that the Propuesta be used for the time being as the basis for joint meetings. Second, the mediation team suggested that a total solution—including the question of the extension of the 1972 treaty—be resolved within the context of the mediation. And, third, a new way of meeting jointly would be sought. Although this plan was never explicitly accepted by either side, it, in effect, became the operational plan for the remainder of the mediation.[74] The major topic of discussion became the so-called *vacuum juris* (juridical vacuum), the juridical vacuum, left by Argentina's denunciation of the 1972 treaty.

Meanwhile, the Malvinas/Falklands war broke out. Although the Argentines were understandably distracted, negotiations did not stop altogether in Rome. Of course, no agreement could be contemplated during the conflict nor during the political turmoil of its aftermath. Nevertheless, in the long run, it appears that the Malvinas/Falklands debacle contributed to a new willingness on Argentina's part to settle the Beagle Channel dispute.[75]

At this time, not all of the domestic trouble was on the Atlantic side of the Andes. Chile was undergoing considerable political and economic strains. It was becoming increasingly isolated in Latin America and generally throughout the international community. European countries, for example, refused to sell it arms although they allowed such sales to Argentina. (The United States resumed arms sales to Argentina in 1983 after democracy was restored but retained its embargo against Chile.) Although political murders and kidnapings that followed the overthrow of Allende in 1973 had virtually stopped by 1979, human rights groups and the Catholic church charged that torture, detention, political imprisonment, banishment and exile were continuing.[76] In another sign of the strains of governing, especially in the midst of an economic recession, in April 1982, President Pinochet dismissed all of his ministers and reappointed military hard-liners in place of civilians.[77]

Foreign pressure on Chile was exacerbated by the Malvinas/Falklands crisis. Chileans speculated that the invasion there was only the precursor to an invasion of the Beagle Channel islands. Moreover, reports that Chile sided with Britain by allowing British forces to operate from Chilean territory, raised additional reports that Argentina had offered to settle the Beagle Channel dispute in exchange for support in the Malvinas/Falklands affair.[78]

The "active phase" of the negotiations began Friday, April, 23, 1982, when the pope addressed the two delegations.[79] He expressed his desire to push the Beagle Channel negotiations ahead to a conclusion despite the troubles in the region. He told the delegations:

> It is needless for me, in the presence of you distinguished members of both delegations, who have borne the weight of the dark daily travail, to devote time to considerations on the laborious road traversed during the last three years. All of us had hoped to see the happy ending in much less time. This has not come to pass and, instead, the anxiety of the peoples has continued. . . .
>
> At certain times there unfortunately have been incidents, sometimes not entirely in keeping with the spirit of the commitments undertaken when my mediation was sought.[80]

The negotiators and the mediators went back to the drawing boards. The challenge for the mediation team was to get the two sides talking again knowing that Chile, in particular, was reluctant to speak, given the *vacuum juris*. So Cardinal Samoré began by using the informal discussions between de Rozas and Bernstein to explore the positions of each side regarding the various provisions of the Propuesta. He tried various methods to encourage movement but soon realized that he had to switch from his goal of getting agreement on the Beagle Channel dispute per se to getting agreement on an extension of the 1972 treaty. Turning to this, the two sides eventually agreed, on September 15, 1982, to accept a formal proposal by the pope to renew the treaty.[81]

This was the first time in nearly four years of deliberation that the two sides had agreed on anything substantial. And while the mediation team tried to capitalize on this fact and push the negotiations forward to agreement, several events thwarted the mediation team's efforts. Bernstein of Chile returned to Santiago because of ill health. Cardinal Samoré himself became seriously ill and had to turn over many of his duties to his assistants. Then, on February 3, 1983, after he had conducted more than five hundred meetings, the last ones at his hospital bedside, Cardinal Samoré died.[82] Secretary of State Cardinal Agostino Casaroli took charge of the mediation as the pope's direct representative. One consequence was a change in the general tone of the negotiations. Casaroli injected a certain forcefulness into the process unlike Samoré's slower, more methodical and patient approach. In addition, because Casaroli was secretary of state and, therefore, the most powerful person in the church hierarchy next to the pope himself, he commanded more influence in the negotiations; he could make demands and insist that each side make concessions. Finally, in February 1983, Argentina's ambassador, de Rozas, resigned his post.

With the Malvinas/Falklands war over and Argentina preparing for a return to democratic rule, negotiations in Rome once again were at a stalemate. Argentina contended and the mediation team agreed, that, for all concerned, it would be better to wait for the new government to take power. But after four months during which nothing happened, the pope decided a new initiative on his part was in order. He proposed that the two countries sign a declaration of peace and nonaggression. This would accomplish the most basic objective of the mediation effort even if a comprehensive solution could not be reached. Argentina, preferring a comprehensive agreement, rejected the idea.

Meanwhile, two Argentine ambassadors stationed in Europe met informally with Chilean counterparts, with the knowledge of the mediation team, to explore how the Propuesta could be modified to meet both sides' interests. The result was a so-called "nonpaper," which became the basis for continued talks. This move outside of the regular Rome negotiations enabled those ambassadors assigned to Rome for the mediation to enter into new talks. As noted, one reason Chile was more willing to negotiate on the Propuesta, which it had already accepted, was that economic conditions in Chile had worsened in recent years.

With negotiations underway again, the mediation team instituted a new procedure. The mediation team would get together with each delegation separately, sound out its position, and, after editing out any strident or potentially inflammatory statements, it would relay the position to the other side. If an impasse should arise, the chiefs of the delegations would meet informally together. If such meetings were not sufficient to break the impasse, Secretary of State Casaroli would intercede and meet with the parties.

The nominal chiefs of the two delegations (who operated mostly from their respective capitals, not Rome), Ernesto Videla of Chile and Marcelo Delpech of Argentina (Ortiz de Rozas's replacement), met informally in their respective capitals in late 1983 and early 1984. They agreed to request that the Holy See bring their two foreign ministers together to sign a Declaration of Peace and Friendship. The mediation team officially invited both delegations with their respective foreign ministers to attend a joint meeting on January 23, 1984, with Secretary of State Cardinal Casaroli presiding.[83]

Addressing the ministers and delegations, Casaroli invoked the memory of Cardinal Samoré and urged the delegations to consider five fundamental points:

1. I want to emphasize before all else, the expectations, the hopes, especially in the two countries, that accompany your eminent work . . . If this occasion is lost, the difficulties for resolving the controversy, in the scope of the mediation, later could become much more serious, perhaps insurmountable.

2. There is a necessity, besides, to maintain and make more patent a climate each day of sincere and mutual trust. The mediation office will spare no efforts to promote such a climate, comforted by the assurance that will follow from having the trust of both delegations and their respective authorities, which will permit it, among other things, to know the fundamental positions of the parties over the diverse issues of the negotiations, so as to be able to offer the most efficacious help.

3. This climate will facilitate the realization of one of the fundamental rules of all negotiation. namely, that one should try to understand the positions and reasons of the other. . . .

4. It does not escape me that some sectors can have, for one reason or another, opinions toward the agreement less favorable than is now delineated, and they can, therefore, appear inclined to demean or obstruct the common proposal of the two esteemed parties and the mediation just as it comes to a just, equitable, and honorable solution.   Before this eventuality, it is necessary that no one be influenced or conditioned by the emotions that elements of this kind can provoke; it is necessary that the true interests of the two nations are viewed calmly and with a clear and objective vision in a global and clearsighted perspective that is known to overcome the passions of the moment.

   We cannot forget that you are working here for history.

5. The aspirations of the public opinion in both nations require that plenty of information is given about the progress of the negotiations, without, however, giving that which damages the necessary reserve inherent in all diplomatic negotiation, especially when dealing with complex and delicate matters as at present.[84]

The meeting of foreign ministers was then consummated by the signing of an agreement of peace and friendship. Although this news was generally well-received throughout the international community, there was some dissent. In Argentina, some observers called the agreement a "treasonous step toward ceding Argentina's interests in the Beagle Channel dispute."[85]

In subsequent negotiations, the two sides appeared to agree to abandon the common zone idea; to grant each other rights to navigational facilities on certain islands; to establish a system for the resolution of future disputes that excluded outside tribunals; and to continue to use the Cape Horn meridian as a point of boundary division. Details for implementation as well as other critical issues remained to be worked out, however.

Keeping the parties separate, the mediation team went through each issue, one at a time, searching for what was possible for agreement. The mediation team asked both sides to be absolutely forthcoming, as if to make "confessions," so that the mediators could assess their true needs. With agreement in sight, the mediation team made it clear that it could not accept any more posturing. The resulting proposals would not be transmitted to the other side but instead would, by the mediation team's judgment, be kept and allowed to "mature." This procedure enabled the mediation team to bring the parties together only at the most opportune moment as well as to provide a means of getting more concessions out of each side. To encourage flexibility, the mediation team also assured each side that any statements would be kept off the record and that any agreements would be binding only when a final agreement was signed. The mediation team also decided to start with those issues considered most important to both sides and to continue the informal meetings between the delegation chiefs. Finally, each side was asked to deliver a proposal indicating how it viewed a final solution.

On April 14, 1984, Casaroli met with each delegation separately. He expressed his concern that certain provisions, such as economic compensation and maritime delimitation, as propounded in the Propuesta would make future difficulties. He asked each country to submit a new suggestion, something concrete and realistic. This they did, and with some modification by the mediation team, the result was delivered to Casaroli.

On June 11, 1984, Casaroli delivered to each team his suggestion for delimitation and economic compensation. The suggestion included a binational commission to deal with all the economic issues. At this time, he made clear that this was the Holy See's final suggestion for a solution; there would be no more. To reject it would be to terminate the mediation effort. Both sides accepted the suggestion.

The exact delimitation, means of setting up cooperative efforts, and a systematic and obligatory process for the peaceful resolution of future disputes were worked out with experts called in especially for this phase of the treaty writing. At this point, the mediation team had little input; only after the details were drawn up was the team informed. With the language of a final treaty in hand, the chief of each delegation traveled to his respective capital for final consultation.

In early October 1984, Argentina and Chile announced they had reached a "full understanding." On October 18, Cardinal Casaroli delivered the "treaty text."[86] Before the final signing by the countries' foreign ministers, Argentina submitted the matter to a yes-or-no, national referendum. On November 25, 1984, Argentines approved the treaty with 77 percent approval and 70 percent participation.[87]

Finally, on November 29, 1984, in a solemn ceremony in the Reggia Hall next to the Sistine Chapel, a place traditionally reserved to receive kings, Foreign Ministers Dante Caputo of Argentina and Jaime del Valle of Chile and the Vatican's Secretary of State Cardinal Agostino Casaroli signed the final treaty.

Not everyone was happy with the treaty. In Argentina, for example, a retired admiral said, "With this treaty they cut the little finger from our body, and the soul of a nation is built on its body. Our nation has never had a coherent, constant, and secure foreign policy."[88] Ricardo Echeverry Boneo, chief of the Argentine delegation from the beginning of the mediation to July 26, 1984, and one who reportedly resigned out of disillusionment with the developments in the mediation, commented:

> I believe it is time to contain the Chilean expansionism. You negotiate under pressure, and this goes against what a mediator does. We have paid a high price for a certificate of good conduct before international public opinion. I did not agree with the 1980 Propuesta, and I agree less with the one now that gives Argentina's boundaries to the south with Chile. . . . I differ with those that say that the result of the mediation that is unfavorable for Argentina owes exclusively to the incoherence of the foreign relations of my country. I believe that there was hastiness and pressure. . . .
>
> We acted under pressure from the Vatican, which was more an arbitrator than a mediator.[89]

And in Chile, the chief of the navy said that Chile's Junta could not accept the treaty as it stood: "Changes must be made."[90]

The treaty granted sovereignty over the three islands to Chile. But instead of granting Chile a 200-mile "exclusive economic zone" extending in all directions from the islands, the maritime boundary line was drawn such that it would extend about 30 miles southeast of the islands, turn south to the latitude of Cape Horn, run west to the meridian of the cape, and then project due south toward the Antarctic. In this way, Argentina could claim that its "bioceanic principle" had been maintained. In addition, maritime jurisdiction in the eastern mouth of the Straits of Magellan and navigation rights for Argentine ships in Chilean waters were established. The pope's earlier idea of a common zone was abandoned. Finally, a permanent binational commission was established to promote economic integration between the two countries.

ANALYSIS OF THE VATICAN INTERVENTION

The Beagle Channel case exhibits two phases of intermediary intervention: crisis management via shuttle diplomacy and agreement attainment
via mediated negotiations. In both phases, the domestic determinants of
the acceptance and entry questions and of the intermediary's problem of
getting movement are prominent. These determinants apply not only to
the disputing parties' constraints but, as in the Camp David case, to the
intermediary's constraints, as well. This case, therefore, allows a detailed
look at an intermediary's decision making and its impact on disputants and
their decision making. I first assess two propositions from part 1 regarding
the parties' acceptance decision and the mediator's entry decision. From
there, I examine four instances of mediator practice in the two phases of
the intervention to assess and expand on the peculiar opportunities and
limitations of a neutral mediator.

Acceptance and Entry

As for the acceptance question, it could be argued that Argentina and
Chile chose mediation only as a last resort. Negotiation and arbitration
had been tried, Argentina rejected adjudication, and so, at the point of an
outbreak of hostilities, a neutral third party was the only remaining alternative. Closer examination suggests, however, that the decision to seek a
mediator was not a simple default decision. By construing the acceptance
decision as a *bargain over process* where the choice of direct negotiation,
mediation, or arbitration is a joint decision between parties, it appears
that mediation was a mutually beneficial compromise.

To ignore domestic politics and internal decision making for the moment, Argentina and Chile were the two monolithic parties in this bargain
over process. Argentina's paramount interest in a process was that it be
"political." As one high-level diplomat involved in the Beagle Channel
negotiations for many years explained, for Argentina, it was not just a
settlement that was important but one that was definitive and durable.
This was a view held by military and civilians alike. It was not enough to
entrust the matter to a court or to an outside power, the results of which
could be overturned at the whim of a future government of either side. A
long-term solution required that both sides make an investment in the
solution, that they hammer out a treaty directly or invest resources in
some other way such that both sides would be truly committed to the
solution. Thus, Argentina's process interest was that the process lead to a
definitive, durable, and committed solution, in short, that it be what the
Argentines termed "political."

Chile's process interests related more to its relatively weak international position. In terms of economic and military power, geography, and population, Chile was the smaller and more vulnerable party. Since Pinochet's coup of 1973 and his well-known human rights abuses, Chile had little support in the international community. Chile also feared the involvement of neighboring countries, especially Peru and Bolivia, should a war break out. Recalling Foreign Minister Cubillos's description of criteria for choosing a mediator, it is reasonable to conclude that Chile needed some kind of overseer, some kind of guarantor to ensure that Chile would not be bullied (a word Chileans commonly used in reference to Argentina's behavior). To do this, the guarantor's authority could be economic, military, legal, or moral. So, in this bargain over a dispute resolution process, Chile's interest was that the process involve an overseer with some authority.

The next step is to assess the bargaining range. In this bargain over process, the feasible agreements, that is, those requiring a joint decision, were negotiation, mediation, and arbitration.[91] Those processes requiring only a unilateral decision constituted the alternatives and thus set the limits to the bargain: resort to the International Court for Chile and use of military force for Argentina.[92]

If the above captures the structure of the process bargain, what mutually satisfactory agreements were possible? Direct negotiation suited Argentina's need for a direct solution whereas arbitration suited Chile's need for third-party authority. But neither process met both sides' interests: direct negotiation lacked the guarantor Chile needed and, for Argentina, arbitration was not "politically definitive." Mediation offered a compromise solution given the two sides' interests. A mediated agreement comes only with a solution signed by both countries and yet it is overseen by an outside party.

By this analysis, the source of the outside party's authority was not particularly important. To the extent national pride and self-determination were important components of the two nations' negotiating positions, involvement of a major economic or military power would be counterproductive. This was especially true for Argentina. Chile actually invited the United States to send observers to the Beagle Channel islands to document events should Argentina invade. Similarly, a legal authority was superfluous to Argentina's needs once tensions rose and symbolic issues became prominent.

This portrayal of the acceptance decision is not meant to suggest that mediation was the only feasible method of resolving the dispute nor that it was especially appropriate at all stages of the dispute. It would be tempting to conclude that, because the mediation was successful in the end, it should have been employed earlier. But this portrayal does suggest that the necessary conditions for a successful intervention include some combination of needs for both a third-party guarantor and a direct solution. Put more generally, parties accept an intermediary when they must accommodate both strong autonomy interests and outside overseer or coordinating interests.

This last point is consistent with the institution analogy discussed in chapter 2. Disputing parties often need third parties—whether institutions in repeated games or intermediaries in one-shot games—to facilitate settlement. In nonsecurity disputes, the third party serves primarily to reduce transaction costs and to allow expectations for behavior to converge. In security disputes, such as those discussed in this book, a third party also guarantees the legitimate participation (that is, without force) of all parties, including the weaker ones.

The above lays out structural factors governing the disputants' choice of a mediator in the Beagle Channel case. Adding process interests enriches the stylized decision problem developed in chapter 5. The acceptance question can be further enriched by examining the two countries' domestic conditions and their actual decision making.

Chile appeared to employ a reasonably rational process to decide on and then to choose a mediator. When negotiations collapsed and Argentina refused to submit the matter to the International Court, Chile set up a committee of senior diplomats to decide what to do. They concluded mediation was the best alternative (although some still wanted to go unilaterally to the court). They established criteria, drew up a list, got the go-ahead from Pinochet, and approached Argentina.

The fact that Chile's move to request a mediator failed raises an additional issue regarding the disputant's acceptance question. Chile likely viewed its overture to Argentina as an act of reassurance, signaling that indeed it wanted to settle the affair and to do so without an armed confrontation. But, given that Chile's previous attempts at reassurance went unheeded (or misinterpreted), a direct appeal to Argentina to seek a mediator likely was not reassuring. In fact, Argentina (and, in particular, the Junta) likely viewed it as little different from Chile's suggestions to go to the International Court, a move Argentines unofficially but repeatedly and emphatically declared would be a casus belli.

This observation suggests that, from a disputant's perspective, the acceptance decision has at least two important components. The first was developed in chapter 5: Is the expected value to oneself of a mediated outcome greater than a directly negotiated one or its best alternative? The second starts with the recognition that the acceptance question is not only a benefit-maximizing one but a strategic one as well. For one party to welcome a third party means it must also get the second party to accept the third party. As in any strategic interaction, part of the difficulty is signaling intentions: Who should initiate the solicitation of the intermediary, and how should it be done? With the value of hindsight, it seems that in this case, Chile would have been better off routing the suggestion through a third party, at least to sound out the real decision makers, the members of the Junta. To approach Argentine leaders directly, as Cubillos did, only forced them into a corner from which it was hard to escape without appearing manipulated by the Chileans.

Argentina's approach to resolution was ambivalent at best. Certainly the decision-making apparatus was in disarray. If the Foreign Ministry evaluated the prospects of an intermediary intervention favorably, it appeared to have little effect on the military leaders. The important question is, Why did the military leaders object to an intervention by the pope or, for all we know, by anyone?

Perhaps a sufficient answer is that they were determined to prevail on this matter, either through intimidation or force. In light of the domestic political situation, it is not surprising that they sought a foreign success. The political system was extremely weak, the leaders themselves were never secure, and the internal power struggles were at times severe.[93] Only two elected civilian presidents in the past half-century had completed their terms of office without being thrown out in a coup. Public support for Videla and the Junta diminished after their "success" against the subversives and the initial stabilization of the economy. With an inflation rate of 187 percent for the fiscal 1977–1978 year and the extreme repression, it soon became apparent to government officials and the public at large that the government had no answers to the serious economic and social problems. Such a weak political situation tended to invite the time-honored technique of seeking a success abroad—whether military or negotiated—to offset discontent at home.

Intermediaries are rarely welcome in such circumstances. They can thwart leaders' plans, weakening their ability to make a credible threat (they would never launch an attack with a peacemaker at work). Or, even if a negotiated—as opposed to a military—success is sought, leaders will be reluctant to share the benefits of a foreign success. Consequently, under the conditions Argentina experienced in the late 1970s, intervenors of all kinds were resisted.

Several additional factors likely contributed to Argentina's rejection of a third party. One was the third-party bias the leaders' would have expected. Given Argentina's poor standing in the international community at the time and the likelihood that any mutually acceptable intervenor would represent that community to some degree, the Argentine leaders could not expect a sympathetic, let alone neutral, outsider. Rejecting the outcome of an arbitration proceeding to which the country committed itself was not good form. Chile was likewise an international pariah but, on this matter, it had done everything right—legally, anyway—which, of course, was the crux of its strategy.

If Argentina's concern for third-party bias was significant, it suggests that Chile, for the strategic purpose of getting an intermediary accepted by Argentina, should have sought not a "neutral" party, but one that may have been somewhat inclined toward Argentina, say, Uruguay (the small country across the Plata River from Buenos Aires). Chapter 5 concluded that a disputant could rationally choose to accept a third party biased against itself if the expected outcome was still better than the alternative. The evidence from this case suggests an additional reason: a biased third party may be necessary to induce the other disputant just to accept an intervention.

Another factor working against acceptance could have been a general psychological resistance to accepting help from others. As Kelman and Warwick observe, "Such resistances are especially likely to arise when the influencing agent is an outsider—a representative of a different country, a different culture, or a different class. In such a case, the need for personal autonomy is augmented by a concern with the self-determination of one's group."[94]

This psychological resistance would be especially pronounced after Argentina's interests shifted from mere islands to questions of sovereignty and national identity. Even though these military leaders considered themselves good Catholics, they did not want some Italian, man-of-the-cloth from the Holy See telling them how to conduct their affairs. Given these views, a less visible or less "foreign" intervenor might have assuaged the Argentine military's concern with self-determination. In retrospect, however, once the Vatican was rejected and the pope intervened anyway, it was the very stature of the Holy See and the pope that made it impossible for the military to carry out its invasion.

Argentina's resistance to an intervention and Chile's failure to get agreement on a mediator can be further understood in terms of the parties' view of the conflict. The aggressor-defender and conflict spiral models of conflict escalation capture elements of Argentina's and Chile's worldviews and their perceptions of each other's intentions and show how these perceptions contributed to a fixation on the distributive aspects of the dispute, the escalation of the conflict, and the resistance to third-party intervention.[95]

In the *aggressor-defender* model, the aggressor, whose goals directly conflict with the defender, starts with mild contentious tactics and, as these fail to influence the defender, proceeds to use heavier tactics. The defender merely reacts, and the conflict escalates until the aggressor wins or gives up.

Given the events of 1977 and 1978 in the Beagle Channel dispute, Chile—and most observers—clearly viewed Argentina as the aggressor. As many Chilean participants explained in interviews, Chile would not provoke the hungry giant next door, but, at the same time, it had to match each of Argentina's moves so as to deter Argentina from attacking.[96] And the more Chile resisted—whether by refusing to negotiate over certain issues or by conducting military maneuvers of its own—the heavier the tactics Argentina employed.

In the corresponding "deterrence" model of international relations, Jervis explains that "Great dangers arise if an aggressor believes that the status quo powers are weak in capability or resolve. . . . To avoid this, the state must display the ability and willingness to wage war. It may not be able to ignore minor conflicts or to judge disputes on their merits. Issues of little intrinsic value become highly significant as indices of resolve."[97]

This view of international affairs, one in which moderation and conciliation are taken as signs of weakness, seems to have been shared among military leaders on both sides of the Andes. For example, one influential Argentine geopolitical theorist and, in 1977, a Beagle Channel negotiator, wrote in 1982: "To give priority to the preservation of the peace over the national interests, would be a sign of weakness. Universal experience shows that the countries that demonstrate weakness in the conduct of their external affairs, do not achieve good results. Weakness brings disregard from an adversary and provokes contempt and systematic aggression."[98]

To the extent such attitudes prevailed among the highest authorities in both countries, when faced with a question of territorial integrity, it is little wonder that decision makers took a distributive, constrained view of the conflict. In their game of "chicken," neither side could back down. This view may have been especially acute for Argentine leaders for whom accepting an intervenor such as the pope was viewed as a concession and, thus, an invitation for further Chilean encroachments. Consequently, both sides appeared to hold a highly conflictual, zero-sum perspective of the dispute in which Chile had to match each of Argentina's aggressive moves.

If this model helps explain events in the Beagle Channel dispute, it does not completely account for the "aggressor's" (Argentina's) motives nor how a seemingly trivial matter took on such grave proportions. The defensive *conflict spiral* model, where a vicious circle of contentious actions and reactions get established between two roughly equal partners, helps do this. In this model, each party reacts so as to protect itself from a threat it finds in the other's self-protective actions. Each retaliation provides a new issue—a new grievance—for the target of this action, feeding the escalation.

Thus, although Argentina's goal—getting the islands—was at complete odds with Chile's, its actions—demanding new negotiations after the Laudo, threatening force—may, from the Argentine leaders' perspective, have been in response to *Chile's* actions. That is, when the Laudo was handed down, Chile immediately accepted the results, refused to negotiate over them, and declared a 200-mile projection from the islands, thus encroaching on Argentina's Atlantic waters. That Argentina's aggression was, at least in part, a reaction to Chile's prior actions, was apparently dismissed by both Chile and outside observers (and later, possibly, by the papal mediation team). As Pruitt and Rubin note, outsiders often "assign the cause of the conflict to actions of the side with which they have weaker relations or the side that has employed the heavier, less defensible tactics. But a careful analysis usually reveals that causation has flowed both directions."[99]

In this case, then, the spiral conflict model complements the aggressor-defender model by showing that, at least from the perspective of the "aggressor," the "defender" contributed substantially to the escalatory dynamic. The aggressor-defender model may be accurate from the perspective of Chile and most outsiders, but the spiral conflict model reveals what was likely part of Argentina's motive—to resist Chile's provocations and intransigence. In effect, then, the spiral conflict model highlights a general feature of conflict: although, from the outside, the aggressor may appear obvious, from each disputant's perspective, the aggressor is the other guy.

For the purpose of understanding an intervention, especially the acceptability of an intermediary, this model suggests that intervenors need not determine which side is "right"—that is, which side correctly perceives the other as the aggressor. The likelihood of acceptance will be higher if the intermediary can demonstrate to each side that it accepts as legitimate that side's view of the conflict.[100] Of course, this presents yet another dilemma for the intermediary: how to accept one side's view when doing so is tantamount to rejecting the other's view and, by association, the other's legitimacy. Theodore Roosevelt did it by supporting each side's position even when that involved obvious contradictions. The pope did it by sending an envoy who assiduously avoided talk of mediation (a process he deemed judgmental) and took great pains to appear even-handed in his shuttling.

These two models of conflict escalation capture major differences between Argentina and Chile in their views of the conflict, the meaning of each other's actions, and their propensity to accept an intermediary. Traditionally, however, the two countries differed markedly in their views of international affairs. As noted, Argentina put great stock in "political" solutions. Chile, by contrast, saw the principle of international law as the highest ideal for managing disputes.[101]

Given such disparate world views, it is not surprising that misperception and confused signaling helped escalate the conflict out of proportion to the immediate issues in dispute. An intermediary can be most effective initially, therefore, in stopping the escalatory cycle, not in attempting to get an overall settlement. A powerful intermediary may be able to serve this function but only if, by its involvement, it does not exacerbate the disputants' interactions. Although not a perfect analogy, several years later in the Falklands/Malvinas crisis, U.S. Secretary of State Alexander Haig appeared to help both Argentina and Britain dig in their heels rather than give them an easy, face-saving way out. A less powerful actor, one without strong relations with the protagonists, and yet one with some international respectability (whether on legal or moral grounds) is more likely to deescalate such a conflict.

Turning to the intermediary's decision problems, the first question is entry. How can the last-minute timing of the pope's intervention be explained? It is possible that he anticipated a formal mediation process at the Vatican and wanted to ensure maximum leverage over the disputing parties once there. Consistent with the entry-timing argument of chapter 4, he would have wanted to wait until the last possible moment short of hostilities to launch his initiative. Of course, if this were his calculation, it was a risky one. Had he waited a day or even a few hours more, hostilities would have commenced, lives and ships would have been lost, the world would have awakened to this threat to regional stability, and the leaders on both sides could have easily ignored a papal envoy. It is likely, therefore, that the pope's decision calculus involved other factors as well, especially institutional and perceptual factors .

The relevant time period for considering these factors and the pope's entry decision is from November 1 to December 23, that is, when bilateral procedures were not in place. A long history of sensitive relations between church and state makes any pope hesitant to intervene in the affairs of state. The implicit, on-going bargain that has allowed the church to survive in the modern world (and, in many cases, thrive, especially in the Third World) has been that the church and the state respect each other's sphere of influence with minimal intrusion. For the church to enter the secular realm, even to promote peace, especially uninvited, would have threatened those fragile relationships. Thus, as church officials stated, there would be no intervention without an invitation. This partly explains the willingness of the Vatican to wait until the two countries came to agreement regarding the choice of a mediator.

But when they did not agree on a mediator, the Vatican still waited a week. This delay could have been owing to the fact that, as Ambassador Landau discovered, the pope firmly believed two Catholic countries would not commence hostilities in the Christmas season. It could also have been owing to the fact that the pope simply did not have the information. Certainly he was alerted to the crisis from the early days of his papacy, but the Roman Curia works slowly. After Nuncio Laghi's December 14 meeting with President Videla, Laghi himself was worried that his message would not get to the top quickly enough to be acted on. As one of more than a hundred nuncios worldwide, he, after all, had to work through channels. Every day the pope receives a multitude of requests for assistance from all over the world. The Curia, a tiny central bureaucracy serving a populous church, has, over the centuries, become adept at filtering and channeling such requests. Despite the urgency of the matter, it is very likely that Laghi's message indeed took some time to make its way to the few who had direct contact with the pope.

The waiting, in sum, can be interpreted in part as strategic maneuvering between the Vatican as potential intermediary and the disputing parties. But it must also be seen in its institutional and bureaucratic context. Given the sensitivities of church-state relations, the difficulty of mobilizing papal action on anything, especially on short notice, and the great uncertainties an intervention would entail regarding the dispute itself, it is not surprising that the pope held out until all other possibilities were exhausted.

Samoré's Shuttle Diplomacy

In bargaining terms, Samoré's shuttle diplomacy gave Chile its best alternative to a directly negotiated agreement. Because Argentina's best alternative appeared to have been force, the intervention appeared to weaken that alternative by adding the potential disgrace to the military of initiating a hostile act in the presence of a papal envoy. Domestic and international reaction to the snubbing of a religious man sent on a mission of peace could have been substantial.

The intervention also changed the Argentine government's channels of action. When the December 12 meeting between Foreign Ministers Cubillos and Pastor collapsed, all of Argentina's decisions fell to the military, especially to the hard-liners. These leaders presumably reasoned that, once Argentina occupied the islands (*Argentina's* islands) and compelled Chile to negotiate (their stated objective), the public would rally behind them. The pope's intervention frustrated those plans and, in effect, exposed the plot. The leadership then could only indirectly enjoy the public's support—in this case, through the popular and respected papal envoy. The intervention thereby conferred new legitimacy on the moderates, Videla and Viola. Consequently, the Argentine Foreign Ministry took front stage in the negotiations, led by the recently "disauthorized" Pastor, this time to conclude an agreement to accept papal mediation.

In addition to worsening Argentina's alternatives and changing its action channels, a third effect of the intervention relates to the psychology of accepting outside help. As discussed earlier, there is a natural tendency to resist influence from outsiders. This tendency can be diminished, however, if the outsider can assure the party that its support structure is not threatened.[102] Moreover, the effect of outside help is less to change minds than to change actions.

In his shuttle diplomacy and in the formal mediation afterwards, Samoré did not challenge the legitimacy of the Argentine leadership itself. In fact, his mere presence was, at least implicitly, a legitimating factor for the leadership. In addition, in Buenos Aires he talked to everyone—the military (hard-liners and moderates), diplomats, academics, church officials. By bringing them on board, he could assure the leaders that, should they accept the idea of papal mediation, they would be broadly supported. Pinochet, it should be added, enjoyed such broad support throughout the entire process.

To successfully rally support for a decision is not to say that the intervention created a fundamental change in attitude. The hard-liners were not suddenly conciliatory. Subsequent events—the renewal of hostile acts against Chile in 1981 and then the Malvinas/Falklands fiasco in 1982—indicate that no fundamental change occurred. Interventions like Samoré's do not effect such transformations by themselves. Their precise impact, it appears from this case, is to influence immediate decisions and to effect marginal changes in action.

That is, the hard-liners' attitudes toward conflict in general and to the Beagle Channel dispute in particular were probably highly resistant to change. For example, in November and early December 1978, the decision makers, the hard-line military members, were being pressured to accept a mediator. These urgings likely came from many sides: the military moderates including Videla and Viola; the foreign minister; the Chilean foreign minister and ambassador; church officials, especially, Nuncio Laghi; and third parties like the United States, other South American countries, the OAS, and the United Nations. Along with the decision makers' apparent predisposition to see conflict in win-lose terms, the social and political context in which they operated provided strong psychological and social support. Because the top officials of government were military appointees, it is likely the Junta members had surrounded themselves with like-minded supporters. Besides, this was a time of national crisis. Drastic measures had to be taken. Those who stood up for the country, who showed resolve, were reinforced. Those who did not were dismissed. In short, under these circumstances, the hard-liners were not likely to change their attitudes and, consequently, they were not likely to "concede" by accepting an intervenor.

As Kelman and Warwick point out, however, a change in attitude is not always necessary for a change in action. In fact, they say, "It might be more effective to begin a change effort at the level of concrete practices and their situational supports, and to leave attitude change—on which the ultimate stability of the new patterns of behavior may depend—to a later stage."[103]

The change effort of the papal intervention was directed at the leaders' choices of a settlement procedure and at their domestic support. No leader was converted to the value of communication or peaceful change or judicial process. But the mere presence of a papal envoy in a Catholic country meant the leaders had to talk. Once they started talking, once "peace was in the air," there was little they could do but "concede" and accept the papal mediation in Rome. To send the envoy home without agreement and then launch an invasion would have been nearly unthinkable. Put differently, whereas an invasion would have rallied public support without a papal intervention, it became unthinkable in the presence of a papal envoy.[104]

The general proposition suggested by this case is that to establish a dialogue or to get an agreement an intermediary need not change hearts and minds. In many circumstances, an intermediary need only change how a party acts and, especially, how it interacts with its opponent. In this case, the uninvited intervention compelled the hard-liners to change course, at least temporarily, and, once they did and were left with little political advantage to squeeze out of the dispute, they accepted measures to reestablish negotiations. The intervention did not change attitudes or compel agreement, it only facilitated some necessary steps toward agreement.

Could any intervenor have performed this task? The counterfactual argument suggests not. A U.S. secretary of state, for example, might have been acceptable to Chile but not likely to Argentina. To accede to a dominant power's suggestions, no matter how reasonable or similar to Samoré's, would have challenged Argentina's very reason for launching an invasion—to demonstrate the leaders' strength and resolve and their ability to manage Argentina's own affairs. A major power would have demeaned that intent; a minor player, especially one so humble and demure as a man-of-the cloth, one with no strategic or economic interests in the Southern Cone, would not have. Cardinal Samoré, once he established his evenhanded, nonjudgmental approach, was not threatening to the integrity of the leadership. In fact, by meeting with everyone and condemning no one, he was quite the opposite. Moreover, he had little to offer but prayers and little to threaten but a failed trip. He did not come to Buenos Aires to bargain because he had little to bargain with. In short, Cardinal Samoré, in his shuttling capacity, was a "neutral mediator" focusing on the disputants' bilateral interactions not on his bargain with each. As such, he could credibly deny any future benefits of his intervention other than to achieve peace and improve overall church-state relations.[105]

Finally, although Samoré's shuttle diplomacy resembled Henry Kissinger's shuttling in the Middle East, the objectives of the two shuttles—mediated talks for Samoré and troop disengagements for Kissinger—and the effects of the interventions were fundamentally different. Samoré sought improved bilateral interaction when, at the height of the crisis, little existed. Moreover, he sought an agreement expressly designed to promote mutually beneficial direct interaction, that is, mediated negotiations. Kissinger, by contrast, sought only a troop withdrawal agreement, leaving a broader settlement to the parties' own devices or to future third-party efforts. He made no effort to encourage direct interaction and, in fact, actively discouraged it. Constantly bargaining with both sides to promote a solution meeting U.S. interests in the region, he could do little to improve the belligerents' relations (other than to get troops withdrawn). In short, Samoré's shuttling focused on the parties' interactions whereas Kissinger's focused on U.S. relations with each belligerent. Being in-between, they both were able to secure a ceasefire but only Samoré got a settlement process established.[106]

This conclusion, then, is consistent with the argument in chapter 2 whereby the neutral mediator's target of intervention is expected to be the disputants' bilateral relationship, whereas the principal mediator's target is each disputant. The effects of such interventions are for the neutral mediator to enhance disputant interactions and for the principal mediator to detract from them. Neither in the abstract nor, as the Samoré and Kissinger instances of shuttle diplomacy suggest, in practice is either effect superior a priori.

Vatican Mediation

Pope John Paul II's mediation of the Beagle Channel dispute in Rome by itself constituted an improvement in the interactions of the two parties because the direct negotiations had collapsed in November. But did the mediation improve communication and understanding, identify a bargaining range, create joint gains, and establish principles for choosing a point of agreement? Or did it simply buy time until domestic conditions changed enough to allow for agreement? Examination of the mediator's practice over those six trying years reveals that, in this case, the impact was primarily to buy time. That, nevertheless, was no mean feat and the long-term result was, indeed, to provide the basis for improved relations.

This section thus goes beyond the argument in chapter 2 that predicts a neutral mediator will improve disputant interactions. It uses the detail of mediator practice to address a range of questions regarding the specific effects of a neutral mediator's intervention. For example, to what extent did the methods employed by the mediation team facilitate resolution and to what extent did they hinder it? How did the timing of the various "interventions" (for example, a speech by the pope or a proposal by Cardinal Samoré) affect the process? How did domestic events in the two countries affect the mediator's work? How did the training, world perspective, and personality of the mediation team affect the process? Why did the mediation take so long when all the facts were essentially on the table from the beginning?

These questions can be framed in terms of the mediator's bases of influence. For the Vatican, that influence is based not only on its ability to make disinterested proposals and to pool information as developed in chapter 3 but on its institutional routines, norms, and procedures and on the operational necessities of conducting a mediation process.

INFLUENCE: INSTITUTIONAL IMPERATIVE

In the Beagle Channel case, the mediator's need to have control over the process and to influence the parties can in part be understood from the historical, spiritual, and organizational position of the Vatican. The Roman Catholic church views itself as the spiritual sovereign of all Catholic peoples. Because peacemaking is seen as being as much a spiritual matter as a temporal one, the Vatican could justify its initial intervention in the Beagle Channel dispute—as well as subsequent steps throughout the mediation—as being part of its mandate to protect and to guide its subjects, those individuals of the Catholic faith. In so doing, it could justify its demands on the parties in religious and moral terms: "God, the Father of all, drove me to make a gesture of peace," said the pope.[107] The Vatican also could legitimately call upon its local parishes to pray for peace or, as it turned out, to garner support for Argentina's national referendum on the final treaty.

The very structure of the church hierarchy and the organizational routines of the Holy See lent themselves to the exercise of tight control over the mediation process. The Holy See, the central government of the church, is organized as a monarchy with the pope at the top, and with the Roman Curia—the administrative apparatus of the government—acting as a papal secretariat. The church as a whole is highly decentralized but the Curia is small and tightly run from above, especially from the secretariate of state. In the Vatican, little of significance happens without curial insiders knowing about it. At the same time, what does happen is often guarded as secret, even when that information seems insignificant. As a small, tradition-bound institution, the Holy See is, therefore, accustomed to keeping things under wraps.[108]

This tradition affected, among other things, the Vatican's approach to the press in the Beagle Channel mediation. From the very beginning, the Vatican required that all press announcements be made jointly and through the mediation team. The ostensible reason was to avoid unduly arousing public opinion, to avoid unreasonable expectations, and to head off any maneuvering on either side that could be justified by misleading press reports. Ultimately, the Vatican argued, strict control of the press was needed to build "trust in the mediator."[109]

Although control over the press is understandable from the Vatican's perspective and would certainly be the envy of other mediators, this approach to the press can be interpreted equally well, and perhaps more plausibly, as a means of building mediator influence over the parties. This interpretation has two aspects. First, controlling public announcements removes from the parties the opportunity to employ the familiar negotiating tactic of using the press to make commitments binding. That is, if in a negotiation, one party must convince the other side (and, for that matter, the mediator) that it cannot budge from a stated position, a public announcement of its position makes it more difficult to find a face-saving means for moving from that position. Second, freeing the parties from the burden of constantly answering to the press makes it easier for the mediator to make proposals and demand concessions from the parties. For example, the mediator can claim that a concession on a given point is not significant if it is only temporary and conditional upon a settlement on all points. Because the party's constituency need never know about such a conditional concession—and the mediator can guarantee confidentiality—it is a low-risk move.

Proposal making thus entails more than relieving the parties of contentious bargaining. It requires finding ways to make it easier for the parties to accept the proposals. One way is to credibly promise the confidentiality of conditional acceptance. The Vatican relied on its institutional traditions—it does not pretend to be a democracy nor an open government and it answers to the outside world only when it wants to—and on its religious authority to enhance that credibility. As it turned out, the Vatican mediation team was able to secure tentative concessions in private that eventually found their way into the final treaty.

INFLUENCE: OPERATIONAL IMPERATIVE

The need to establish firm control can be further established by examining four examples of the Vatican mediation team's practice: the Vatican's stated position of seeing the process through to the finish; its manner of controlling information; its handling of the parties' positions and interests; and its attempts to alter the parties' alternatives to a mediated agreement.

The mediator's repeated statements that it would never abandon the mediation put the burden on the parties to withdraw. If at any time one party decided to give up, that party would suffer the opprobrium of sacrificing a peace effort for some uncertain, probably contentious, process.

And, given that the two sides could agree on virtually nothing on their own, it was not likely they would agree jointly to abandon the mediation. Thus, with the mediator committed to staying indefinitely, unilateral withdrawal could easily have been condemned by the other side, by the Vatican itself, or by other third parties. The cost in international standing could have been high.[110]

A second example of the Vatican's attempt to gain control in order to avoid failure can be found in its practice of keeping parties separate and strictly limiting the flow of information. On the principle that information is power, the effect was to enhance the mediator's influence. What is important with respect to mediation, however, is how such tight information control either furthers or hinders the mediation process.

One effect of controlling the information flow in a negotiation is to allow the mediator to learn the issues and the parties' interests in a manner unencumbered by strategic play between the parties. This was the reason given by the Vatican. Parties are more likely to reveal information and less likely to protect their positions or be tempted to act strategically vis-à-vis each other if they are not facing each other in the same room.

A second effect of information control is to influence the interactions between each disputant and the mediator. In the Beagle Channel mediation, Chile's case rested largely on standards of international law and propriety, and so its strategy in Rome was to convince the mediator that everything it did was consistent with the notion of playing by the rules. In turn, because controlling information facilitated the mediator's ability to act as a "rules manipulator,"[111] the mediator could use Chile's stance to encourage strict adherence to the rules of the mediation as written in the 1979 Accord of Montevideo and as later interpreted by the Vatican. The result was not only a willingness on Chile's part to be forthcoming in providing information and revealing its positions but also to pursue imaginative paths for a solution. For example, Chile did accept the pope's concept of a "common zone," a jointly administered region for the cooperative exploitation of natural resources.

Argentina, on the other hand, was primarily looking for a concession from Chile. It seems clear that given the political turmoil in Argentina throughout the period of the mediation and the risks of deviating from a hardline view, no Argentine negotiator could return home without major concessions from Chile.[112] Thus, the Argentine strategy in Rome was to give little but to get the mediator to extract a lot from Chile.[113]

Dealing with Argentina's stance was certainly more problematic for the mediator than dealing with Chile's. Even if the mediation team could extract a concession from Chile, it felt compelled to balance it with one from Argentina. Attempting to do this, nevertheless, required control over the process. For example, to seek concessions, the mediator would naturally feel compelled to work separately with each party, knowing that each party would never on its own be the first to move. And once movement was detected, the mediator would have to guard that information carefully so as not to jeopardize securing the concession.

While the mediation team appeared to pursue such a strategy, in time it seemed to realize that simply squeezing out concessions would not necessarily lead to agreement. In fact, such concessions may have inhibited progress if any concession on the part of an Argentine negotiator endangered his or her position back home. This result would make that negotiator all the more cautious about any subsequent move, whether concessionary or integrative. This interpretation of the effect of urging concessions seems to suggest that an incremental approach to achieving a settlement—especially with a focus on concessions—may, under some circumstances, be counterproductive. It suggests that negative dynamics, such as increasing cautiousness, can develop and then feed back to make resolution more difficult to achieve.

Once the mediation team came to realize the dilemma of the Argentine negotiator, the response of the mediator was to protect the negotiator. One means was to restrict press coverage. Another was to make direct public appeals to the negotiator's leadership and public. Still a third method was to do all possible publicly to appear absolutely fair and impartial, thus enabling the negotiator to argue that a settlement package involved a balanced process of making concessions. All these methods, once again, required a degree of control over the process.

A third example of the mediator's attempt to build influence in order to avoid failure can be found in the Vatican's otherwise inexplicable stress on positions. The mediation team dwelled on the parties' stated positions to such an extent that the search for underlying interests was inhibited. This process started at the very beginning of the mediation with the mediation team's request for written statements from both sides and continued throughout much of the mediation when the mediation team asked for position statements on major issue areas and when it asked for draft solutions. All this had a legitimate purpose for the mediator, of course, namely, to acquire information and see how far apart were the two sides. But acquiring information in this way invites rigidity and an unwillingness to explore creative options.

Why would the mediation team have taken such an approach? One reason could have been that, lacking any experience in mediation and with essentially nothing to serve as a guide, the mediation team simply did what seemed logical. Cardinal Samoré did do some reading on the matter and it is possible that with so little written on actual procedures of international mediation, he may have adopted what appears to be a labor model of mediation: start with each side's last bid, determine how far each can go, and then press both sides to converge to a midpoint.

From an institutional perspective, another reason could be that this is standard operating procedure for the Holy See. When disputes arise within the church, say a difference between a bishop's local practices and the official doctrine of the church, the Holy See adopts an adjudicatory role rather than a neutral intermediary role. In the adjudicatory approach, those charged with resolving the dispute collect information and make a decision, a decision that presumably meets everyone's interests. The Vatican view of mediation initially could have been similar; its role was to collect information and make a *suggestion* that met both sides' interests. Because in the beginning the mediation team had every reason to believe that the two sides would accept the pope's proposed solution, especially given the mediator's demonstrated efforts to be fair, equitable, and impartial, the only difference in procedure was a decision rather than a suggestion. To the Vatican, that difference may not have appeared to be much. But as the mediator was soon to find out, when Argentina did not accept the pope's Propuesta, a difference in decision-making authority—between making a decision and a suggestion—can have profound effects.

A third possible reason for the focus on positions comes from the mediator's need to maintain control over the process. Given the risks to the Vatican of losing control, the mediation team's inexperience as a mediator, and, at least for Argentina, a lack of support back home, any attempt by the mediator to engage the two countries in a seemingly open-ended process of exploring underlying interests and searching for joint gains could have jeopardized the parties' faith in the Vatican's ability to effect a settlement. The mediation team often stated that it took such measures as restricting press coverage and holding separate meetings to "build trust in the mediator." Although this enigmatic phrase can be taken at face value, it can also be interpreted as indicative of more strategic concerns of the Vatican.

That is, the mediation team entered this process with a sense of considerable uncertainty and risk: the team members had never conducted such a process; the dispute had eluded solution for a century; an unexpected twist of events in South America could have easily upset the mediation team's best efforts; and failure to reach a settlement could have made war likely and could have impeded the pope's ability to conduct foreign affairs on other fronts. It is not surprising that members of the mediation team, once thrown into such a situation, would adopt a risk-averse approach, an approach that would strive to give the appearance of being in charge, one that would avoid direct confrontations between parties, and one that would put control of the process as much as possible into the hands of the mediation team. Moreover, given the initial positions of the two sides— Chile wanted a juridically sound solution and Argentina wanted concessions on land—it is reasonable to conclude that, in the beginning, the two negotiating teams themselves would have balked at anything but a very formal, highly structured process.

The fact that the mediation team continued to demand written positions when such a process achieved little in terms of movement appears to confirm this interpretation of mediator control. If the mediation team only had been seeking factual and positional information by requesting written position statements (something, by the way, that could have been achieved in other ways), once it had such information it would have moved on to exploring interests and crafting solutions. The mediation team did, of course, do these things, but it also regularly reverted to a process of requesting statements on new positions, each time hoping one side or the other would move enough to provide the basis for agreement. Assuming the mediation team did learn over these six long years that requests for position statements rigidify positions and inhibit creative problem solving, the best explanation seems to be that this was the only conceivable means of maintaining some control given external events.

The previous three examples primarily involve the mediator's efforts to control procedures. A fourth example of control involved attempts to influence the parties themselves, in particular, their alternatives to a mediated agreement or their perceptions of feasible agreements.

When, after one year of effort, the mediation team realized progress toward agreement was not forthcoming, Cardinal Samoré raised some unpleasant alternatives. He suggested that if the parties did not significantly change their positions, the pope could either suspend the mediation or offer them a take-it-or-leave-it solution. When this produced no movement, the Vatican considered sending a papal representative to each country's president or simply calling in each country's foreign minister for talks. Finally, the two sides were given an audience with the pope in which John Paul underscored the seriousness of the great distance still existing between the two sides.

All these moves can be seen as attempts to change the parties' perceived alternatives to a mediated agreement. That is, if the parties originally were convinced that the pope would never abandon the mediation, the best alternative to "agreement now" was continued mediation. Suggesting that the pope might reverse his promise was an attempt—albeit an ineffectual one—to change that perceived alternative.

The mediation team also stressed alternatives at the very end of the mediation when a solution was in sight. First, the mediation team insisted that posturing could no longer be tolerated and that their positions, their truly inflexible ones and their flexible ones, had to be revealed truthfully, "as if in confession." Then, when the last objectionable feature of the pope's Propuesta was excised and the mediation team determined there was nothing else that could be done to improve the proposal for either side (presumably without simultaneously hurting the other side), the mediation team said that this was the final proposal: to reject it would be to terminate the mediation effort. This threat to cease the mediation was more credible this time because it was clear to all that the mediation team could do no better and was tired and frustrated with the entire ordeal. Moreover, in Argentina in 1984, with the return of democratic rule, existed the most favorable climate ever for resolution, and in Chile there was an increasing urgency to settle the matter and claim a foreign success. And, finally, the mediation team made its take-it-or-leave-it offer public. Conditionally imposing upon itself the public image cost of retracting such a pledge, this time the Vatican made a binding commitment.

In conclusion, the desire—or the need—for control can explain much of the Vatican's approach to conducting an international mediation. To identify control as a major concern of the Vatican is not, however, to ascribe motives any less noble than working for peace. Rather, the Vatican viewed strict control as a necessary means to achieve a peaceful resolution. Furthermore, although the means of establishing such control may be unique to the Vatican, the perceived need is probably felt universally by international intermediaries. They enter a dispute on an ad hoc basis, experience great uncertainties and possibly risks, and immediately search for means of getting on top of the situation. Thus, the general proposition is that intermediary behavior can be understood not as the application of techniques or as the search for mutually beneficial solutions but, first, as finding ways to take charge in a highly precarious, ill-defined situation.

Explaining Delay

One question remains regarding outcomes and the ultimate impact of the pope's intervention: Why did the Beagle Channel mediation take so long? If mediation is a process of identifying issues and interests, finding a suitable bargaining range, and helping parties move to agreement, then why did the Beagle Channel mediation take six years and not six months as expected? Certainly the facts were on the table—for the most part they had been since the arbitration of the early 1970s—and it appears the negotiators from both Argentina and Chile were experienced, competent individuals.

Part of the explanation relates to the mediation team's inexperience with the process, which is probably a common feature of international mediation. The mediation team was searching for a method and had little guidance in procedure. The procedures they did use were developed ad hoc. In addition, it appears that Cardinal Samoré's slow methodical approach, in which no stone could be left unturned, each party was given ample opportunity to explain everything, and each nuance was carefully explored, contributed to the delay. If either party had reason to delay—and Argentina evidently did at several points—Samoré's style was well suited to allow for it.

A second factor was the apparent distributive view both sides took of the negotiation. Both saw their primary objectives as getting islands and as much of the sea as possible. This is how the dispute was viewed from the beginning, and there is little evidence that the perception changed during the mediation. Although the mediation team sincerely tried to unbundle issues and to add new issues to find integrative solutions, they had little success. In part, this was owing to the very nature of the dispute—it was primarily distributive as long as high-value interests, such as territorial integrity and national sovereignty, were attached to the otherwise straightforward issues of territorial and maritime delimitation. Public opinion was concerned largely with who won and who lost. And, finally, the mediation team's methods, such as requesting position statements, tended to focus the negotiation on the distributive aspects.

A third factor, and unquestionably the most important for final settlement, was the effect of domestic events on the negotiators' ability to agree. This was particularly pronounced for Argentina. As in any negotiation with representatives, an agent-principal division occurred. Here that division seems to have been a major source of frustration for the Vatican mediation team. All the painstaking work of mastering the facts and exploring interests, crafting a solution that seemed to meet those interests, and winning the negotiators' acceptance, was repeatedly defeated either intentionally by decision makers or inadvertently as a result of tumultuous domestic events.[114] The Argentine negotiators received conflicting demands from different sectors of the military governments throughout this period. Furthermore, during the mediation period, Argentina had five presidents and five Vatican delegation chiefs. All told, it is little wonder that an Argentine negotiator would not dare recommend agreement. This would have been the case no matter how reasonable the proposed solution, no matter how balanced the process and how fair the results, no matter how much creative problem solving took place, no matter how many joint gains were extracted.

So were the Vatican's efforts ultimately for nought? Was the mediation team playing the wrong game, engaging in details in Rome when the real problem was in South America? These are the kinds of questions any intermediary must ask when a dispute appears unresolvable, when a serious division exists between negotiators and their constituents. A preliminary answer is that if maintaining a peace is the foremost objective of any mediation effort—whether for instrumental or intrinsic reasons—the Vatican's efforts contributed to six years of such peace. This was no mean feat given the tensions between the countries at the time of the pope's intervention and the military's propensity to seek an external success to compensate for its internal failures (witness Argentina's renewed provocations against Chile in 1981 and then the invasion of the Falklands/Malvinas islands in 1982). On this count alone, it seems the Vatican mediation can be considered a success. It was not just that a settlement was reached but that a peace was maintained through some very rough times.

This conclusion does, however, raise an interesting question. Suppose the Vatican could have foreseen the course of events, the intransigence of the parties, the domestic upheavals. Would it have acted differently? Should it have? Accepting the above conclusion that a peace was maintained, the answer would have to be no. But then that suggests that the mediator's true task is not so much to move parties toward agreement but rather to keep the parties busy. And because sophisticated negotiators cannot put up with busyness, even on expense accounts, they must do at least what *appears* to be the work of negotiation under the guidance of a mediator.

Thus, an alternative interpretation of the seemingly endless meetings typical of many mediated negotiations is that such meetings serve primarily to keep the parties at the table and not at each other's throats. But in order to keep them there, the mediator must convince them that they are doing something worthwhile. The most convincing activity is, naturally, "negotiating." But, in fact, they are doing nothing of the kind—they are just biding time. This, of course, is a rather ungenerous view of what mediators do. But, at least in the Beagle Channel mediation, it may partly explain why the mediation team plodded along, day after day, year after year, continuing to request position statements, sound out variations on old themes, and look for new angles.

Even if this view is close to the mark—that is, even if it helps explain much of the day-to-day activity of the Vatican mediation—it does not deny the value of the fruits of those labors. Continuing to work on details when agreement on a package was impossible set the stage for an expeditious settlement when domestic conditions changed. The pope and the mediation team seemed to realize this and never let up, even in the worst of times (e.g., during and after the Malvinas/Falklands crisis). As a result, when Argentina was ready for a solution in the Beagle Channel dispute— the time of which, by the way, no one could have predicted more than a few months in advance—so was a settlement package. This being the case, the day-to-day activities are indeed more important than just biding time. But contrary to popular concepts, such activities may actually do little to bring parties closer to an agreement. The paradox, once again, is that a mediator still must convince the parties that what they are doing is what they are supposed to be doing—getting an agreement. If this concept of what a mediator actually does in the day-to-day activities of a mediation is true, it highlights yet again the difficulty of mediating, the contradiction and ambivalence such a role demands.

Two prescriptions for mediators follow from this line of reasoning. First, although getting agreement may appear to be one's mandate, achieving a temporary peace is, in many circumstances, no small matter and is a worthy achievement in its own right. Doing so may well be the necessary precursor to a more comprehensive solution. It is worth noting that, even in the final solution of the Beagle Channel case, a comprehensive solution was not achieved. This was left to the "Binational Commission" that in 1985 began work on matters of "regional integration."

Second, in the course of a mediation, mediators must continually ask themselves whether or not to continue. It would be tempting to quit when it appears the success of the mediation (defined as getting agreement) is out of the control of the negotiators and that everything depends on constituencies and external events. The proper decision, however, pertains to the alternatives the mediator and the parties face. If abandoning the mediation is likely to lead to hostilities, continuation, even if it appears futile (in the sense of reaching an agreement) makes sense.

Another way of saying this is that, for continuing the mediation, the relevant calculation is at the margin: if the cost of continuing one more time period is less than the expected value of discontinuing (where all the possible consequences including hostilities are factored in with their respective estimated probabilities), the mediator should continue. Notice, by the way, that this calculation by the mediator can be thought of in either a strictly altruistic sense (What are the parties' expected costs?) or in a self-interested sense (What are the costs to the *mediator* if the parties incur these costs?). Thus, this is the proper calculation whether the mediator claims to be operating strictly in the interests of the parties or whether the mediator sees its own interests as paramount.

CONCLUSION

The Vatican's intervention in the Beagle Channel dispute, although unique in many respects, provides a preliminary test of several key propositions of part 1. Furthermore, by incorporating political, institutional, and psychological factors into the explanation of events, additional general questions about the nature of international mediation arise. Five propositions result.

One, the disputants' acceptance question was not a neat cost/benefit calculation but, as noted in chapter 5, involved well-known ambiguities of signaling and offering reassurance. Domestic conditions also weighed heavily on the acceptance question, especially in Argentina where an intermediary intervention would thwart or depreciate the sought foreign success. Moreover, in the leaders' strategic calculation vis-à-vis Chile, an intermediary intervention would only weaken the credibility of their threat and undermine their already shaky political base. Possibly the most important insight from this case, however, was the fact that although an intervention can threaten leaders, it need not convert them to be successful. From the perspective of the intermediary seeking acceptance, the intervention need only influence immediate decisions and effect marginal changes in actions. This conclusion points up yet again how limited yet, at times, how critical an intermediary's intervention can be.

Two, the art of proposal making entails more than making nonstrategic offers that parties presumably welcome as a way out of contentious bargaining, as discussed in chapter 3. It requires finding ways to make it easier for the parties to accept the proposals. One way is credibly to promise the confidentiality of conditional concessions. The Vatican relied on its institutional traditions—it does not pretend to be a democracy or an open government, and it answers to the outside world only when it wants to— and on its religious authority to enhance that credibility. Other mediators with little need for public accountability can operate similarly. In general, however, in the modern state system, few major actors have such latitude.[115] Those that do tend to fit the category of "neutral mediator" as developed in chapter 2. Small states, transnational actors, and private individuals can commit to a limited, nonbargaining role in part because they can draw on institutional factors to aim their intervention at promoting constructive interactions. They help the parties resist pressure from the press and public opinion that otherwise denies them the confidentiality necessary for effective negotiating. They, in effect, recreate an environment that diplomats in the classical European great power system enjoyed because they were insulated from domestic constraints. In this way, then, intermediary intervention compensates for the confidentiality missing in modern diplomacy.

Three, the labor mediation model of urging concessions and seeking convergence to a midpoint has limited applicability in most international conflicts. Rather than generating momentum, the experience of the Argentine negotiators in this case suggests that, when mediators employ a labor model, negotiators become cautious and increasingly anxious about the concessions they make. The analytic implication is that where a bargaining range concept helps explain the focal point effect of a mediator's proposals (see chap. 3), the concept can be misleading when it comes to concession/convergence because such an approach may hinder, not promote, movement toward agreement.

Four, this case reveals the compelling need of neutral mediators and, possibly, principal mediators as well, to gain control over the process once in the dispute. In chapter 4, the need for process control was assumed in developing the link between entry timing and control. The detail on mediator practice afforded by this case enables an examination of institutional and psychological determinants of the need for process control. Although some of these may be unique to the Vatican—its closed door history, its tenuous church-state relations—at least one general proposition can be posited.

That is, mediators operate under conditions of high uncertainty, sometimes even risk. Much of their behavior, consequently, can be understood as attempts to gain control. The means will depend on the institutional and decision-making factors most prominent for that mediator. But, contrary to prescriptive approaches that stress technique—especially those that promote open-ended, problem-solving techniques—in practice, a mediator is likely to seek control first, creative exploration second. Thus, in this case, we saw strict controls placed on press coverage and heavy use of position statements. Based on in-depth interviews of Vatican mediators, I can say that the Vatican fully appreciated the need to engage the disputants in problem-solving efforts and to seek innovative solutions. That need, however, was only second to the need to gain control and reduce uncertainty. In sum, *explanations* of mediator behavior, as opposed to idealized *prescriptions* for mediator behavior, will be stronger to the extent they account for mediator interests in general (as stressed in part 1) and for the sources of and responses to mediator uncertainty and risk in particular.

Finally, this case elaborates on the question of measuring success. In part 1, and in the subsequent case studies, I argued that an intermediary intervention should not be viewed as a major determinant of a conflict outcome, that marginal change, helping tip decisions from contention to collaboration, is the most once can expect. Here it is evident that a mediator can succeed by holding parties at bay. As long as a pretense of negotiating and making progress is maintained, the mediator fulfills a valued service, maybe not what the realists would demand to take the process seriously nor what the negotiation advocates would claim is its significance, but only what can be expected of a limited role in the settlement of international conflicts.

Chapter Nine

BIAFRA: THE OAU, THE BRITISH, AND THE QUAKERS MEDIATE IN THE NIGERIAN CIVIL WAR, 1967–1970

FOR MOST PEOPLE, the Nigerian Civil War of 1967–1970[1] conjures up images of mass starvation and attempted genocide. For others, it was a not unexpected consequence of decolonization in an ethnically diverse country blessed with oil. Either way, the conflict between the Nigerian federal government and the secessionist eastern region of Biafra was extremely costly in lives and material resources. It was never strictly a domestic affair, however. From the earliest signs of civil strife until the federal government's victory, the international community was actively involved, especially in its humanitarian efforts. Some of the third parties—especially, the OAU, the UK, several African neighbors, and various religious groups—also intervened to manage or resolve the conflict. The OAU supported Lagos; several religious groups, Biafra; and the Commonwealth Secretariat and the British tried to stay in the middle. Only a group of Quakers traveled to both capitals and relayed messages directly between the leaders. Over thirty months, Adam Curle and two other Quakers, John Volkmar, and Walter Martin, became well known in top government circles in the Nigerian capital, Lagos, and in Biafra. They consulted with representatives of the disputing parties in New York, Washington, London, Paris, Geneva, and Lisbon and were called in to consult with officials of Britain and the United States and a number of private organizations. In all, they consulted seven times with the Nigerian federal government's leader, General Gowon, in Lagos and made four trips into Biafra, often under dangerous conditions.

This, then, is an account and analysis of these interventions with special attention given to the Quaker effort. By dwelling on the Quakers' role, I do not mean to suggest that their efforts were major factors in the conflict. They were not. As Mike Yarrow writes, their intervention was a "footnote." The Quaker intervention, nevertheless, is particularly revealing of the particular advantages of a "neutral mediator," especially as it contrasts in this conflict with the other third-party interventions. In fact, the Quaker intervention comes closer to the limiting case, the "ideal type" delineated in chapter 2, than virtually any other intervention conceivable. This case, therefore, offers a more stringent test of the principal/neutral mediator distinction than that afforded by the Beagle Channel case where, in its church-state relations, the Vatican had something of a bargaining relationship with the two states. The Quakers strive to limit their role and, in so doing, impose norms of interaction between disputants that other third parties cannot achieve.

THE CASE

Nigeria gained independence from Great Britain in 1960 amid intense rivalries among three large ethnic groups in three major regions—the Muslim Hausa-Fulani in the North; the Christian/Muslim/animist Yorubas in the West; and the Christian Ibos in the East. The government created a fourth region to ease tensions but, as each group maneuvered to gain control of the federal government, the pressures only mounted, culminating in violent and fraudulent elections in 1964 and 1965.

In a 1966 coup, an Ibo took power. Although the coup received broad public support, other ethnic groups feared that Ibos, long dominant in economic and governmental affairs, might take over entirely. Such fears eventually led to demonstrations and then riots against Ibos in the North. A countercoup brought Lt. Col. Jakubu Gowon, a Northerner, into power. Despite appeals for unity, soldiers joined civilian mobs in the North in October killing 10,000 Ibos and other southeastern people and sending 1.5 million fleeing to the southeast. There, the regional military governor, Lt. Col. Chukwuemeka Odumegwu Ojukwu, became leader of the Ibo secessionist movement.

As conditions continued to deteriorate, British and American diplomats encouraged Gowon to meet with Ojukwu outside the country but Gowon refused. Ghana's head of state worked quietly behind the scenes for five months and finally convinced Gowon, a personal friend, to meet with Ojukwu and the other military governors in a hilltop retreat in Aburi, Ghana. The January 1967 meeting, as it turned out, was to be the two leaders' only face-to-face encounter in the conflict. At the meeting, Ojukwu surprised everyone with a carefully planned agenda and a series of resolutions. Among these was the renunciation of force to settle internal conflicts and an extensive decentralization of the Nigerian federal government. Eventually, Gowon accepted Ojukwu's vaguely worded proposals, but his government subsequently issued its own interpretations including the retention of a strong federal government.

In the coming months, Ojukwu used the so-called Aburi Accords as the basis of even greater demands for regional autonomy.[2] When leaders of the western region also began speaking of greater autonomy and even secession, Gowon, desperate to save the federation, made further concessions. It was still not enough; Ojukwu moved closer to secession. In late May, Gowon decided to divide the country into twelve states. This would have shifted political power to the many minority tribes who comprised 40 percent of the country's population and who resented Ibo domination. Moreover, if Ojukwu had accepted the twelve-state structure, his government would have lost 60 percent of its agricultural revenues and 95 percent of its petroleum income. Cut off from the coastal provinces, Ojukwu's government would have been landlocked and impoverished. Within 48 hours of Gowon's announcement, on May 30, 1967, Ojukwu officially declared the creation of the state of Biafra. One week later war broke out.

Until this time, the Quakers had no organized involvement in Nigeria. Adam Curle, a professor of education at Harvard and, for three years, head of a Ghanaian university Department of Education, had recently returned from a Quaker conciliation mission in India and Pakistan. In December 1966, he contacted Walter Martin at the Quaker's UN headquarters in New York to see if his conciliation experience could be applied in Nigeria. Martin arranged a meeting with Nigeria's UN ambassador, who knew of the Quakers through their conferences for diplomats. In their meeting in January 1967 at the United Nations, Curle expressed his concern for the situation and asked if the Quakers could be used as channels of communication. The ambassador was interested but indicated that the Nigerians were sensitive to outside meddling. He did, however, welcome an unofficial visit on school-related business.

Curle got clearances from the Quaker committees in Philadelphia and London to travel to Nigeria as they described it, to express concern, to listen, and to find ways of helping through conciliation or relief. With Volkmar, he visited the major areas of Nigeria in April and May 1967. Many of the people they contacted knew of the Quakers, and some had been involved in Quaker programs. In all, they met with seventy-eight individuals, thirty-five of whom had been exposed to Quakers, twenty-seven who had been in touch with a Quaker organized program, and eight who knew Quakers in other connections, usually as students.

They did not see Gowon but met with his principal secretary and Dr. Okoi Arikpo, who later became commissioner of external affairs. In the East, they met directly with Ojukwu and most of the key people involved in presenting the Biafran cause to the international community.

Just one week after their trip, Ojukwu declared secession. The Quakers were, therefore, unable to establish the peace work as envisioned, but the contacts made on the trip did establish the basis for message carrying over the ensuing two and one-half years. Moreover, in Yarrow's words, this initial trip "gave the Quakers a balanced understanding of the total situation and established a firm base for conciliation. Because of their overall knowledge, helped by the reporting of Curle and Volkmar, the Quaker organizations did not yield to the pro-Biafra sentiments that swept the churches of Europe and North America."[3]

In October, Arikpo and several Nigerian officials at the United Nations met at Quaker House in New York. The Nigerians suggested that the Quakers pass the following message to the Biafrans: If Ojukwu and his immediate associates abdicated, the federal government would grant amnesty to all other rebels; there would be no reprisals or executions; Gowon would restrain his troops from the East; and an Ibo would be appointed to administer the East Central State. The Quakers viewed such terms as tantamount to a demand for surrender and declined to convey the message, concluding that to do so would contravene the role of a neutral mediator. Instead, they decided that the Quakers' first move would be to support the mediation effort of the Organization of African Unity.

In its annual summit conference in September 1967, the OAU created a "Consultative Committee" to deal with the Nigerian situation. At the insistence of the Nigerian federal government, the OAU deliberately avoided any mention of mediation. The committee, composed of the heads of state of four African countries led by Ethiopia's Emperor Haile Selassie, traveled to Lagos in November 1967 to "consult" with the federal government. Although the committee's purpose was to assure Gowon of the OAU's "desire for the territorial integrity, unity and peace of Nigeria," the Nigerian government was nevertheless apprehensive about the trip. It feared the Committee would press for negotiations on terms it would deem unacceptable but which would be presented in such a way that to refuse would discredit the federal cause."[4]

In Lagos, Gowon welcomed the African leaders and explained that "Your Mission is not here to mediate . . . your consultations with the Federal Military Government can be fruitful only if we all recognize the nature of our crisis. There was fear of domination by one region over the other and by one ethnic group over the rest. The only way to remove this fear and the structual imbalance in the Federation is by creating more states. . . . We cannot cease current military operations to end the rebellion . . . until the rebels renounce secession."[5]

With no agenda and no diplomatic precedent, neither the Nigerians nor the committee knew how to proceed. Despite the committee's desire to establish communication with the Biafrans, in the end, the committee sided with Gowon and sent a message via two-way radio to the Biafran leaders, calling on them to renounce secession and to accept the federal government's offer of peace. The committee's position came as no surprise because most of its members were themselves threatened with secessionist movements. As a result, no one from the committee visited rebel territory, and Ojukwu simply ignored their call for Nigerian unity.

The failure of the OAU Consultative Committee to establish talks between the two sides prompted other third parties to intercede. For example, in December 1967, Pope Paul VI sent two envoys on a tour of Nigeria's three ecclesiastical provinces. Going first to Lagos, they declared that their mission was not political, religious, or diplomatic, but merely humanitarian. When they asked Gowon if he would agree to a temporary cease-fire, he declined, even after a public appeal from the pope for a Christmas truce. In Lagos, the Vatican was already viewed as pro-Biafran. This impression was reinforced when the papal envoys arrived in Biafra, a predominantly Catholic region. Ojukwu announced a unilateral cease-fire, and huge throngs of people turned out to celebrate the visit. This was the first official delegation to breach the federal blockade. In their final communiqué, the papal envoys called on the world to prevent a general massacre of innocent civilians. Five weeks later, a delegation from the World Council of Churches came to Biafra and experienced a similar reception.

On March 20, 1968, the Vatican and the World Council of Churches issued a joint appeal to the federal and Biafran governments and to the entire international community. They called for an immediate cease-fire, mediation by African leaders, and assurances of security to both sides. The appeal was precisely what the federal government feared and what Ojukwu had hoped for. It was a major victory in Biafra's attempts to gain international attention and eventual recognition. Ojukwu supported the appeal in its entirety but, in private conversations with the papal envoys, ruled out negotiations unless Biafran independence was recognized. Gowon, in a public statement, argued that the Biafrans would use the cease-fire to rearm and that Nigerian unity had to come before any negotiations.

The Quakers, meanwhile, began exploring a different kind of third-party role. Shortly after the Consultative Committee meeting in Lagos, Quakers in Philadelphia debated a suggestion by the president of Niger that the Quakers set up secret low-level meetings. They agreed that an unofficial, nonpolitical group might be able to arrange talks that could lead to formal discussions. Curle argued that they should aim for a meeting of high-level officials, but the Philadelphia staff felt seminars among lower level officials would be best. They agreed to authorize a trip to both sides and, in the Quaker tradition, to proceed "as the way opened." They would try to set up a meeting and would provide a chairman and observers if desired. The Quaker position of relating openly to both sides was made clear from the beginning and, on this basis, representatives of the federal government and Biafra in New York agreed to a visit. Curle and Volkmar were selected to go.

Leaving for Africa in late January 1968, Curle and Volkmar decided they needed to reach the top people on each side. They felt that if they divulged too much to lower level officials about their intention of convening a meeting, their efforts could be sidetracked by hard-liners. An early interview with Gowon would be essential. Because they had not met with him on their first trip and they did not have the institutional support of, say, the Catholic church, they had to begin from scratch. Once in Lagos, after a number of false leads and an unsuccessful attempt to raise interest through a letter, they contacted the permanent secretary of the minister of External Affairs who was close to Gowon. For the first time, they confided their intentions. The minister thought that a Quaker role might be useful and so overrode others' opposition and arranged a meeting with Gowon for February 3.

Curle and Volkmar prepared for this meeting by role playing and trying to anticipate Gowon's objections. They drafted a nine-point proposal for convening an open-agenda meeting with persons appointed by each side. These representatives would not have policy-making authority but they would have direct access to those at higher levels. In the proposal, the Quakers stressed the internal nature of the conflict and their awareness that initiatives of this sort had been used by the other side for propaganda purposes. The Quakers would, therefore, be very reticent concerning any positive suggestions the federal government might make with regard to such talks. In other words, all communications would be strictly confidential.

Curle began the meeting with Gowon by describing his message-carrying work in the recent India-Pakistan conflict. Gowon said he had studied about Quakers in school and knew of their concern for justice and peace. He then described at length the government's position regarding the conflict, stressing the rebels' guilt. He was skeptical about an unpublicized meeting because other attempts to get the parties together had failed. For example, the Commonwealth Secretariat had tried and failed to arrange meetings in London in October and November 1967.[6] Gowon explained that rebel propaganda had misconstrued his overtures for peace, and he was afraid the Quaker effort would be treated similarly. He said he would not oppose a Quaker trip to the other side if they were willing to take the risk, but he could not guarantee their safety. In fact, he said that his planes would have orders to shoot down their plane.[7] Curle said both he and Volkmar had been under fire before and were willing to take the risk.

Gowon then said he was willing to have an unpublicized meeting and that the two could tell Ojukwu that as soon as a cease-fire was agreed upon, he would stop his troops' advances and would bring in a third party to police the lines.

This last concession took the Quakers by surprise. To this point in the conflict, the government had asserted that the war was strictly an internal affair and, indeed, the government continued to say so publicly. To agree to outside policing of a cease-fire contradicted this assertion.[8] But in this meeting, Gowon was telling the Quakers he would agree to talks and that he would accept a peacekeeping force of some sort, and he said this in the context of encouraging the Quakers to transmit this information to the Biafrans. He ended the meeting by telling them that he would be very interested in their report from the other side.

Gowon's response was especially encouraging given that the federal government had spurned similar mediating offers by the World Council of Churches and the Presbyterian church of Canada. In New York, the Nigerian representative contacted the Quakers to report that he had received positive reports on their visit and proposal. He praised the Quakers' emphasis on the internal nature of the conflict and the fact that the team revealed their work to so few people.

Curle immediately applied for a visa to Biafra. He contacted Biafran leaders in London, Paris, and Geneva and explored the possibility of using the Geneva Quaker center for a meeting. He conferred with members of the Commonwealth Secretariat who were eager to hear of the federal government's openness to a third-party policing force.

After a month, Curle secured his visa and was joined by Walter Martin for the trip to Biafra, March 4, 1968. This trip was less dangerous than later trips because the airport was still under Biafran control.

They were greeted by the Biafran chief justice who arranged a meeting with Ojukwu for March 9. In that meeting, Curle explained the purpose of their visit and described their meeting with Gowon. Ojukwu said the idea of a secret meeting was acceptable in principle. Talks without preconditions, he said, should be held as soon as possible. He said the auspices of a nongovernmental, nonpolitical organization might make the other side more willing to talk. He asked the Quakers to take back the message that secret talks without preconditions should be held as soon as possible and on neutral ground. A cease-fire would help, but he would not insist on it. The representatives to such talks should not be low-level officials. Finally, he added that it would be important to have the Quakers there as honest brokers.

Curle did not press Ojukwu on peace terms that Lagos was repeatedly issuing. At this early stage, the Quakers were not trying to find common points but merely trying to offer an unofficial setting for talks. They were fully aware that such talks were likely to be inconclusive, but they seemed to be the only hope of reducing suspicion and exploring the possibility of compromise. At this point, then, the prospects for a Quaker-sponsored meeting looked good.

Owing to wartime conditions, it took Curle and Martin one week to get back to Lagos. In a meeting with Gowon, his foreign minister, Dr. Orikpo, and the head of the navy, they reported that Ojukwu was favorable to the Quaker proposal of a secret meeting in a neutral place, that it should involve senior people, and that it should be with no preconditions. No publicity was given to their visit, the Quakers reported, an indication that the Biafrans might be serious in wanting talks. A channel for return communication to Ojukwu through his delegate in London had been established.

Cowon said was he touched by the Quakers' willingness to risk their lives and by their diligence in coming back to see him, something other mediating groups had failed to do. He said it was clear the rebels appreciated the seriousness of the visit because they made no reference to it in their radio broadcasts. He said that the visit showed him that the Quakers were discreet and that the rebels were willing to use the Quakers as a channel of communication.[9] But, he said, two preconditions still had to be met: the rebels must renounce secession and accept the twelve-state division. With these, there could be an immediate cease-fire and talks could begin. Gowon still feared that Ojukwu would use such a meeting as he had in Aburi, Ghana. There, Ojukwu not only surprised Gowon with a list of demands, but thereafter used the event to rally international support for the Biafran cause. Arikpo questioned the Quakers about Ojukwu's ideas for an agenda but was not satisfied when all they could say was that Ojukwu's concern was to end the war quickly through negotiations. The Quakers were asked to report back to Ojukwu regarding the two preconditions.

In this meeting, the Quakers did more than just convey messages. They also relayed their general impressions of the situation in Biafra, some of which conflicted with prevailing views in Nigeria. For example, although severe food shortages were widely reported, the situation was not as bad as many believed. Moreover, morale was high and Ojukwu enjoyed broad support and not just from the Ibos. He was a charismatic leader who represented the people's only hope of creating an independent nation and escaping annihilation. After the wanton slaughter of Ibos in the north and the brutal acts carried out by the federal government and its troops, the fear of genocide was firmly planted. The Quakers also said their attempts to convince Biafrans that the federal government did not intend to commit genocide were ineffective in light of aerial bombardment and the food blockade.

In assessing their meetings in Biafra and Lagos, the Quakers felt the Biafrans' eagerness for open-ended talks accentuated suspicions and led to demands for preconditions from Lagos. If Ojukwu did not accept those preconditions, the most likely response, they might suggest a meeting to examine the implications of preconditions. The Quakers felt the war would be a long one and any effort to change perceptions would be worthwhile because propaganda and suspicions accentuated the two sides' differences.

The two Quakers returned to London and delivered a letter to the Biafran representative, who evidently ignored it because two months passed before they received a reply, and then only a polite but inconsequential one. Ojukwu was moving on other fronts, including making contacts with the Commonwealth Secretariat and sending diplomatic missions to other states to gain recognition.

Since mid-1967, the secretary general of the Commonwealth Secretariat, Arnold Smith, worked behind the scenes in London and New York to arrange direct negotiations between the Nigerians and the Biafrans. Given that the UN would not interfere with a regional authority and that the OAU's Consultative Committee failed to establish itself as an intermediary, the Commonwealth Secretariat remained the only intergovernmental body actively engaged in trying to arrange a peace conference. But unlike his counterparts at the UN or the OAU, the secretary general had no legal mandate for intervening. Smith tried to use this fact to convince both sides that he was acting entirely in his personal capacity. Neither the Nigerians nor the Biafrans took this contention seriously, however, viewing, in Stremlau's words, "the Commonwealth secretary general to be little more than a stalking horse for British interests."[10] And those interests were substantial. In addition to British arms sales to Nigeria, British companies had more than $250 million invested in oil installations around Port Harcourt, Nigeria's next military objective in late 1967. In addition, Britain feared that a prolongation of the war could result in greater Nigerian dependence on Soviet military supplies and an increased Soviet presence in West Africa.

Against this background, Arnold Smith invited the federal government to send representatives to London for secret talks. The Nigerians were dubious but did not want to offend the British,[11] so Gowon sent three members of his kitchen cabinet for two meetings in January 1968. There, Smith assured the delegates that he was not acting as an arbitrator and that his actions should not be interpreted as conferring parity on the Biafrans. The Nigerians first wanted to know about the Biafrans' position, and Smith said his contacts assured him they would welcome his proposals and would be flexible. He also indicated that the Biafran representatives feared personal reprisals should they deviate from Ojukwu's instructions.

Smith then tried to elicit concessions from the Nigerians on substantive issues. They reiterated their standard, nonnegotiable position that a cease-fire could only take place after Biafra resolutely renounced secession and embraced the twelve-state structure. As the first meeting ended, one Nigerian official warned that the federal government "could not afford to give much in advance in an attempt at political bribery."[12]

Despite their intransigence on this issue and others, Smith tried to find a face-saving formula to permit the Biafrans to renounce secession without really appearing to do so. He secured Nigerian approval to maintain informal contacts with Biafran representatives. In their second meeting in January, the Secretariat asked for the Nigerians' minimum needs for a cease-fire, but they would only repeat their previous position. They were most interested in learning whether the Biafrans had made any new concessions. The Nigerians did say that direct talks could begin immediately while the fighting continued, but the Secretariat knew this was unacceptable to the Biafrans.

In April 1968, after Tanzania recognized Biafra and the British were becoming increasingly impatient to get a cease-fire, Nigeria's External Affairs commissioner, Okoi Arikpo, declared that Nigeria was prepared to talk with Biafran representatives any time and any place. At a press conference, Ojukwu responded to the offer by dropping his insistence on a prior cease-fire but demanding that the question of a cease-fire be the first item on the agenda of any negotiations. As if to one-up Gowon, he proposed that the talks commence within 48 hours, that they be conducted at the ministerial level, at a venue in Africa mutually agreed upon, and that they be held under the joint chairmanship of two African heads of state selected separately by each side. The federal government labeled Ojukwu's proposal unrealistic and stated that the question of a cease-fire would have to be the last, not the first, item on the agenda.

With the possibility of negotiations looking increasingly unlikely, the British prime minister, Harold Wilson, took a more active role. He met with Arikpo in London, who declared that the Nigerian government was prepared to begin talks without preconditions within five days. But back in Nigeria, the Ministry of Information clarified his statement by reiterating the government's positions regarding the acceptance of a unified Nigeria and a twelve-state structure. The Biafrans labeled Nigeria's proposed agenda "terms of surrender" and issued a blanket rejection.

Undeterred and with strong backing from the British government, which was receiving heavy domestic criticism for Nigeria's intransigence and for British complicity in the war, Smith pressed forward with "technical" talks in London. In these, the two sides agreed that any further talks would take place in Kampala, Uganda. They could not agree, however, on who would serve as chair of the talks nor on a detailed agenda. The

Biafrans were looking for an open agenda to maximize the international impact of the meeting and to press their cause whereas the Nigerians wanted to begin with the acceptance of a "one Nigeria" concept. Leaving these questions ambiguous, the Commonwealth Secretariat convened talks in Kampala, May 23, 1968.

By the time the Kampala talks commenced, Port Harcourt, vital to Biafra's economic viability with its airport, docks, oil refinery, and commercial facilities, fell to Nigerian forces. This was a major military victory, but contrary to the Nigerians' hopes, the Biafrans did not surrender in the coming talks.

In Kampala, the two sides met in nine formal sessions between May 23 and 31 but without result. With fifty members of the world press in attendance, this was the Biafrans' first opportunity to present its case as a sovereign power. Each side's opening speeches were predictably strident and replete with hardline demands for settlement.

On the Biafran side, the loss of Port Harcourt meant that communications with Ojukwu were even more difficult than before. The Biafran representatives, already under strict orders not to stray from their written instructions, had little leeway for negotiating. As a result, they emphasized Nigerian brutality and the need for an immediate cease-fire. They did concede that "although only sovereignty can guarantee to Biafra the minimum security required, the Biafran delegation will be prepared to examine any other formula put forward by Nigeria which equally and effectively guarantees to Biafrans, by clear and inviolable institutional arrangements, the control of their own security."[13]

On the federal side, the chief delegate acknowledged that the real issue for the Biafrans was security, not sovereignty. He delineated the government's plan for a settlement, a solution that the Biafrans viewed once again as terms of surrender. With reports of Biafra's imminent collapse, the Nigerians were in no rush to make concessions.

With the talks at an impasse, Arnold Smith intervened to seek a formula vague enough to obscure the fundamentally conflicting demands. The chief delegates went along and agreed that Nigeria would eventually be united and that a cease-fire should be the first order of business. Despite the apparent movement, talks were stalemated after Gowon sent word that nothing of substance, including the twelve-state structure, could be conceded. One day later, Ojukwu publicly denounced the federal government for its commitment to a military solution. Despite attempts to revive the negotiations by Smith and the Ugandan government, the negotiations collapsed. Both sides turned to convincing the world that the other side was to blame.

With the collapse of negotiations in Kampala, the British government came under increasing pressure to terminate arms shipments to Lagos and to end the war. After a spirited parliamentary debate, the British government sent an emissary, Lord Malcolm Shepherd to Nigeria to press for a cease-fire. The Nigerian government was irritated by the mission because they assumed it implied a threat to discontinue arms sales. Shepherd proposed that talks begin in London out of the glare of the press and that because the Biafran representatives could only carry messages back and forth from Ojukwu, it was important that Arnold Smith be allowed to go to Biafra to talk sense to Ojukwu. Shepherd told the Nigerians that the British government was "in a position to apply pressure for concessions" and that it was necessary for him to return to London with "some positive result, that is, at least the promise of talks beginning soon."[14]

The federal government's reply was as follows:

1. Not to accept a cease-fire until the rebels accept a United Nigeria. . . .
2. Not to approve a visit by Arnold Smith to the rebel-held territory because it would be used by Ojukwu to portray a measure of recognition and might offend the OAU Consultative Committee which the federal government already had dissuaded from sending representatives to Ojukwu.
3. That the chairman of the British Red Cross be allowed to visit the rebel-held area at his own risk.
4. That informal talks be commenced in London as soon as possible without preconditions and, if they succeeded, fuller talks would be resumed in Kampala.[15]

Shepherd returned to London somehow convinced that talks could begin. That was short lived, however, when, several days later, Ojukwu denounced Shepherd, likening his efforts in Lagos to Chamberlain's 1938 visit to Munich. The Commonwealth Secretariat, like the OAU's Consultative Committee before it, subsequently lost contact with the Biafrans.

As the situation in Biafra became increasingly desperate under a total blockade by Nigerian forces, the OAU once again intervened. The president of Niger met on separate days in Niger's capital, Niamey, with Gowon and Ojukwu. In subsequent private sessions with their representatives, the two sides agreed to establish a "mercy corridor" for relief and to conduct further negotiations in Addis Ababa, Ethiopia, under the chairmanship of Emperor Haile Selassie.

The ensuing conference in August 1968 was a highly formal affair with the delegations addressing each other across a large hall and Emperor Haile Selassie acting as little more than a convenor. Because by this time only three major cities remained in Biafran hands, the prevailing question was not whether one side could win but whether the Biafrans would continue warfare indefinitely with a guerrilla force.

The Quakers had sent a delegation, Curle and Martin, to the Addis Ababa conference to assist quietly behind the scenes. But seeing no opportunity for progress there and concluding that a disastrous guerrilla struggle was likely, they went to Lagos to see Gowon. This time, they realized, they would have to present more of their own point of view than before. Although they would approach Gowon as tactfully as possible, they felt it was time to speak out even at the risk of offending him.

Just before leaving Addis Ababa, the chief Biafran negotiator, Dr. Njoku, revealed to the Quakers what terms the Biafran government could accept yet were unable to state openly for fear of appearing weak. Njoku maintained that his government was willing to become part of a Nigerian union. The concept of sovereignty, more a symbol of defiance than a political necessity, could be diluted. He said the Biafrans were willing to be flexible on cease-fire lines, boundaries of the eventual state, composition of a peacekeeping force, and even on the name of the state. On only two points would they insist strongly: an army under Biafran control must be maintained within the cease-fire boundaries, and the resulting state must have international standing.

On August 14, in Lagos, Curle and Volkmar gave Gowon copies of a paper they had drawn up describing Njoku's proposals. They also made their own suggestions for meeting the Biafrans' two demands. The army could be a militia or a homeguard, armed only with defensive weapons. International standing might be met with membership on international or regional commissions. For his part, Gowon questioned the degree to which Njoku represented Ojukwu and the Biafran hard-liners. The Quakers told Gowon that Dr. Njoku had spoken openly of the items about which he would need to persuade others and, in any case, the only way to test his influence and reliability was to respond in a positive, although tentative way.

Apologizing for their temerity, the Quakers expressed their hopes for a negotiated settlement and the avoidance of a guerrilla war. Gowon answered that his men knew how to deal with guerrillas and that, without a good supply line from the outside, such guerrilla activity could not be sustained. At the end of the meeting, Gowon said he would study carefully what they had said and might call on them to speak to other officials.

As the Quakers left, it appeared that, despite the possibility of an opening to negotiations, the final military drive was being planned. Volkmar stayed in Lagos while Curle went to London and the United States. Volkmar later learned that the Quaker report aroused considerable controversy in the inner councils of the federal government. Some officials maintained that the message from Njoku constituted significant concessions, but others thought there was little new. In the end, the hard-liners prevailed.

On August 16, Volkmar was called in by two high-level officials to inform him that the federal government decided to pursue the war into the heart of the East Central State to crush the Biafran movement. On August 24, Gowon announced the "final push." The talks in Addis Ababa were still in session, but they seemed more and more futile. The Quakers turned their attention to relief efforts.[16]

ANALYSIS OF THE BIAFRA INTERVENTIONS

The Nigerian civil war has been called the most mediated conflict in recent history. From the meetings in Ghana in early 1967 to last-ditch efforts by Pope Paul and Emperor Haile Selassie in late 1969, a host of third parties intervened in a variety of capacities. None, of course, ended the war. Nor did any precipitate negotiations effective enough to limit the violence. If a military solution was inevitable as, in hindsight, it appears to have been, then all attempts by third parties to effect a negotiated settlement were ultimately hopeless. But complex conflicts of this sort are rarely, if ever, so neatly determined. Leaders do recalculate, and they do change preferences. In the face of horrible losses and uncertain prospects for victory, the singleminded pursuit of a goal—say, secession or national reunification—gives way to a multiple-path search for settlement. Throughout a conflict, opportunities for the cessation of hostilities open up as military, diplomatic, and economic conditions change. From the perspective of intermediary intervention, the important question is whether the intervention capitalizes on these opportunities. Does the intervention facilitate or hinder the leaders' desires to bring the conflict to an end? Does it put sufficient pressure on one or both sides to cease hostilities and break the escalatory cycle? Does it create conditions conducive to nonaccusatory communication, to testing each other's sincerity, and to exploring alternative solutions?

With these questions in mind, in this section I analyze the interventions of three intermediaries in late 1967 and early 1968 to show how their different effects were owing in part to their different roles. Although this case lends itself to a direct comparison between neutral and principal mediators, it also allows for a more differentiated view of mediator roles. In particular, the peculiar intervention effects of intergovernmental organizations—here, the OAU and the Commonwealth Secretariat—can be explored. First, however, it is necessary to put negotiations into perspective as a viable alternative to violence. In this case, like the Portsmouth case, leaders were faced daily with the agonizing choice of pursuing the hostilities or seeking a negotiated solution. Moreover, in both cases, the contention-versus-cooperation calculation was influenced in part by third parties. Thus, the disputants' acceptance question is conditioned by factors much different from those the leaders at Camp David and the Vatican faced where hostilities were not on-going. The implications are developed in the context of the three third-party interventions.

In the Nigeria-Biafra civil conflict, the aims of the two leaders—Nigerian unity versus Biafran secession—may have been so strictly opposed that only total victory by one side could have brought the conflict to an end. As a unity-versus-secession question, the conflict was strictly zero-sum and the bargaining range consisted of only two, mutually exclusive points. The failed conference negotiations and the never-ending statements of intransigence and maneuvers for one-sided gain would appear to support this all-or-nothing view. For the purpose of understanding conflict resolution processes, however, especially the potential of intermediary interventions, it is critical to see beyond such "facts." Both third parties and analysts must be wary of accepting at face value the necessarily strategic posturing of leaders faced with dire choices. As in the Portsmouth case, a leader's decision to negotiate often occurs well before such thinking is publicly known. Here, then, I give weight to the possibility of a negotiated solution in early 1968, to the prospect that both sides revealed enough flexibility to render unnecessary and avoidable the hundreds of thousands of deaths in the succeeding year and a half.

Two points about conflict resolution thus underlie the analysis: one, leaders' public statements are poor indicators of underlying flexibility, and, two, changes in preferences often occur well before they are reflected in official positions. Leaders have strategic incentives to regularly and forcefully pronounce their willingness to pursue the conflict to its bitter end. To assure their constituents and supporters, they must consistently show their resolve even if it takes them past the point of net expected benefits. If leaders do wish to signal their intention to negotiate, they must do so covertly, obliquely, and deniably. Even then, the message will always be ambiguous and subject to varying interpretations. The problem for the analyst and the decision maker alike is that information of this sort is difficult to come by, even when leaders are desperately looking for a way out of their dilemmas. Only the insider or the inquisitive investigator or the well-placed third party are likely to be privy to such information.

In the Nigerian conflict, consequently, one can expect to find only hints, ambiguous at that, that the leaders were looking for multiple paths to end the conflict and that their preferences changed enough to open opportunities for third parties.[17] For example, in an interview after the conflict, Ojukwu says he did communicate to the Commonwealth Secretariat in late 1967 Biafra's willingness to reunite with Nigeria. In a separate interview, Arnold Smith confirmed that he had received the signals through his contacts in London.[18] From those early discussions at the end of 1967, Arnold Smith concluded that sufficient flexibility existed for a negotiated settlement, at least for a cease-fire.

Perhaps the most convincing evidence of underlying flexibility was the acceptance by both sides of the confidential missions of the Quakers. First was Gowon's initiation of a message-carrying function for the Quakers. It should be recalled from the case that the Quakers originally went to Gowon to propose a secret conference, not to convey messages. It was Gowon who asked them to send the feeler for talks (unlike the previous request in New York to convey a demand for surrender). And when Ojukwu did not exploit the trip or Gowon's message for propaganda purposes, Gowon expressed his satisfaction that the message was conveyed confidentially and taken seriously by the Biafrans. This minor but positive interaction between the two sides was soon overtaken by events, of course. But it does reveal that behind the bellicose statements and the military assaults, the two sides were searching for alternatives, however hesitantly.

The second revealing incident occurred initially in Kampala in May 1968 when the Biafran lead negotiator asked the Quakers to convey a confidential message to the leaders in Lagos. If the Biafran gesture was only an attempt to score propaganda points, it would had to have been public. If it was a delaying tactic, it could have been played out in the on-going negotiations in Kampala. It may not have been reflective of Ojukwu's exact position, but it was consistent with his long-standing overtures to negotiate a cease-fire. The difference here was that, through this overture, the Biafran negotiator separated Ojukwu's necessarily strategic posturing (recall the games of oneupmanship he played every time Gowon did agree to talks) from his willingness to explore a negotiated settlement. The message reached the Nigerian side during or shortly after a decision to pursue an all-out military solution. It obviously did not change their calculus but the controversy it stirred suggests that the military option was not unanimously supported. The point here, it should be stressed, is not that the third party was or was not effective but that, amid the overwhelming "evidence" that the two sides were implacably committed to a single course of action, they did appear genuinely to be seeking alternatives.

If the two leaders indeed were willing to negotiate and compromise, why were third parties so unsuccessful in bringing about negotiations? From the federal government's standpoint, peace conferences and peace missions favored the Biafrans because they easily became publicity stunts or exercises in arm twisting. Direct contacts by third parties with leaders in Biafra only added ammunition to Biafra's propaganda barrage. The Nigerians, consequently, could not risk allowing a third party like the secretary general of the Commonwealth Secretariat to travel to Biafra for fear Ojukwu would exploit such a trip. And certainly, neither Gowon nor his representatives could meet Ojukwu directly for fear of implying equal status. If a third party was to be useful to Gowon other than as an ally, it would have to be one who neither tried to coerce him nor offered Ojukwu more propaganda advantages.

The Biafrans were in a similar bind regarding negotiations but for different strategic reasons. The Biafrans felt that, by avoiding negotiations and publicizing Biafran suffering, international pressure would build against Nigeria for a cease-fire. According to Ojukwu's chief secretary, in mid-1968, Ojukwu had concluded that "as long as the impression was given that talks were going on, no country would take action [favorable to Biafra] for fear of being accused of trying to undermine the success of the peace talks."[19] Ojukwu's primary strategy was to wage psychological warfare; a third party was, therefore, useful primarily for its propaganda value, not its facilitation of negotiations.

Even if Ojukwu had changed preferences, he could not reveal this change without assurances that Gowon would reciprocate. Such an exchange would have been extremely delicate. It could not have been carried out over the airwaves (the dominant means of communication between the two sides) nor in a conference hall under the gaze of the world's media. Third parties might have been helpful but not by supporting one side and condemning the other, acts that only exacerbated tensions and forced the leaders into proving their resolve. Even trusted representatives may not have been trusted enough to do any more than send out easily retractable feelers.

Effective negotiations, that is, negotiations aimed at reaching an agreement—whether for a cease-fire or an overall settlement—were, therefore, extremely difficult to conduct. And owing to the dynamics of the conflict, third parties tended to exacerbate these difficulties. When negotiations did take place, the leaders gave little authority to their representatives. The Biafran representatives even feared for their personal safety should they contravene Ojukwu's wishes.[20] If a negotiated solution were possible, it had to be reached directly between the leaders (or, presumably, between plenipotentiaries). But with the stakes so high—for Gowon, the dissolution of Nigeria or, quite likely, indefinite guerrilla warfare; for Ojukwu, the oppression, if not genocide, of his people—each leader had to appear absolutely resolute. In this environment of posturing and intransigence where the opportunities for promoting effective communication were few, ambiguous, and fleeting, what then, were the specific effects of the third parties in late 1968 and early 1969?

OAU and the Consultative Committee

The OAU created the Consultative Committee with little idea of what it should do other than to "consult" initially with Lagos. Emperor Haile Selassie was concerned that secession in Nigeria would threaten the integrity of all African states and appealed for greater international involvement to find a peaceful settlement. As for the committee's role, he proposed that, "to discharge effectively the mandate we hold, it is necessary to somehow, I do not know what particular procedure, communicate with Col. Ojukwu. Through that communication we hope to be in a position to persuade the secessionist group that the consequences of their actions are inconsistent, not only with the interest of the Nigerian people but the interest of all of Africa."[21]

Other leaders on the committee also pressed for an OAU-Biafra dialogue, arguing that communication with Ojukwu was essential to an agreement. What transpired, however, was anything but dialogue.

In Lagos, Selassie asked Gowon to "elucidate further about the ways and means of achieving initial contact" with the rebels, adding that such contact "does not mean that we hold any sympathy for them."[22] Gowon said he accepted the need to transmit a message to the rebels on behalf of the OAU but certain conditions had to be met, namely, that the rebels accept reunification, the twelve-state structure, and new Ibo leadership. He insisted that any contacts with the Biafran regime not be construed as the first round of substantive mediation. In addition, the message should be given publicly to "avoid misinterpretation."

In other words, Gowon would use the OAU to convey demands amounting to surrender but not to establish a "dialogue." Communication would not be an exchange of positions (let alone of interests, intentions, perceptions, needs, and fears) but a one-way, public declaration. As it turned out, the committee members accepted Gowon's conditions and, in effect, foreclosed any kind of dialogue. For them, the alternative was to appear to be—or to allow Gowon to portray them as—sympathizers with secessionists, something anathema to the norms of African unity and postcolonial sovereignty. They were in no position to discuss, let alone "mediate," the substantive issues. As one leader argued: "Basically it is the territorial integrity of Nigeria which is of concern to us. The rest is entirely a domestic affair. How can we in our contacts with the rebels discuss the number of states within the territorial boundaries of Nigeria itself? How can we really talk to them about the status of this or that Nigerian citizen or of this or that region?"[23]

In the final communiqué, the committee reaffirmed the OAU's support of the territorial integrity of Nigeria, including the twelve-state system,

and called on the rebels to renounce secession. The communiqué was
relayed to Ojukwu via a two-way radio link, and Ojukwu, not surprisingly,
ignored the message. The Biafran government later condemned the decision as "an attempt by a few African states to use their position in the
Committee to blackmail and discredit the Organization of African Unity.
By so doing these African states have fallen prey to the British-American
imperialist conspiracy to use the Committee's recommendation as a pre-
text for a massive arms support for their puppet and tottering neo-coloni-
alist regime in Lagos."[24]

Even after discounting for hyperbole and propagandizing, it is clear the
OAU's mediation did nothing to enhance communications or understanding. It did not even meet its objective of softening Biafra's position; if
anything, quite the opposite: Ojukwu hardened his public stance and used
the communiqué to convince his people of the conspiracy against Biafrans.

In sum, the only communication the OAU established in its trip to
Lagos and its radio message to Biafra was a vituperative exchange of accusations and demands. If a precondition for a negotiated settlement was a
dialogue between leaders—possibly through an intermediary—they
failed to achieve this. If the committee members felt they could advance
the peace process by lining up on one side to pressure the other side into
making concessions, they failed on this count too because Ojukwu became
only more obdurate. Why the failure? According to the principal/neutral
taxonomy of chapter 2, the OAU was primarily a principal mediator and,
hence, its target of intervention must be bilateral deals with one or both
sides. As an intergovernmental organization, the explanation is more complex, though. The OAU was constrained by the very nature of its membership and its raison d'être as a regional organization, namely, to promote
African unity—that is, the unity of the existing state structure in Africa. It
may have been able to mediate substantive issues in a conflict between
existing states but not within a state. Thus, although the Nigerian civil war
was highly "internationalized," the OAU could not act except to denounce
the secession. As a result, it not only missed an opportunity to establish
effective communications but even exacerbated tensions.

Commonwealth Secretariat and the British Government

The Commonwealth Secretariat managed to establish communications
with both sides and to avoid overtly supporting one side. Beyond this, the
London talks were notable only for the fact that representatives from the
two sides met and that they agreed to meet again in Kampala. The London
talks did nothing to effect direct communications between the leaders let
alone to set an agenda or ground rules for the subsequent negotiations. In
fact, Smith had to allow so much ambiguity in the conditions of the Kam-

pala negotiations that both sides were able to use them entirely as they wished. As it turned out, not surprisingly, the Nigerians used Kampala to press for terms of surrender, and the Biafrans used it to rally international support. Thus, although the Commonwealth Secretariat succeeded in establishing exchanges between the two sides, the effect was little different from that of the OAU mediation: there was virtually no dialogue and, of course, no movement toward agreement. International pressure may have brought them together, but such pressure could not force a compromise nor even keep the talks going.

What was needed, it seems Smith discovered almost too late, was direct contacts between the two leaders. International conferences with large negotiating teams may work when the parties conform to the norms and practices of classical diplomacy—that is, when plenipotentiaries from culturally homogeneous backgrounds meet under well-defined rules of accommodation to work out compromise agreements involving territorial adjustments and reparations.[25] But intense civil conflicts are of another sort. Survival and national and ethnic identity are the primary concerns, not the realignment of a balance of power. Leaders cannot afford to confer complete negotiating authority on their representatives when the primary issues are essentially nonnegotiable. Under these conditions, the international community is useful to a protagonist not for the norms it sets but for the unilateral support it can provide. Conferences thus tend to aggravate difficulties, not surmount them. At best, they provide a public forum to validate prearranged agreements. But for the purpose of settlement, it is the *prearranging* that matters, not the signing. Smith seems to have appreciated this after London and Kampala. What he and the British government did not appreciate was their own limitations as intermediaries for this particular kind of intervention.

The Commonwealth Secretariat was limited by its perceived link to British interests, a perception reinforced by Britain's subsequent request to send Smith directly to the belligerents' capitals. The British, in turn, were limited by the distrust they engendered on both sides. To the Biafrans, the British were imperialist warmongers propping up discredited neocolonialists; they could be useful only to the extent that they forced concessions from their puppet regime. To the Nigerians, the British were unreliable supporters subject to the whims of an emotional public and manifesting few qualms about selling out Nigerian (that is, federal) interests to advance their own interests; they did, nevertheless, have to be appeased to keep the arms coming.[26]

Consequently, each side might deal with the British to pressure the other side or to enhance its own position. The Biafrans would make their appeal via British public opinion, and the Nigerians would threaten to bring in the Soviets or to jeopardize British investments. These schemes might have worked in the sense that one side might have prevailed, a cease-fire would have been compelled, and, eventually, substantive negotiations would result in a settlement. In hindsight, it appears that had Britain come down hard on one side or the other, much of the bloodshed could have been avoided. But Britain did not play it this way. Instead, it chose to have it both ways—avoid any threat to British interests and mollify its public over Biafran suffering—by attempting to merely facilitate, not coerce, negotiations. Of course, Britain's intention to merely facilitate was not matched by the parties' intention to use the British to advance their primary objectives. Moreover, merely to facilitate required a peculiar relationship with the parties—that is, as a "neutral mediator," not as a "principal mediator"—a relationship the British did not have.

In short, both parties related to the British in terms of hard bargaining. In that game, Gowon had to preserve his relationship with the British and prevent or downplay British contacts with the Biafrans. On these terms, Gowon succeeded by blocking the British attempt to send Smith to Biafra. In so doing, he also blocked effective communications and cut off what benefits might have accrued from direct contacts with the Biafrans. Assuming he did see value in direct communications (witness his willingness to allow the Quakers to travel to Biafra), that was the trade-off he made. In a game of hard bargaining, building a coalition with the third party and excluding one's opponent overrides all other considerations. Gowon won his bargain with the British but lost a chance to move toward agreement with his principal opponent.

In sum, the Commonwealth Secretariat and the British government, linked together in the eyes of the protagonists, could use their bargaining weight to convene a conference. But they could neither compel an agreement there nor subsequently assume the mantle of neutral mediator in attempts to promote a dialogue between the leaders. The nature of their relationship precluded anything but hard bargaining between each disputant and the third party. The effect was to detract from, not contribute to, the disputants' direct interactions. The Quakers, by contrast, did contribute to positive interactions, however minor their overall impact. Understanding the limits and the potential of these neutral mediators' contribution helps illuminate a brand of international diplomacy—sometimes called unofficial diplomacy[27]—that, in part by its nature, is little known and, where power politics is the only conceivable game, even less appreciated.

The Quakers

As noted, the Quaker mediation was more a footnote in the entire conflict than a major chapter, owing in part to the obvious smallness of the Quaker church and the missions it sponsors. But it was also owing to the Quakers' deliberate attempt to limit their involvement, not to be inconsequential but to carve out a special niche as a third party. That niche focused on establishing the *preconditions* for effective negotiations, not the formulas and forums of formal negotiations. Thus, the Quakers were significant not so much for their ability to establish substantive negotiations (although they did deal very much in substantive issues with the leaders) but for their ability as "powerless" intermediaries to encourage a mode of interaction necessary to counter the norms and practices that exacerbated tensions. The important analytic task is to spell out how the Quaker intervention encouraged a kind of interaction that, under more favorable military, economic, and international conditions, might have led to effective formal negotiations. The first step is to examine how, in general, the Quakers define themselves as neutral mediators and how they interpret their role, processes that begin with the entry and acceptance decision problems.[28]

In gaining access to decision makers in a conflict, Quakers define themselves as message carriers or, at most, mere convenors of informal talks. Seeing themselves as vehicles of communication, they neither set deadlines nor offer formulas for settlement. Deadlines, they say, would give the impression that they have something to gain, that they have their own agenda. They explain to disputing parties that in similar situations decision makers want to talk directly yet cannot and that experienced message carrying can help. As members of a small religious group with a long history of commitment to nonviolence and peace, they have no personal vested interest in the outcome of a conflict beyond the reduction of violence and the attainment of peace.

Quakers intervene knowing, even expecting, that their message carrying will be used by each party for its own purposes, especially as sources of information about the other side. In conflicts like Nigeria-Biafra, the Quakers often gain access to locations and people that the protagonists' best intelligence networks cannot. For this reason, it is not surprising that leaders effectively interrogate the Quakers upon their return from the other side. The Quakers' intention of facilitating communication is not, therefore, necessarily matched by the disputant's intention of enhancing intelligence gathering. The Quakers reconcile these conflicting objectives by drawing on their position as a small religious group and on specific practices as mediators to impose conditions of interaction on the parties.[29]

In defining their limited, neutral role, one condition the Quakers impose on the parties and themselves is confidentiality; they insist that no one make public statements about the Quaker mediation. This stance was particularly critical in the Nigeria-Biafra conflict when the Quakers traveled to Biafra. Had the trip been publicized, the Quakers felt, they would have become part of the struggle itself. So when they arrived in Biafra without fanfare and met with leaders on a confidential basis, their meetings necessarily took on a special character. With the no-publicity condition, the Quaker mission had no propaganda value and was good for only one thing—establishing a different kind of interaction via confidential message carrying.

A second condition is to insist that each side accept the other side's ability to terminate the Quaker intervention at will and without repercussions. They explain that this condition is necessary to ensure that neither side feels coerced. A third condition is to recognize that, if the Quakers ever feel they are being used for purposes other than to reduce the violence, they will on their own refuse a request or discontinue the message carrying. Although they try to avoid making moral judgments of leaders, they reserve to themselves the right to judge whether their own actions contribute to more or less violence. Thus, when the Nigerians asked them in New York to pass a message that, in the Quaker view, was tantamount to a demand for Biafran surrender, they refused. They made a judgment that *their* objectives—reducing violence and respecting the aspirations of all parties—would not be advanced.

A fourth condition is that all sides must be heard. From the beginning of their involvement in the Nigeria-Biafra case, the Quakers took pains to hear and respect the positions of federal and Biafran officials. They were careful to recognize the legitimacy of each side's concerns—if not their means—and to avoid supporting or condemning one side. And they did so with the parties' full knowledge. This stance contrasted greatly with that of virtually all other third parties in the conflict.

By imposing these four conditions, Quaker mediators do more than avoid the spotlight or keep themselves removed from the dynamics of the conflict. By eschewing publicity, giving each party a veto over the continuation of the message carrying, and hearing all sides, they effectively say: This is *your* dispute, not ours. We have no interests in your disputed issues beyond seeing violence stopped and peace achieved. If we did, we would want others to know of our valiant efforts. We demonstrate this by giving you veto power—indeed, insisting that you have it. If we had a vested interest in a particular outcome, we could not afford to let one side veto our work without consequences. In fact, in principle, we Quakers could become a key ingredient in a resolution process (whether a move toward negotiations or some other piece of an overall settlement process), and you could use us right up to the final step and then drop us. You would get the glory of being a peacemaker, and nobody would be the wiser. There is no public record to show otherwise. And, once again, we have demonstrated that we have no overriding interest, not even to claim credit for a settlement, and, thus, we have no incentive to expose your claim as a peacemaker.[30] In addition, the communication and reconciliation process we bring is *yours*; you have complete control over this process in the sense that you can single-handedly cancel it at any time by either exposing the operation or by quietly asking us to leave. In addition, if you were to ask us to leave, you need not jeopardize any progress made. No one can accuse you of blocking a peace process because no one knows it is going on. You have perfect deniability.

In short, these conditions—in combination with the historical, religious, and personal factors Quakers bring to an intervention—make a Quaker intervention a very low-risk enterprise for disputants. The messages disputants send need not be ambiguous and disguised and easily retracted. One party can float a new idea or test the other side's idea with a provisional acceptance. When reputations and lives are at stake, getting hostile parties to communicate in this way rather than through bullets and press releases is no small achievement. How, then, do leaders come to accept such an intervention and the conditions it entails when the imperative to continue the struggle is so strong?[31]

First, for leaders with vital interests at stake and few options—all of them bad—low-risk communication can be quite attractive. But to be low-risk, leaders have to be convinced that the process is indeed confidential and deniable. They must trust the intermediary in a way they cannot possibly trust their opponent or an interested third party, that is, another disputant or a principal mediator. Quakers foster such trust by binding themselves to a very limited role. They do not and cannot demand benefits for themselves nor push a particular solution. As predicted in chapter 2, neutral mediators must expend great effort to demonstrate that they are unlike most international actors and, in this case, they must demonstrate that they are even unlike other religious groups.

Second, the Quakers initially gain acceptance by approaching the parties with very modest objectives and proposals. In the Nigeria-Biafra conflict, they originally only asked to make a trip to the country to learn more about the conflict. Concerned about the suffering, they explained that they wanted to do what they could, but they did not raise the possibility of mediating. Only once they were in the country and had secured access to high-level officials did they broach the topic of a secret conference. The problem the Quakers find, as Adam Curle explains it, is that, once the idea of a conference or message carrying is broached, its value as a secret operation is lost. Moreover, lower level officials can easily block such efforts before they are presented to the real decision makers.[32] In sum, Quakers gain entry by involving themselves gradually and by making initially modest requests and proposals that convey little threat yet offer a real possibility of advantage to the protagonist.

The process of gaining entry serves another purpose. It allows the Quakers to resist efforts by either side to use them in ways inconsistent with Quaker values and objectives—that is, with their commitment to using nonviolent means to achieve a state of peace. They effectively say to the parties: Whether or not you share our values and objectives, we Quakers have to live by them. This commitment puts a constraint on you at least with respect to the message carrying: the alternative to accepting our conditions is to call it off.

This self-binding nature of the Quaker intervention and the implied threat is, then, the essence of the "power of powerlessness" Quakers often speak of. It also expresses in practice the essential nature of the neutral mediator role. A Quaker mediator is powerless to impose terms of agreement. Unlike powerful, or "principal mediators," the "powerless" mediator cannot change the disputants' cost-benefit calculation through threats of pain or promises of aid. But it can change the nature of the disputants' interaction. It can set the standards for the intervention process—the message carrying, in this case—and, thus, influence the interactions between parties.

In bitter, protracted disputes like the Nigeria-Biafra conflict, this standard-setting effect can be significant. It can change the norms of disputant interaction: the parties can refrain from accusing each other of malevolent intent because they need not fear looking weak; they can reveal their inner suspicions and fears with low risk; they can "play" with alternative approaches to a solution, again, at low risk. In short, with these norms of interaction, conciliatory and nonbelligerent gestures are easier to make. This is a form of influence that principal mediators like the British and even other African states mostly did not have. They play the game of power politics whether they like it or not. Everything they say and do is strategically tinged. And everything the parties say and do carries enormous risks. Not so with "powerless" or "neutral" mediators like the Quakers. They cannot impose a solution, but they can guarantee a low-risk means of communication and impose certain standards of interaction.

Quakers do more than this, however. In a limited way, they try to change misperceptions about each others' intentions and motivations, and they suggest ways of reassuring each other. For example, Gowon firmly believed that his government's bombing of civilian targets was breaking the will of the Biafran people to resist. Instead, what the Quakers found and what they conveyed to Gowon was that the Biafran people and their leaders were becoming more resolute after each bombing episode, not less. Similarly, in this and other conflicts, when the Quakers propose direct talks and at least one side says it cannot talk when the other is committing such horrendous crimes (which, of course, may be true), the Quakers point out that having talks is not absolutely incompatible with continuing to fight. In other conflicts the Quakers have mediated, Adam Curle has used the example of Zimbabwe where the entire time negotiations were being conducted the two sides were trying to score points on the battlefield. It is possible to talk *and* fight, the Quakers respond, if not wholly desirable. Finally, the Quakers resist promoting specific, substantive proposals, but they do engage leaders in lengthy substantive discussions regarding, for instance, methods of reassuring parties without appearing weak.[33]

From this assessment of Quaker mediation, it follows that so-called message carrying is not merely transmitting words from one side to the other. Quakers are not human telephones. They do set conditions at entry that constrain disputants' behavior in an eventual mediating process. They do have influence, influence based not on great resources but on the very absence of such resources. Furthermore, that influence is targeted not at party payoffs but at party interaction as predicted in the propositions of chapter 2. To the extent existing party interactions set up dynamics that perpetuate and escalate the conflict (e.g., communication by public pronouncement, bombing missions designed to break the will of the people), a Quaker intervention, therefore, can serve to counteract those dynamics and contribute to an overall resolution process.

CONCLUSION

We will never know if negotiations were indeed possible in the Nigeria-Biafra conflict, or if, by some kind of intervention (or, better, some combination of interventions), the terrible suffering of the war could have been averted or limited. But to ascribe third-party failures merely to leaders' intransigence misses important dynamics of decision making and third-party intervention. It ignores information, however tentatively or secretly put forward, that reveals opportunities, however uncertain and fleeting, for an earlier conclusion.

As a tiny, transnational actor, the Quakers did what other third parties could not do. They physically went to each side, talked at length with the respective leaders, avoided publicity, and returned with confidential messages. Arnold Smith, in his capacity of secretary general of the Commonwealth Secretariat, could not, by his own admission, do the same.[34] Britain might have effected a different kind of process through its leverage as a major power, but it, too, was limited in what it could do to promote direct and effective negotiations. And the OAU was constrained by its mandate to preserve the existing African state system.[35] The comparative analysis of these three interventions substantiates and builds on the principal/neutral distinction, the entry/acceptance questions, and the nature of mediation and diplomacy generally. Four results stand out.

One, with respect to neutral mediators, small actors, not just Quakers but states like Sweden and Algeria, can be effective as mediators *because* they are small. They may have to refrain from taking the seemingly high moral ground of supporting the most aggrieved party (witness the failed "mediations" in this case of the Vatican and the World Council of Churches), but they can use their relative "powerlessness" to set conditions and impose norms of interaction. In so doing, they can offer what most larger actors cannot: low-risk opportunities to explore alternatives to force.

Two, with respect to principal mediators, three-way coalitional bargaining may work better in theory than in practice. To form a coalition, the third party offers support—moral, political, economic, or military—to one side. The theory, presumably, is that such support will compel the other side to negotiate or to negotiate in good faith or, simply, to give in. This case study suggests that, at least in intense civil conflicts where secessionist or rebel groups seek autonomy or enhanced status, lining up on one side can be counterproductive. It may have been morally right to support the Biafrans (although even the church groups began to question this presumption when it became increasingly apparent that they were being used to prolong the fighting) or, in the case of the OAS and Britain, politically necessary to support the federal government. But none of these efforts promoted serious negotiations. In fact, for the most part, they heightened resolve and encouraged intransigence. In general, locating oneself "in between" morally and politically may be an uncomfortable and risky position to take. But, whether for a neutral or a principal mediator, it may be the only position that provides the preconditions for effective negotiations. Although in this case the Quakers may have been the only ones to act truly in between, others, most notably the British, could have adopted an intermediary position at the opposite end of the neutral-principal spectrum. They could have played an intermediary role much like that of the United States in the Middle East and, bargaining with both sides, brought an earlier end to the conflict.

Three, in this case, entry timing appeared less important than the conditions the third party imposed at entry. The OAU and the Commonwealth Secretariat imposed few if any conditions and, as a result, were easily used by the parties for purposes other than promoting negotiations. The Quakers imposed strict standards in the context of their message carrying and succeeded in changing disputant interactions, albeit with minor overall impact.

Four, the arguments of part 1 took the nature of the conflict as given; interventions affected disputants' calculations regardless of the source of the conflict. This case reveals that direct negotiation and third-party intervention in intense civil conflicts is fundamentally different from that of classical diplomacy. Conference negotiations, especially, are ineffective when parties do not conform to the same norms and practices. When survival and national and ethnic identity are the primary concerns, not the realignment of a balance of power, and when attentive constituencies and important third parties follow every move through the media, leaders can ill afford to be flexible and confer complete negotiating authority on their representatives. Under these conditions, the international community is useful to a protagonist not for the norms it sets but for the unilateral support it can provide. Conferences thus tend to aggravate difficulties, not surmount them. At best, they provide a public forum to validate prearranged agreements. But for the purpose of settlement, it is the *prearranging* that matters, not the signing. In short, the diplomacy that contributes most significantly to an overall conflict resolution process is more likely to be quiet, behind-the-scenes negotiating, not noisy, media-driven conference negotiating.

Chapter Ten

CONCLUSION

UNDERSTANDING an intermediary's practice requires an understanding of the inherent contradictions in the intermediary's role: the need to stay removed from the parties' positions on issues yet, at some point, make proposals that challenge those positions; the need to act as a purveyor of process but also to act to change the parties' perceived alternatives; the need to set appropriate expectations and in so doing risk challenging vital interests; the need to foster cooperation and yet to resort to contentious acts to urge movement. In short, an intermediary must walk a thin line between being a neutral catalyst and a power broker. Some intermediaries are, by their position in the dispute, better as neutral catalysts, what I have termed neutral mediators. Others use their weight as major powers to get results; these I have termed principal mediators. But, to gain entry, to enhance communications, to structure negotiations, and to move parties toward agreement, all intermediaries must engage in some kind of influence process. The specific nature of that influence depends critically on the intermediary's position in between.

In this book, then, I have endeavored to develop a logic of "in betweenness." I have relied in part on deductive reasoning and in part on focused comparative case analysis to explicate the nature of intermediary influence. Although intermediary intervention may be viewed as a technique, as an add-on to extant negotiations, or as a corrective to leaders' typically imperfect attempts to settle disputes, my focus has been on influence—not just the influence of traditional power politics, the threat of harm or the exchange of concrete resources, as important as these instruments are, especially for principal mediators but also the influence of more subtle means such as making neutral proposals, pooling information, imposing standards of interaction, providing moral or legal endorsement, and ensuring deniability and confidentiality.

Intermediary intervention, it turns out, is a method of conflict management distinguished by the intermediary's peculiar role of being neither party to nor completely removed from the dispute. Regardless of the intermediary's motive, its position in the middle means that its immediate objective is to get agreement (or movement toward one) and, because intermediaries do not (or cannot, by definition) impose settlements, their only means of getting agreement is to promote communication, exchange, and, ultimately, substantive negotiations—in other words, a process of cooperation. Principal mediators do it with carrots and sticks behind them, neutrals with a focus on disputant interaction. Either way, the parties must cooperate enough to agree, whether or not they realize all potential gains or achieve an equitable outcome.

The fact that intermediaries must promote cooperation to achieve their objectives can easily be confused with altruism: that is, that intermediaries intervene to serve the disputants' interests. A purpose of this study is to show that intermediary behavior is best understood in terms of an intermediary's own interests and, as a result, the intermediary's relationship with each party. Intermediaries do promote cooperation, but they do so in the context of strategic interactions with each disputant. More precisely, their strategic aim is to move each party away from its preferred unilateral solution—which would exclude the intermediary—to a negotiated one. Whether their motive is to get a solution favorable to themselves or to enhance their international standing or to reduce violence and achieve world peace, intermediaries are best seen as self-interested actors. To assume altruism or to stress technique only obscures the essential nature of intermediary intervention, especially the intermediary's primary objective of getting agreement. In short, intermediary intervention is a subtle form of bargaining among self-interested actors, each—the disputants and the intermediary—interacting strategically with the other.

Put differently, intermediaries may be promoters of cooperation, but they are not necessarily cooperative. Their intervention objective—a negotiated agreement—may directly conflict with the disputants'—namely, unilateral victory. Their attempts to seek joint information from the parties to package a deal or to create realistic empathy may conflict with the disputants' intention of employing intermediaries to improve intelligence. Their desire to be "neutral" may conflict with the disputants' desire to acquire an ally. Their attempts to discourage threats and ultimatums from disputants may be contradicted by their own threats to withdraw services or to reduce aid or to denounce the party in the court of world opinion. And so on. The point is that one misses a lot about what intermediaries do and why they do it if one ignores the self-interested, strategic components of the intermediary's behavior. Moreover, not only do we miss a complete explanation but a complete prescription, as well. Policy recommendations based on assumptions that discount the intermediary's interests and motives will also discount the peculiar tensions an intermediary necessarily experiences acting in between. If, for example, a prescriptive framework tells one how disputants can interact better and which third-party techniques will presumably promote such interactions, then it tells the *intermediary* little about *its* interactive difficulties. It tells the intermediary little about gaining the parties' acceptance or timing its entry or committing to a neutral position or building procedural control or timing a proposal or threatening to withdraw. The purpose of part 1 was to explicate these tensions to provide a basis for improved explanation and prescription.

THE PRACTICE OF INTERMEDIARIES

The four case studies of part 2 reveal the considerable variation in intermediary intervention, variation attributable to historical, institutional, and individual factors. Systemic factors—the balance of forces, the number of actors; domestic politics—leadership struggles, bureaucratic politics, public opinion; and individual differences—personal views of conflict and conflict resolution, decision-making style—all not only create variation but confound the analysis of intermediary effectiveness. Nevertheless, the four cases, examined comparatively, provide a preliminary test of the propositions of part 1 as well as raise important additional questions about intermediary intervention.

Principal or Neutral

The principal/neutral mediator distinction, as with any ideal construction, was not perfectly replicated in real-life situations. In the cases, the half-dozen third parties fit variously along a continuum, not at the extremes. The United States role in Camp David best approximated the principal mediator and the Quakers in the Nigerian conflict, the neutral mediator. The significance of the distinction, however, lies not in where the mediator fits but in the behavior predicted by its structural position.

Jimmy Carter, try as he might merely to facilitate Israeli-Egyptian negotiations, targeted his intervention at, and achieved his success by, rearranging the disputants' payoffs. Theodore Roosevelt, although less direct in his intervention, did likewise. The Vatican and the Quakers were constrained in their ability to rearrange payoffs but used that "weakness" to alter disputant interventions. Moreover, as predicted, the two neutral mediators went to great lengths to demonstrate that they were not playing the usual game of power politics and, especially for the Quakers, not even manipulating public opinion to pressure one side as other religious groups had done.

As for prescription, the cases demonstrate in different ways that a comprehensive conflict management strategy requires policy coordination among third parties, not simply the choice of a single third party. The Nigerian case was most revealing in this regard. It is hard not to conclude in a retrospective analysis that, had both Great Britain (with its surrogate, the Commonwealth Secretariat) and groups like the Quakers coordinated their interventions, much of the bloodshed could have been adverted. Together, they could have rearranged payoffs, making unilateral victory demonstrably impossible, and improved communication to advance the time when leaders could publicly renounce unilateral approaches. Thus, in most complex disputes, there is no "best" intermediary, only combinations of intermediaries carefully chosen and sequenced to increase the likelihood of overcoming obstacles to negotiations.

Proposals and Information Pooling

The power of a mediator's proposal was evident in all cases as much of the parties' tactics vis-à-vis the mediator could be understood as attempts to encourage, discourage, or delay such proposals. Jimmy Carter's proposals had considerable bearing on Menachem Begin's behavior as did Roosevelt's on the Japanese. The Vatican's most effective initiative was Samoré's uninvited trip. But even if the Pope's Propuesta, delivered after eighteen months of formal mediation, did not achieve agreement, it did serve as a focal point for subsequent negotiations and helped keep the parties at the table. The Quakers made no formal, substantive proposals in their limited message-carrying capacity. In other conflicts, however, their proposals to hold secret meetings have prompted movement by disputing parties.[1]

Information pooling as an influence-building technique was most evident in the Portsmouth and Vatican cases. In different ways, Roosevelt and the pope acquired exclusive information about party interests and used that to pressure the parties as well as to craft solutions. The fact that Jimmy Carter tried but failed to gain the information he sought can, in part, be explained by what the parties perceived was the nature of the game—that is, hard bargaining. The Quakers also acquired exclusive information—namely, credible indications of each leader's willingness to negotiate a solution—and used that to maintain access when others could not be assured of such access. In their limited role, they never bargained with the two sides over substantive issues.

Entry and Exit

These cases suggest that the entry question is rarely a simple yes-or-no, now-or-later proposition nor is acceptance a rational calculation of advantage. In practice, intermediaries insinuate themselves into a dispute (Roosevelt) or accelerate an on-going process (Carter) or start with mere message carrying (the Quakers). Occasionally, intermediaries are presented with a clear-cut, entry-timing choice (the pope in 1978).

Timing, nevertheless, does appear to affect intervention effectiveness: the worse the parties' alternatives become, the better becomes the mediator's leverage. Had Jimmy Carter entered at a time of higher conflict intensity when Begin could not sit comfortably and wait for the president's window of opportunity to close, Carter might have been able to counter Begin's maneuvers. In the Nigerian civil war, it is not possible to say how, for example, Great Britain's effectiveness varied with the waxing and waning of the federal government's military situation. It is conceivable, however, that, had Britain intervened forcefully when the federal government's prospects for victory were at their lowest, it could have made unilateral options untenable.

On the whole, well-substantiated generalizations are not possible with the entry-timing question. And, yet, the cases do suggest that mediator timing affects mediator effectiveness, if not in the bargaining sense developed in chapter 4, then at least with respect to the level of vulnerability and receptivity to change that leaders experience as the conflict progresses.[2]

The mediator's view afforded by these case studies confirms the general proposition that mediators experience considerable tension performing "in between" and that much of their behavior can be interpreted as attempts to resolve that tension, not necessarily to resolve the parties' dispute. Certainly much of a mediator's tension derives from its own stake in the dispute. But the contradictions of role, the central argument of chapter 4, were also borne out by the cases. Carter wanted to be a problem solver and Roosevelt a mere convenor but neither could avoid being a power broker. The Vatican resisted making threats but eventually did so when movement was not forthcoming. Would-be international mediators—from major powers to private individuals—would be well advised to take into account these inevitable tensions because acting in between is unlike promoting one's own interests in disputed issues, the accustomed practice in international affairs.

Acceptance and Role Bargaining

As for the final set of propositions from part 1, these cases substantiate the proposition that disputants cannot fully know what they are getting with an intermediary intervention. Acceptance indeed entails uncertainty and risk. Menachem Begin thought he was getting yet another hard sell from a U.S. president, one that would be diluted or dropped as the U.S. elections approached. The Japanese thought they were getting an ally in Roosevelt, one who would ensure their "fruits of victory." The Chileans thought they were getting an advocate of international law in the Vatican, not one who would push for a political compromise. General Gowon thought he was getting mere message carrying in the Quakers, people who would not dare to lecture him on the psychological effects of bombing civilians. In short, from the perspective of the disputants, especially of those determined to prevail, not to engage in problem solving, acceptance of an intermediary brings new dynamics to the dispute. The disputants may do better with the intervention but in ways that cannot be predicted at the time of intervention. Once engaged in the dispute, intermediary roles do evolve, as discussed next.

THE CHALLENGE OF INTERMEDIARY INTERVENTION

In addition to providing a preliminary test of the propositions of part 1, the four case studies reveal additional features of intermediary intervention and raise new questions about its fundamental nature. Among both are the fact that the role is negotiated, that preparing the process is as important as conducting it, that domestic politics cannot be ignored, and that an intervention's most important contribution may be to reduce the gap between leaders' decisions to negotiate and their actual negotiating.

A Negotiated Role

In all cases, the uncertainty surrounding the intermediary intervention meant that, unlike the role of the protagonists or of, say, an international organization such as the World Court, the intermediary's role was never obvious from the start: Was it mere convener as the Japanese and Russians appeared to want of Roosevelt? Was it arm twister as Egypt wanted of the United States or the Biafrans wanted of the British? Was it decision maker as the Chileans wanted of the pope? Was it message carrier as the Nigerians wanted of the Quakers? Was it an intelligence source as, in some ways, all wanted of the third parties?

These functions may be prescribed by international law but, in practice, they are jointly decided by all the parties; that is, they are themselves subjects of negotiation. Disputing parties accept an intermediary intervention because other options are foreclosed or because it is one of many options to pursue simultaneously. But because the outcome of the negotiation over the intermediary's role is as unpredictable as the outcome of the substantive negotiations, the disputants accept an intermediary with little idea of its impact. Where one party expects to get a table and coffee, it gets someone pushing for concessions. Where another foresees support for its position, it gets pressure to accommodate. Where one expects mere message carrying, it is beseeched to see its actions from the enemy's perspective. Where a party anticipates facilitation, it gets another bargain, one over information if not substantive issues. And, possibly most significantly, where a party enters mediated negotiations with no intention of making concessions but only a desire to appease opponents or rally inter-

national support, it finds itself negotiating and acceding to the demands of
the third party.

In sum, an overriding characteristic of intermediary intervention that
emerges from this study is that an intermediary's role is negotiated and it
is evolutionary. What starts as mere good offices becomes an effort to
build international pressure. A multilateral conference aimed at facilitating a rational, comprehensive solution to a regional problem ends in a
limited, bilateral agreement sweetened with the intermediary's aid and
guarantees. A fact-finding mission becomes a formal mediation process. A
simple message-carrying effort leads to substantive proposal making. Because of the indeterminacy of the role (not to mention the bargaining process itself), therefore, intermediary interventions are full of surprises. Negotiators go into a mediation expecting to buy time or appease domestic
opposition, and they come out with a cease-fire or a peace treaty. When
both sides are deemed intransigent, when everyone knows they prefer to
fight it out, when a nation's reputation for resolve is on the line, intermediaries sometimes achieve the unexpected.

But why, it is worth asking, is one surprised? Maybe the intervention is
coincidental to larger forces that bring disputants to the table, and so one
misattributes the cause. But quite possibly, the reason intermediaries'
successes are surprising is that prevailing assumptions about conflict and
conflict resolution tend to discount the impact intermediaries can have.
Disputing parties, it is assumed, negotiate when they are ready, and settlement occurs when unilateral options are foreclosed. At one level, these
assertions are always true: one always wants the most for oneself and one
accepts compromise only when forced to. But what was force when the
Japanese and the Russians wanted a negotiated settlement but could take
the first step only through an intermediary like France or the United
States? What was force when Jimmy Carter persisted in his mediating
efforts beyond anything imaginable for an election-sensitive U.S. president? What was force when Cardinal Samoré traveled to South America
and averted a war? What was force when the Quakers elicited a major
concession from the Biafrans? None of these instances of change and
movement toward agreement are entirely explicable through conventional notions of power or cost-benefit calculation. But from an expanded
concept of influence, one that incorporates the decision-compelling effect
of creating a focal point, of offering nonstrategic proposals, and of pooling
information; one that takes seriously the impact of challenging enemy perceptions, the importance of reinforcing moderate elements through moral
or legal example, or the value of promising confidentiality when no one
else can; from this view, the means of influence is not so mysterious, just
less predictable than calculations based on power and motivational
factors.[3]

Having said this, it is important to stress that the case studies, despite their focus on intermediary interventions, do not diminish the role of systemic and domestic factors as the major determinants of a conflict outcome. A treaty between Egypt and Israel was not likely until Egypt and Syria reconfigured the balance of power in the Middle East in the 1973 war and until Egypt agreed to recognize Israel. A settlement between Argentina and Chile was not likely until radical changes occured in the Argentine government. The changes an intermediary can effect do not override these factors. What intermediaries can do is help parties overcome the difficulty of initiating and continuing a negotiation process. They can counter the interactional norms and practices that perpetuate and escalate conflicts. They can promote incremental steps toward a settlement and eventual resolution.[4] In short, when, owing to larger forces, parties are poised on the brink of taking either a confrontational or a cooperative path to settlement, intermediaries can tip the balance. An intermediary intervention, this study suggests, can make a marginal, although not trivial and, quite possibly, a critical, difference.

A different way of saying this is that intermediary success cannot be defined as simply getting agreement.[5] An intermediary does not merely push for concessions until parties converge on an agreement point. Nor does an intermediary necessarily find a "win-win" solution by probing underlying interests and discovering joint gains. In practice, an intermediary's impact is more nuanced. An intermediary may do little more than provide a sight and restrict the press. It may open a line of communication where none existed. It may clarify perceptions and intentions when each side was convinced it understood the other side but the other side did not understand it. An intermediary may provide a sounding board, an audience, and, thus, grant a sense of legitimacy to a besieged party. It may suggest a timetable or an agenda. It may rally public opinion—domestic or international or both. It may delve into the issues, find the dispute as intractable as the parties had found it, but, in the process, help prolong negotiations and avert hostilities. It may worsen alternatives, add incentives, or simply persist in its efforts until the parties eventually find agreement the only rational choice.

No single one of these activities or even a combination will necessarily lead to agreement. It so happens that in three of the four cases, agreement was reached. But a major finding of this study is that the effects of intermediary activities are more subtle than those necessary to ensure agreement (such as imposing a settlement). Intermediaries may do all of the above activities and accomplish little more than to get negotiations started or to keep negotiations going. The final outcome, agreement or not, who gains and who loses, will be a product of larger forces. An intermediary intervention, therefore, may not be a major determinant of outcomes, but when the alternative to sitting at the table is fighting, or when the alternative to gaining new information about the enemy is to operate on the basis of enemy images and biases, then intermediaries do make a difference. Success, in sum, cannot be measured by agreement alone but by the incremental impact of the intervention.

Intermediary Intervention as Negotiation Preparation

The case studies indicate that what the intermediary does before formal mediated negotiations is critical. Entry timing may affect the intermediary's process influence as argued in part 1. But the cases reveal that much more is involved. For Theodore Roosevelt, quiet but persistent diplomacy set the stage, once military and economic conditions were right, for his entry and the commencement of negotiations at Portsmouth. Not only did he gain entry through his persistent diplomacy but, from the belligerents' perspective, his early lobbying provided a ready alternative to continued fighting (as well as to a major power conference that both sides dreaded). For Jimmy Carter, whether intentional or not, his attempt to convene a multilateral conference at Geneva gave Menachem Begin incentive to make incremental concessions—including coming to Camp David itself—that eventually led to agreement. For Pope John Paul II, Cardinal Samoré's shuttle diplomacy not only secured a cease-fire, it set the conditions for Vatican mediation. For the Quakers, an early trip to both sides of the Nigeria-Biafra conflict not only established contacts but added credibility to their claim of neutrality, which no other third party could make.

In many instances, especially those of unofficial intermediaries like the Quakers, the interventions only set the stage for formal talks. In rare instances, such as Jimmy Carter's recent private diplomacy in the Horn of Africa, intermediaries actually conduct formal negotiations as well. In general, much of what intermediaries do can be viewed as attempts to wean the parties away from assisted negotiations to direct negotiations and, possibly, to improved ongoing relations. This was certainly true in the Beagle Channel case where the Vatican kept the parties at the table until domestic conditions changed. Much of the mediated negotiations then gave way to direct negotiations and, after the treaty was signed, the two countries were able to move rapidly to improve relations.

Domestic Politics

Contrary to the unitary actor assumptions of part 1, the case studies reveal the important role domestic politics play, both as constraints and as opportunities, in an intermediary intervention. A U.S. president, for example, must be constantly looking homeward as he conducts foreign policy. As Jimmy Carter's domestic base weakened and elections loomed closer, he became increasingly vulnerable to hard bargaining by the disputants, a fact Begin especially exploited. A pope, although elected for life, must operate through an ancient bureaucracy in Rome and a far-flung, often rebellious church spread around the world. At the time of the Beagle Channel crisis, Pope John Paul II was just beginning to consolidate his position as a new pontiff in a church increasingly dominated by the Third World. The crisis gave him an opportunity for a victory in Latin America, but it also presented the possibility of a crisis in the church and in church-state relations. This fact Argentina and Chile later used to render impotent the pope's threats to withdraw from the mediation. In the Nigerian conflict, the OAU was constrained by its members' strategic interest in dissuading secessionist movements. Despite the Consultative Committee's desire to create a dialogue, the members' support for the federal government precluded an effective intermediary role. The British government was forced by domestic pressure to mediate because it was reluctant to halt arms sales or to apply other pressures. But domestic pressure was not enough to establish an effective mediating role when both sides were highly distrustful.

Just as domestic pressures provide constraints on intermediaries, their absence affords opportunities. The Quakers had no significant domestic constituency and, hence, enjoyed considerable latitude as intervenors. They could, for example, credibly claim that they did not "need" a settlement to assuage people back home and, as a result, were better able to set the conditions of their involvement. Roosevelt, unlike Jimmy Carter, was relatively secure at home and, hence, had little to risk in his venture into world diplomacy. He, too, could manipulate the conditions for negotiations with little fear of the disputants directing counterpressure at his domestic base.

The domestic conditions of the disputants are major determinants of intermediary effectiveness, as well. To illustrate with the Beagle Channel case, Cardinal Samoré exploited Argentina's internal disarray to insert a key provision regarding force withdrawals as a condition of Vatican mediation. Once the mediation began, however, that same disarray confounded the mediation team's efforts to discover a consistent, and flexbile, Argentine position. When agreement was finally near, the pope and his mediators, exasperated with Argentine intransigence, went over the heads of the Argentine government and appealed to the people through the parishes to approve the referendum.

In general, it appears that large countries with representative governments will be more constrained as intermediaries by their domestic concerns. They have constituencies to please and elections to prepare for, factors disputants can use to their advantage. This observation thus provides a counterpoint to the common notion that only a powerful country like the United States can mediate effectively in a place like the Middle East. It may be true that the incentives a major power offers are essential to getting movement toward agreement, but it is not necessarily true that such a power will prevail in its specific bargains with the disputants. Diffuse power resources do not necessarily translate into specific bargaining advantages. This is especially true when a disputant can afford to sit while the intermediary faces deadlines.

In sum, unitary actor assumptions miss important dynamics of an intermediary intervention. From the intermediary's perspective, the bargain it establishes with each disputant is not strictly bilateral. It must deal with the negotiator's own two-way negotiating, that is, its negotiation across the table and its negotiation back home.[6] And, in some cases, the intermediary must deal directly with decision makers and their constituencies, not just representatives. At the same time, intermediaries with significant domestic constituencies must keep an eye on both the dispute abroad and one's political base at home. Thus, a comprehensive modeling of an intermediary's bargaining must be multifaceted and multidirectional.

Narrowing the Negotiation-Hostilities Gap

In many conflicts, the difference between when a leader searches for alternatives to force and when negotiations actually commence can be large—large, that is, in time, lives, and material resources. The costs can also be large in the sense of delaying ultimate reconciliation because bitterness and hatred mount during such times. The reason for this difference may be technical or bureaucratic—messages are delayed in their transmission or translation; policies take time to formulate. But it may also be owing to strategic factors (leaders cannot request negotiations for fear of appearing weak; first offers are high-risk moves when their interpretation is so variable) and to perceptual factors (the opponent's overture is deemed insincere given the horrendous things it has done; reciprocation is not expected because the other side has given no sign of moderation). These factors were involved in varying degrees in all the cases and contributed to missed opportunities for early settlement.

In the Russo-Japanese conflict, Japan and most observers thought that, given Czar Nicholas's nationalistic intransigence, Russia would never agree to negotiate without an invitation from Japan. For some time, only France knew of the czar's early willingness to commence peace talks. And on the Japanese side, few knew of the genro's intentions from the very start of the conflict to negotiate a settlement. In the Beagle Channel case, Chile and most outside observers thought Argentina was committed to a military solution. Only Nuncio Pio Laghi and a few insiders knew that, among the Junta members, Videla and Viola sought to avoid the use of force.[7] In the Nigerian case, the Biafrans originally sought complete and unilateral secession. When a federal victory looked likely in the first year, the Biafrans appeared to shift preferences and accept limited autonomy. But two and one-half years of devastation and suffering ensued without serious negotiations. Biafran persistence was in part fueled by their belief that the Nigerian government was bent on genocide, and federal intransigence was owed in part to Gowon's belief that Ojukwu would only embarrass him in talks. In all cases, then, there was a sizable gap between when parties were willing to talk (and when each recognized when the other was willing to talk) and when negotiations actually commenced (let alone when hostilities or other contentious behavior ceased).[8]

Intermediary interventions may not be able to determine outcomes, but they can be key factors in reducing this gap and, thus, reducing the costs of conflict. One reason relates to the dynamics of intense conflicts. Leaders are often impervious to evidence of changes in their opponent's behavior, and they themselves send ambiguous signals of their own changes.[9] Outsiders react to such signals in much the same way protagonists do: they see reasonableness in their preferred side and intransigence and belligerence in the other side. Moreover, principal parties and observers rely upon public pronouncements that are necessarily designed to prove resolve and are aimed at constituencies and third parties, not opponents. Often, then, it is only those who are "in between," those who engage the decision makers on both sides and witness first-hand their views, who are best positioned to assess when the possibility of negotiations actually begins.[10]

This notion of a gap between a decision to negotiate and the commencement of negotiations can be further refined by considering that the gap occurs in two stages. The first stage is from the decision maker's private decision to seek negotiations (or, at least, explore their feasibility) until the decision is publicly stated. The second stage is from the public expression until the time negotiations actually commence.

The first stage involves cautious testing, floating of trial balloons, and disavowals should overtures not be reciprocated. Because feelers are made at the same time hostile acts are being carried out (or threatened), their credibility is easily questioned. Communication is extremely delicate. Public pronouncements, especially those aimed at one's constituency and other third parties, tend to obscure rather than clarify intentions. As a result, leaders wait until costs mount or the likelihood of unilateral success diminishes significantly before acting and moving into the second stage with a public expression of a willingness to negotiate. It is precisely the rationality of this waiting that intermediaries can challenge during the first stage by carrying messages, exploring options, testing intentions, providing disinterested information and analysis, and doing all this not as a belligerent or an ally, but as one in between.

The conclusion that intermediaries are well suited to closing this gap, I should stress, comes not merely from a wish to reduce the costs of conflict (although that is certainly a policy aim of this entire study). But it also comes from the empirical observation, often missed in studies that discount the role of intermediaries, that even when leaders act to perpetuate a conflict, they are, at the same time, looking for a way out. Moreover, they are often seeking negotiated solutions well before their opponents (and, possibly, before members of their own government) know it. This is the kind of opportunity intermediaries can exploit to promote negotiations, not because they are smarter or wiser or more rational than the decision makers but precisely because they are in between the decision makers.

NOTES

CHAPTER ONE

1. Dominguez, "Mice that Do Not Roar," 191–93.
2. Cited in Bercovitch, "International Mediation," 157–58.
3. The usual distinction between arbitration and mediation is that the parties grant the arbitrator, but not the mediator, the authority to decide the outcome. Hence, arbitration resembles a judicial process much more than mediation, which is thought of as facilitative rather than determinative. The point of view in this book is that international mediation is best viewed as *political*, that is, as a special kind of negotiation in which the bargaining relationship between the mediator and the disputants is critical.
4. Cot, *International Conciliation*, 31–38, 40–41.
5. Ibid., 9–10. The one exception was the Vatican. Divested of its temporal powers in 1870, the Holy See was considered the natural mediator of disputes between temporal powers. In the late nineteenth century when some states were looking for alternatives to arbitration, a number of states requested papal mediation. Consequently, in 1885, Pope Leo XIII served as a mediator between Germany and Spain to settle a dispute over the Caroline Islands. Papal mediation also led to an Anglo-Portuguese settlement over the frontiers of East Africa in 1891 and a territorial settlement between Peru and Ecuador in 1893. These instances of papal mediation represent the first attempts in modern times to choose a mediator with no political authority (pp. 38–40). Despite its apparent successes, the Hague Peace Conference of 1899 and subsequent events in Europe rendered the practice of formal papal mediation obsolete, at least until 1978 when Pope John Paul II intervened in the Beagle Channel dispute between Argentina and Chile (see chap. 8 this volume).
6. In this chapter, I use the terms "mediation" and "intermediary intervention" more or less interchangeably. In the literature and in popular usage the terms mediator, intermediary, conciliator, facilitator, go-between, arbiter, third party, and peacemaker are all used, usually without precise definitions and with overlapping meanings. I make no attempt in this study to resolve this confusion. Rather, in chapter 2, I define terms precisely and for analytic purposes only.
7. Keohane, *International Institutions and State Power*.
8. For discussion of the application of game theoretic concepts to international affairs, see Axelrod, *Evolution of Cooperation*; Keohane, *After Hegemony*; Oye, *Cooperation under Anarchy*.
9. I use "it" for intermediary throughout this book in part to get around the gender problem and in part to suggest that, by intermediaries, I mean states and other organizations as well as individuals.
10. Another way to view the role of intermediaries is as a precursor to the building of conventions, regimes, and organizations. Because, in an intermediary intervention, the disputants must negotiate not only over the disputed issues but over

the role and procedures advocated by the intermediary, the results of the procedural negotiations helps lay the groundwork for more regularized relations on other issues. An intermediary can thus be a critical seed for establishing the negotiating expectations necessary to create more durable institutions. The extent to which this occurs will depend critically on the nature of the intervention. Intervenors who detract from the direct interaction between disputants, what I call "principal mediators" in chapter 2, will be less likely to set such precedents.

11. Hoffmann, *Janus and Minerva*, 5.

12. For discussion of the "diplomatic revolution," see Craig and George, *Force and Statecraft*; Hoffmann, *Janus and Minerva*; Lauren, *Diplomacy*; Nicolson, *Diplomacy*.

13. See Winham, "Negotiation as a Management Process," for an analysis of this transformation in the context of multilateral trade negotiations and U.S.-Soviet arms control negotiations.

14. Craig and George, *Force and Statecraft*, 159. In recent negotiations in civil conflicts in the Philippines, El Salvador, Nicaragua, and Cambodia, ideological differences appear to be less encumbering than questions of representation, venue, and agenda setting.

15. I owe this term to Ralph White. I use it because it minimizes connotations of sympathy and emphasizes the real needs—both cognitive and affective—of protagonists.

16. Jervis, "Rational Deterrence," 198.

17. In the context of coercive diplomacy, Craig and George, *Force and Statecraft*, 202 note that advances "in communication and intelligence-gathering have not appreciably reduced the problems of diplomatic decision-making despite the increased pace of international events and the flood of information now available to statesmen. As a result, misperception remains a severe problem in the application of coercive diplomacy. Time is compressed, the number of influences that must be considered has multiplied, and the military superiority of the superpowers has proven to have limited usefulness and awesome risks. Other forms of power and the influence of smaller states have assumed increased significance as a consequence."

18. This is *not* to say that conflict is a result of misperception and inadequate information. The starting assumption of this study is that international conflicts typically evolve out of real conflicts of interest, whether over territory, natural resources, national sovereignty, and identity, or ideology and religion. What prevents resolution is not the real conflict because both sides have an overriding shared interest in avoiding a dangerous escalation or in prolonging hostilities. Rather, it is the ability to arrest the dynamics of conflict that perpetuate and escalate the conflict and make compromise difficult. Changing these dynamics, then, requires effective communication and realistic empathy. For further discussion of this approach to conflict resolution, see Kelman, "Interactional Approach to Conflict Resolution."

19. In this book, I do not address conflict situations in which one party is strictly committed to prevailing and is willing to suffer extreme costs. Mediators are irrelevant to the designs of Hitlers and Pol Pots. I do, nevertheless, address conflicts

that have the *appearance* of absolute intractability. That is, in many conflicts, what often passes in public pronouncements for unbending belligerence only masks a complex, high-stress, decision-making process. Behind the scenes, not only are there typically more accommodative factions but those leaders with real authority and those who make the bellicose statements are also those who seek alternative means to force. Thus, an operating assumption in this study is that what passes for absolute bellicosity is often only the public manifestation of a leader's difficult situation. The implication for understanding and promoting nonviolent dispute resolution is that opportunities for, let alone the prevalence of, intermediary interventions are considerable.

20. For simplicity, I assume a bilateral conflict throughout this study. Multilateral negotiations add complexities but, for the most part, the conclusions drawn regarding intermediary intervention apply to disputes involving any number of disputants. On multilateral negotiations, see Sebenius, *Negotiating the Law of the Sea*; Touval, "Multilateral Negotiation"; Winham, *International Trade*.

21. In chapter 9 I elaborate on the ineffectiveness of regional organizations as intermediaries by arguing that the regional organization carries neither the advantages of the major powers or concerts—it does not have the bargaining capacity—nor that of the "neutrals"—it does not have the "neutrality."

22. For discussion and data analysis of League of Nations and United Nations interventions, see Brecher and Wilkenfield, *Crisis, Conflict and Instability*, 57–73.

23. For a concise summary of the literature on mediation in the major substantive areas and from the major disciplinary perspectives, see Kolb and Rubin, "Mediation through a Disciplinary Kaleidoscope"; for an extensive bibliography, see Lakos, *International Negotiations*.

24. Like all but the most strictly mathematical of axiomatic theorizing, the approach I take in part 1 is not purely deductive. My starting assumptions are based on the study of numerous mediators ranging from the interpersonal to the interorganizational (e.g., environmental) to the international as well as on my own experience as a small claims court mediator. Thus, although the presentation of the book is divided between the mostly deductive theorizing in part 1 and the inductive generalizing from case studies in part 2, the two necessarily interact in the theory-building process. Moreover, neither method is necessarily superior in its ability to generate useful propositions. A general theory of the sort found in the natural sciences or in economics or of those attempted at the level of international systems cannot be expected here. If a broad theory emerges from this book, it can only be in the sense of developing a set of contingent propositions and questions that make more systematic one's understanding of intermediary intervention and that distinguishes it in useful ways from other forms of conflict management.

25. For discussion of the methodological trade-offs involved in comparative case study compared to correlative methods, see George, "Case Studies and Theory Development." For discussion of the relation between deductive theorizing and case studies, see George and Smoke, *Deterrence in American Foreign Policy*; Keohane, *After Hegemony*; Oye, *Cooperation under Anarchy*.

26. Holsti, "National Role Conceptions."

Chapter Two

1. Notable exceptions are Bercovitch, *Social Conflicts and Third Parties*; Curle, *In the Middle*; Rubin, *Dynamics of Third Party Intervention*; Touval, *Peace Brokers*; Touval and Zartman, *International Mediation*; and Young, *Intermediaries*.

2. For details, see, for example, Schofield, *Evolution*.

3. See Princen, "Security and Conflict Management." There, I show that, outside the East-West context, disputing parties regularly turn to third-parties for assistance—or, influence—in settling their disputes. On third-party conflict resolution in Africa, see Zartman, *Ripe for Resolution*.

4. I am associating interests in the disputed issues with capabilities: an "interested" third party also has the capability to offer or deny resources whereas a "neutral" does not. The remaining combinations of interests and capabilities constitute intermediate categories between the polar cases of principal and neutral. Analytically, these intermediate categories are not particularly interesting, and empirically they are probably inconsequential. Thus, an intervening party with capabilities but no interests—direct or indirect—in the disputed issues is unlikely to intervene. A party with interests in the dispute but no capabilities will not be the subject of bargaining with the disputants but must still be suspected of manipulating common pool information, the use of proposals, and the like, to meet its interests. As will be evident in the discussion to follow, for analyzing the effect of an intervention, both of these intermediate cases essentially fit the principal mediator category.

5. What exactly U.S. interests in the Middle East are, of course, is a matter of debate. As with this entire discussion, I use these two issues, Soviet presence and oil, as illustrations only.

6. This inability to foster trust and open communication between leaders is particularly evident in the Camp David case study in part 2. President Jimmy Carter dearly wanted to bring Egyptian President Anwar Sadat and Israeli Prime Minister Menachem Begin together: "There was no prospect for success if Begin and Sadat stayed apart, and their infrequent meetings had now become fruitless because the two men were too personally incompatible to compromise on the many difficult issues facing them" (Carter, *Keeping Faith*, 316). His attempt failed in part because of the conflicting personalities but also because Carter was, foremost, a U.S. president. Confronting a "principal mediator," Begin and Sadat had to consider everything Carter said, everything he proposed, as strategic. Friendship and understanding were difficult to foster in such a climate. In fact, I argue that he was structurally incapable of building trust and effective communication between disputants. As the case study reveals, however, the process at Camp David did contribute to important, although unanticipated, changes in attitudes and preferences that eventually led to agreement. Nevertheless, the final peace treaty was arranged only when, as is typical of a principal mediator, the United States provided substantial incentives by way of military and financial aid and threats to cut off or reduce aid.

7. See chapter 3 for a more extensive treatment of strategic behavior, strategic interaction, and the effect of an intermediary's intervention.

8. For the purposes of the present argument, the joint problem solving need not be face-to-face. Just as Jimmy Carter never brought Sadat and Begin together at Camp David for any significant direct exchanges, the neutral mediator may only engage each party separately in problem-solving activities. The point here is that, unlike with Carter, the neutral mediator will be far more likely to elicit true preferences and encourage the "playful" exploration needed to expand alternatives. This increased likelihood is primarily owing to the fact, as I argue further below, that the disputants need not fear—and react to—the strategic gaming of the principal mediator. The argument aside, there are, nevertheless, good social psychological reasons for bringing disputants together face-to-face, especially in the "prenegotiation" phase of a conflict resolution process. For further development of this point, see the analysis of the Camp David case in chapter 6.

9. Of course, not all neutral mediators are constrained in the same way a religious group like the Anglicans is. Sweden, for example, can employ more conventional diplomatic techniques while remaining essentially neutral, that is, unable to exchange value on the issues in dispute. Such a bargaining definition of neutrality is developed further in this chapter and in chapter 4. In principle, the United States or the Soviet Union should be able to perform the role of neutral mediator in certain conflicts. But as superpowers, there has been virtually no spot on the globe that does not have strategic interest for them. Consequently, for all practical purposes, superpowers as known for most of the post–World War II period can only be "interested mediators" or "disputants." This may change, of course, as they become increasingly disengaged from some parts of the world. Middle powers may or may not fit neatly into the categories of mediator presented here, these categories being "ideal types." Nevertheless, most *neutral* mediators will be small nations, international organizations, some multinational corporations, academic institutions, religious groups, private individuals, and so forth—in other words, not the traditional subjects of international relations theories.

10. Throughout this discussion and that of the succeeding chapters of part 1, I treat disputants and intermediaries as unitary actors. Many of the factors that limit effective negotiating are domestic, including political, institutional, and bureaucratic factors; or individual, including cognitive and affective factors. Because these factors are best accounted for in detailed case studies, I take them up in part 2.

11. The other effect—the risks of being excluded or of being forced to accept an inferior outcome—I consider in chapter 3.

12. For discussion of this three-way, circular bargaining dynamic with the United States in the aftermath of the 1973 war, see Touval, *Peace Brokers*, 281; and Stein, "Structures, Strategies, and Tactics," 333–34. For discussion of Henry Kissinger's bargaining style, especially his deliberate attempts to channel all exchanges through him, see Quandt, *Decade of Decisions*; Rubin, *Dynamics of Third Party Intervention*; and Sheehan, *Arabs, Israelis, and Kissinger*.

13. For a similar argument regarding the interventions of both Henry Kissinger and Jimmy Carter in the Middle East, see Stein, "Structures, Strategies, and Tactics," 333–34.

14. Notice that, although I often use the terms bargaining and negotiating interchangeably, in much of this discussion I am suggesting a difference. Bargaining

is more inclusive and often encompasses tacit and confrontational interchange, such as the exchange of threats and denials through the media. Negotiating entails what happens at the table (whether or not face-to-face) and implies more of a joint problem-solving effort. Although precise distinctions could be drawn, I find it unhelpful for this discussion.

15. Of course, all mediators have interests. But it is the particular interests that matter. A principal mediator has indirect interests in the issues in dispute, and a neutral has none. But they both may have broader interests in the dispute—namely, the desire for peace, efficiency, fairness, and so forth. The critical difference is that these broader "public" interests are not subject to bargaining; the private, "extractive" ones are. Chapter 4 spells out this distinction in detail.

16. In chapter 5, I argue that, from a disputant's point of view, impartiality is not necessarily a rational criterion for choosing an intermediary. In fact, it may be a "third best choice."

17. Raiffa, *Art and Science of Negotiation*.

18. In principle, a third party can create joint gains between itself and each of the disputants as well as between the disputants themselves. The basis of such an intervention is not simply "sweetening the deal" by adding resources. It also includes trading on differences in interests, in forecasts, in risk aversion, and in discount values. See Lax and Sebenius, *Manager as Negotiator*, 88–116, for a comprehensive discussion of the bases of joint gains.

19. Jervis, "Rational Deterrence"; Jervis, *Perception and Misperception*; Janis and Mann, *Decision Making*; Simon, *Administrative Behavior*.

20. Institutional factors also contribute to biases that impede agreement. Bureaucratic bargaining and leadership struggles can lead to policies that are either more intransigent than those espoused by the negotiators or that deviate in implementation from that intended by the leaders. These factors are important for understanding the effect of intervenors on internal decision making—and vice versa. Because their effect is best seen in their proper historical and institutional context, I treat them in detail in the case studies of part 2.

21. Kelman, 1979, "An Interactional Approach to Conflict Resolution," 107.

22. Of course, there are other interests that a constituency does want to know are being advanced. These may relate either to privately held values like enhanced prestige or public values like making peace. I discuss these interests in more detail in chapter 4.

23. I owe this term to Ralph K. White. Empathy alone often connotes friendly and even sympathetic understanding. These qualities, although perhaps desirable, are not necessary to address underlying interests and needs.

24. Max Weber, quoted and discussed in Keohane, *After Hegemony*, 70.

CHAPTER THREE

1. The concept of bargaining range comes out of the microeconomics literature, especially from the concepts of the Edgeworth Box and the contract curve. For discussion of this approach and the implied bargaining tactics, see Buchanan and Tullock, *Calculus of Consent*; Young, *Bargaining*; and Raiffa, *Art and Science of Negotiation*.

2. This result is, in part, because the better the alternative, the higher the reservation value and, hence, the narrower the bargaining range—narrower, that is, in favor of the one with the improved alternative. It is also owing to the fact that the best predicted outcome of a simple bargain characterized by mutual concessions and convergence is the midpoint of the bargaining range. Constraining the range by improving one's alternative shifts the expected convergence point in one's favor. See Raiffa, *Art and Science of Negotiation*, and Lax and Sebenius, *Manager as Negotiator*, for elaboration of these points.

3. For a comprehensive treatment of tactics for shifting the perceived bargaining range, see Lax and Sebenius, *Manager as Negotiator*, 119–22.

4. For the classic discussion of these tactics, see Schelling, *Strategy of Conflict*.

5. I say "first cut" definition of bargaining because I do not want to suggest that this is all there is to bargaining. For one thing, at this point, I have not yet introduced integrative and distributive bargaining. More importantly, when one looks in detail at real-life negotiations, it is apparent that the assumptions employed here are inadequate. For both explanatory and prescriptive purposes, it is critical to introduce political, institutional, and psychological factors. Indeed, this is a primary function of the case studies of part 2. The analytic approach adopted here derives from game theory and microeconomics. At this point, I use it as a baseline from which to add these other factors. For a discussion of the rationale for this approach in the context of deterrence, see Jervis, "Introduction," 1–12. See also Jervis, *Perception and Misperception*; and Stein, "International Negotiation."

6. Young, *Bargaining*, 5–6.

7. Ibid., 14.

8. Walton and McKersie, *Behavioral Theory*, first developed this distinction with respect to labor negotiations. Much of the popular literature accepts the distinction and sees the aim of negotiating to be to move from the distributive to the integrative. Raiffa, *Art and Science of Negotiation*, argues, however, that some bargains have no integrative potential, and the tactics inherent in distributive bargains cannot be ignored. Lax and Sebenius, *Manager as Negotiator*, conceive of integrative bargains as simultaneously having integrative and distributive components; even when an integrative solution is possible through the use of value-creating tactics, the value-claiming tactics necessary to distribute the gains must still be employed. Thus, what I argue here with respect to distributive bargains is also true for integrative bargains. A focal point, for example, is still useful in an integrative bargain when it comes to either locating a starting point or dividing joint gains.

9. For discussion of these techniques in the labor-management context, see Kolb, *Mediators*. In the public disputes context, see Susskind and Cruikshank, *Breaking the Impasse*; Cormick, "Strategic Issues." In the international context, see Fisher and Ury, *International Mediation*; Winham, "Negotiation as a Management Process"; Young, *Intermediaries*; Zartman and Berman, *Practical Negotiator*.

10. This notion of "principle" is a key ingredient in the prescriptive approach to negotiation advocated by Fisher and Ury, *Getting To Yes*; Susskind and Cruikshank, *Breaking the Impasse*; and others. "Objective standards," "external referents," or "principles" are proposed as methods of fairly dividing gains. Although

the notion is grounded in a legalistic view of conflict resolution, by the strategic view I take here, "principles" are no more than convenient focal points. Even Fisher acknowledges that one should seek the best principle and hope that one's counterpart does not come up with a better one. In other words, there really is nothing inherently "right" or "principled" about any given principle. Such negotiating tactics are, therefore, very much a matter of strategic move, not a search for some universally recognized standard of rightness, as in domestic law.

11. Throughout part 1, I assume that an intervenor's primary objective, its primary means of meeting *its* interests, is to get agreement. In practice, of course, mediators have other, possibly more overarching, objectives as well—securing a durable peace, realizing all efficiencies, protecting future generations. Seeking agreement is a useful first-cut assumption, however, for the kind of stylized argument presented here.

12. In this argument, I am assuming that all parties see a uniform probability distribution over all possible agreement points. That is, no point is more likely, *ex ante*, to lead to agreement than any other point. This follows from the assumption that no point in the bargaining set has prominence.

13. The proposal may still be suspect if a link can be drawn between this issue and those in which the United States does have interests. So, for example, if the relevant issue is the rate of Israeli troop disengagement, then the United States may prefer a faster rate, knowing that once withdrawal is complete, the Saudis will be more cooperative suppliers of oil to the United States.

This discussion refines the principal-neutral distinction of chapter 2. The intervention effects of principals and neutrals differ according to the extent to which mediator interests are linked to the disputants' interests on each issue. On many issues—both substantive and procedural—the principal may be sufficiently detached to make "neutral" proposals. It, nevertheless, is still in a position in which it must prove its neutrality. The perfectly neutral mediator will find this easier to do because it can make neutral proposals on *all* issues. Thus, although the above discussion suggests that mediators fall along a continuum from principals to neutrals (depending on their degrees of interest in the disputed issues and their level of bargaining capability) rather than the "either-or" stylization of chapter 2, there is still something of a discontinuity between principals and neutrals.

14. For experimental evidence of "anchoring"—that is, the power of first suggestions—see Kahneman and Tversky, "Judgment under Uncertainty."

15. In bilateral negotiations between the Philippine government and insurrectionist forces in 1986 and 1987, food service during the negotiations was a divisive issue. As a gesture of good will, the government made all arrangements for meals. The opposition forces, however, viewed the government's unilateral decision to provide the food as a maneuver to demonstrate their weakness. At the national level, no third party was present to decide these "trivial" issues. But at the regional level, local priests served as convenors and, presumably, handled many such questions. The local negotiations were partially successful but the national negotiations collapsed without accomplishment.

16. In confidential interviews, a Quaker mediator describes how, time and again, parties in conflict would appeal to him as if he were in touch with and had

influence on world opinion. The sense was, he explained, that just because this Quaker was an outsider, he could make a difference on the outside. It made no difference that he carefully explained to the party that all his mediating was behind the scenes and that he shunned contact with the press. The result, nevertheless, was that the parties would talk to and listen to the mediator. The mediator, by virtue of his position, did, it seems, create an important audience in the eyes of the protagonist.

CHAPTER FOUR

1. For excellent descriptive work on labor mediators, see Kolb, *Mediators*; and on community mediation, Silbey and Merry, "Mediator Settlement Strategies." Rich descriptive work on environmental and international mediation is more difficult to come by. For domestic environmental mediation, see Bingham, *Resolving Environmental Disputes*; Ticc, "But What Does a Mediator Really Do?" For international studies, in addition to the case studies in this book, see Touval, *Peace Brokers*; Touval and Zartman, *International Mediation*, Zartman, *Ripe for Resolution*. For prescriptive works, see Fisher and Ury, *International Mediation*; Fisher and Ury, *Getting To Yes*; and Susskind and Cruikshank, *Breaking the Impasse*.

2. By this characterization, intermediary intervention is very much an ad hoc process. Surely there are international actors who mediate more regularly, however. The United Nations is the obvious example. But even here, legal definitions of mediation and conciliation do not dictate a role. When a person like Count Folke Bernadotte or Ralph Bunche or Diego Cordova is appointed as a UN mediator, that person may be a professional diplomat or an international legal scholar, but he or she is not necessarily experienced in operating in the middle of a dispute. Nor do the parties necessarily accept the niceties of legal prescription when vital interests are at stake. Rather, they accept the UN mediator if they feel their political objectives can be advanced. In a balance of power system, the parties may indeed accept what they must from a powerful "mediator" who is prepared to impose terms. But, as discussed in the introductory chapter, this book is primarily about conflicts that do not fit the multipolar or bipolar mold, that is, those conflicts that by their sheer numbers prevail in the late twentieth century. Finally, even when the secretary general intervenes, he must negotiate a role for himself. His official position may be an asset, but, unlike with judges, legislators, and managers, it does not define an intermediary role nor does it dictate when to become involved or how to influence the parties to reach agreement. These are all separate matters outside the mandate of the office.

3. For discussion of the levels of analysis question and its relation to international affairs and social change, see Jervis, *Perception and Misperception*; Kelman, *International Behavior*.

4. In personal communication, Roger Fisher states that the advice one gives to a mediator should be no different from that given to a negotiator. This may be true for those mediators committed to nothing more than facilitating negotiations, regardless of the outcome. But at least in international relations, this amounts to a rather generous assumption about mediator motives. My position is that a theory

of "facilitation," like one of cooperation, is stronger if it starts with less generous assumptions. See Axelrod, *Evolution of Cooperation*, for a similar argument regarding cooperation among "egoists."

5. A notable exception is the work of Touval and Zartman. They start with the assumption that mediators like the United States in the Middle East have significant interests that, in turn, significantly affect outcomes. But, in part, their analysis is driven by their choice of mediators. They are virtually all major powers or their surrogates (e.g., the United Nations in the 1950s). When they do consider the intervention of smaller players like Algeria in the U.S.-Iran hostage crisis, interests of the mediator disappear. See Touval, *Peace Brokers*; Touval and Zartman, *International Mediation*.

6. Recognizing that no intermediary actually goes through each step of the decision portrayed here, I am assuming either that a rational intermediary would want to systematically consider these elements of the decision or that the intermediary, having made the entry decision, has implicitly accounted for these elements.

7. A disputant's choice of action may be influenced not only by its own alternatives, but by its perception of the other's alternatives. As is common in intense disputes, each disputant may perceive the other's alternatives to be worsening at a faster rate. Believing that "time is on our side," the disputant will be inclined to persevere with the status quo and shun alternative dispute resolution processes, such as negotiation and mediation. On the other hand, if the disputant perceives its own alternatives to be worsening at the fastest rate, a sense of increasing vulnerability may lead the disputant to the same conclusion, namely, that the status quo is better than a process that could force a "surrender." Either way, mutual perceptions of asymmetrically worsening alternatives can lead the disputants to reject negotiation and the assistance of a mediator.

Thus, the discussion in this chapter, as in chapter 3, assumes a level of rational behavior and sufficient information that may not exist in many real-life situations. Of course, one function of mediation, especially, of the "neutral mediator" is to provide the information that can dispel mirror images of asymmetrically worsening alternatives.

8. See Sick, "Partial Negotiator," for an account—at least, from the U.S. perspective—of this mediation. Sick does not draw the same conclusions about mediator control, however.

9. This principle is most easily seen in the context of a simple bargain, for example, the buying of a car. If, in the course of my negotiations with the car owner, I discover that an identical car is available on the next lot for a lower price, my bargaining "power" in *this* bargain has increased. My bargaining power also increases if the dealer loses an offer from another buyer. For a lucid discussion of this principle, see Lax and Sebenius, *Manager as Negotiator*, 249–58.

10. I am assuming the intermediary's alternative to intervention is constant. The disputants' alternatives, therefore, become the critical analytic focus.

11. Of course, a disputant's claim that not all joint gains have been exploited may well be true. The strategic problem for the intermediary, as discussed in the following, is, nevertheless, the same. That is, because there is a disparity in information between the intermediary and a disputant and because an intermediary

must keep some of that information confidential, the intermediary can never fully convince a disputant that all joint gains have been squeezed out (assuming the intermediary indeed does know this). Therefore, like a negotiator who can never fully convince an opponent that its stated reservation value is the true one and, therefore, must find a means of committing to that value, the intermediary must also find a means of committing to the fact that the efficient frontier has been reached. By committing, I mean steps taken that visibly, irreversibly, and credibly bind one to a stated course of action. A disputant's intransigence may revolve not so much around substance as its need to satisfy a constituency. Once again, the strategic problem for the intermediary is the same, only the commitment must translate into something the *negotiators* can use vis-à-vis their constituencies.

12. The mediation literature is replete with examples of how mediators attempt to urge parties toward agreement. See, for example, Kolb, *Mediators*; Kuechle, "Note on Mediation"; Rubin, *Dynamics of Third Party Intervention*; and Silbey and Merry, "Mediator Settlement Strategies." The stylized choice I am posing here assumes that all these have been tried and found wanting. The second option—leave the dispute—thus becomes a "last resort" tactic and, as such, implicitly underlies all other tactics.

13. Roger Fisher claims that this is indeed only a warning and that, as such, it is legitimate. He considers threats, especially threats of violence, to be illegitimate. Here, I make the distinction not on moral grounds but on strictly strategic grounds.

14. Schelling, *Strategy of Conflict*, 123–24.

15. This is certainly much truer of the "neutral" mediators than the "principals." But as I have asserted before, even the powerful mediator must wrestle with problems of procedural control. To the extent that they hope to create a joint problem-solving environment (as Carter tried, but Kissinger did not), they must face the same contradiction of counseling conciliatory behavior while issuing "threatening" statements.

16. Sick, "Partial Negotiator."

Chapter Five

1. I assume in this discussion that the disputants have some say over the intervention of a third party. In practice, of course, this may not be the case with some third parties. A third *disputant*—one with direct interests in the issues in dispute—may intervene unilaterally and, whether by force or as a fellow bargainer, the third disputant creates a three-way game. Only a third party as an intermediary must be acceptable by both parties. This follows from the analytic distinctions laid out in chapter 2.

2. A higher "expected outcome" can be thought of informally—simply, that the disputant will come out "better" with an intermediary than without. Or it can be thought of more formally using utility theory. The "expected values" of the two choices—intermediary intervention and the best alternative—can be assessed in terms of all possible consequences of each course of action; the probabilities (subjectively assessed) that each consequence will occur; and the "utility" (the value to

the actor adjusted for risk) of each consequence. The formal approach is especially valuable for prescriptive purposes. Even if the calculations are never made, the formulation encourages the actor to think of all possible contingencies, to consider the likelihood of each occurring, and to consciously weight them for their value to the actor.

3. Quakers often talk about "balanced partiality" rather than impartiality. By this they mean that they see themselves as advocates for *both* sides or, more precisely, for overarching goals such as the reduction of violence that both sides presumably prefer. Because mediators, especially powerful ones with strong interests, are often seen by each party as favoring the other side (see the Camp David and Portsmouth cases in part 2, for cases in point), maybe the better term is "balanced bias."

4. One could take the intermediary's perspective on the question of impartiality. But, a priori, it is difficult to see any inherent value in a position of impartiality. The only reason the third party would prefer an impartial position would be to increase the chances of a successful intervention. To predict the chances, one would have to know the impact on the disputants. Thus, the best perspective from which to judge the impartiality question—aside from someone's definition of a "world view"—is that of the disputants.

5. I thank Howard Raiffa for bringing this problem to my attention.

6. I am assuming here the possibility of some kind of interparty comparisons.

7. See chapter 8, the Beagle Channel case, for a discussion of the difficulty of signaling intentions when one party (in this case, Chile) initiates the solicitation of an intermediary.

CHAPTER SIX

1. Carter, *Keeping Faith*; Quandt, *Camp David*; also, Touval, *Peace Brokers*; Dayan, *Breakthrough*.

2. Quandt, *Camp David*, 79.

3. Ibid., 80–81.

4. Dayan, *Breakthrough*, 102.

5. Carter, *Keeping Faith*, 311, from his diary of March 21, 1978.

6. Carter, *Keeping Faith*, 312–13.

7. Dayan, *Breakthrough*, 155.

8. Carter, *Keeping Faith*, 329–30.

9. Quandt, *Camp David*, 277.

10. Ibid., 280.

11. Ibid., 302.

12. See Silbey and Merry, "Mediator Settlement Strategies," 7–32, for evidence of this tendency in the domestic context.

13. Carter, *Keeping Faith*, 277.

14. Quandt, *Camp David*, 317.

15. Carter, *Keeping Faith*, 276.

16. Quandt, *Camp David*, 202.

17. Carter, *Keeping Faith*, 342.

18. Carter did engage in hard bargaining eventually as discussed further in this chapter. He conceded as much in his description of the coalitional bargaining both Sadat and Begin tried to play. What is most revealing, though, is his phrase, "I must admit that I capitalized on this situation," as if he was embarrassed to admit that he indeed engaged in such behavior.

19. Dayan, *Breakthrough*; Sadat, *In Search of Identity*; Fahmy, *Negotiating for Peace*.

20. Dayan, *Breakthrough*, 102.

21. Ibid., 213–14.

22. Sadat, *In Search of Identity*, 362.

23. Quandt, *Camp David*, 224.

24. Dayan, *Breakthrough*, 182.

25. Fahmy, *Negotiating for Peace*, 196.

26. Carter, *Keeping Faith*, 291.

27. Ibid., 352–58.

28. Ibid., 352–58. Recall also Begin's earlier comment to Carter that he was "wounded in the heart" when his December 1977 plan offering to withdraw from the Sinai had first received words of praise but later faded away.

29. On this point, see Burton, "Track Two." On the importance of diagnosis in the context of foreign policy making, see George and Smoke, *Deterrence in American Foreign Policy*.

30. Kelman, "Interactional Approach to Conflict Resolution," 108.

31. Carter explains his notetaking as follows: "Because of the historic importance of the negotiations and the unique personal interrelationships at play within Camp David, I kept meticulous notes, recording verbatim some of the more significant statements made in my presence" (p. 327).

32. In general, Carter was severely constrained by his domestic political position as Quandt demonstrates so convincingly in his book. The point here, however, is that, aside from his domestic structural constraints, he was structurally constrained by his capacity to bargain. As argued in part 1, a *bargaining* capability limits an intermediary's *facilitating* capability. Here it is clear that, although the concrete incentives Carter had at his disposal were not regularly on the table, they always lurked in the background and cast a shadow over the disputants' expectations. They may not be explicit topics of bargaining, but when the hard decisions are imminent, they are elevated from the implicit to the explicit. Thus, in Carter's Middle East mediation, when either side was especially intransigent or when agreement was in view, the concrete incentives did emerge as bargaining issues.

33. Carter, *Keeping Faith*, 352.

34. It can also be argued that the major psychological barriers had been already broken. Sadat went to Jerusalem and Begin reciprocated by going to Egypt. In addition, Israel's willingness to return the Sinai and Egypt's willingness to formally recognize Israel were established by the respective parties well before Camp David. Thus, in some sense, Carter's task was, indeed, only to work out the details. That it was not just a technical task soon became apparent, however. Many political factors had to be accounted for and, it seems from their private encounter with Carter, perceptions of each other's needs and intentions were not clear.

35. Carter, *Keeping Faith*, 356.

36. Dayan, *Breakthrough*, 183. Carter's comment at the beginning of the direct talks between Sadat and Begin reinforces Dayan's view: "I knew what they had to say—I could have recited some of the more pertinent passages in my sleep" (Carter, *Keeping Faith*, 343). The question I raise here is, Did he really know? Sure he knew the "facts" and all the position statements, but did he understand what lay behind them? Did he comprehend the parties' fundamental fears for security and identity? Apparently not.

37. Settlements—that is, formal agreements—can be reached without addressing underlying needs and concerns. Provisional agreements are common in international affairs when the conflict cannot be "resolved." And, given the seemingly intractable nature of the Middle East conflict, it is probably too much to expect that Jimmy Carter or any other U.S. leader could get a comprehensive agreement, let alone effect a complete resolution of the conflict. In fact, many would argue that only principal parties through their direct interactions and their personal and political commitments can achieve resolution.

38. Carter, *Keeping Faith*, 321–22.

39. Of course, the return home can be, and usually is, portrayed as regrouping, reassessing, and planning for the next mission. But everyone knows that when Henry Kissinger or Cyrus Vance were sent abroad, they were expected to come back with something. This is especially the case when a president is publicly staking so much of his political capital on such an effort.

40. Increasing costs also worked in reverse, of course. The further into the Middle East miasma Carter got, the harder it was to extricate himself without something to show. Begin was able to use this reverse entrapment most effectively not at Camp David but in the ensuing negotiations to conclude the treaty. This is where Carter truly appeared to be "giving away the store."

41. In fact, one can argue that if Carter were known for being more politically sensitive—that is, to his reelection and to his party's success—he might not have convinced Begin of his intention of seeing out the mediating effort.

42. Carter, *Keeping Faith*, 366.

Chapter Seven

1. The primary sources for this account are Esthus, *Double Eagle and Rising Sun*; and Okamoto, *Japanese Oligarchy*.

2. Esthus, *Double Eagle and Rising Sun*, 16.

3. The idea of forming a military alliance with one's bitterest enemy may appear farfetched. But Witte had seriously discussed the matter with the czar before leaving St. Petersburg for the United States. If anything, the idea was just a bit premature. By secret entente agreements in 1907, 1910, 1912, and 1916, the two powers did, in fact, form such an alliance. Nineteenth-century alliances were formed less out of ideological or cultural affinity and more out of a perceived need to maintain, or change, the balance of power.

4. Esthus, *Double Eagle and Rising Sun*, 133.

5. Jacob Schiff, an American financier who was a key figure in many of Japan's wartime loans, did write to Takahira on August 25 to explain the financial conse-

quences of continuing the war. He expressed concern that, although Russia could draw on its substantial gold reserve, the money markets of the United States, England, and Germany would no longer be able to finance Japan's war to the previous extent. Schiff said, nevertheless, that his own firm would do all it could to continue to provide financing. There is no evidence, according to Esthus, that the letter was related to Roosevelt's peacemaking efforts.

6. Esthus, *Double Eagle and Rising Sun*, 174.

7. See chapter 2 for discussion of the primary differences between the "principal mediator" and the "neutral mediator." For a more nuanced distinction with dynamic considerations, see the discussion of chapter 3, in particular, the two dimensions of bargaining and proposal making.

8. See Luttwak, *Strategy*, for a lucid discussion of the "culminating point of success" which is easily surpassed by a victor when it fails to appreciate (or, in the argument above, is unable to act upon) the logic of military strategy.

9. As seen in the Camp David case, this works the other way, too. Both Begin and Sadat played on Carter's domestic problems and their own respective constituencies in the United States to extract concessions from him. Neither Japan nor Russia had such constituencies nor were domestic factors so important then. And Roosevelt had a much freer hand in international affairs.

Interestingly, although Roosevelt appears to have been weaker as a mediator than Carter, he was also not domestically constrained in the way Carter was. The advantages of having minimal domestic constraints will be even more evident when the "neutral mediators" are taken up in chapters 8 and 9. The conclusion, chapter 10, develops further the role of domestic politics in international intermediary interventions.

Chapter Eight

1. Recall from chapter 2 that "neutral," as I have defined it, does not mean without interests nor without impact nor without bias. It simply refers to the fact that a third-party intervenor has no bargaining capability with the disputants nor any interest—direct of indirect—in the disputed issues. So, for example, a neutral mediator's proposals are neutral in that they are not simultaneously part of a strategic bargain with the disputants as is the case with principal mediators.

2. Interview, Lanusse, Buenos Aires, 1986. Author's translation.

3. Because the closest English equivalent to the term *Laudo* is "arbitration award," I use the Spanish term here.

4. Barros, *Chilean-Argentine Relations*, 116.

5. Confidential interview, Argentine official, Buenos Aires, 1986.

6. Lanus, *De Chapultepec al Beagle*, 515–16. Author's translation. When questioning both Argentine government officials and the "man on the street" for one month regarding the dispute, not once did an Argentine express any doubt that the Beagle Channel islands were Argentine. They had read it in their textbooks since childhood.

7. This view was articulated in a confidential interview by a high-level Argentine diplomat who was legal counsel to some of the early negotiations.

8. Villegas, *La Propuesta Pontificia*, 99. Author's translation.

9. Barros, *De Chapultepec al Beagle*, 140.

10. Goñi Garrido, *Crónica del Conflicto*, 57. Author's translation.

11. *El Mercurio* (Santiago), February 10, 1978. Author's translation.

12. Lanus, *De Chapultepec al Beagle*, 521; Goñi Garrido, *Crónica del Conflicto*, 69.

13. Confidential interview with Chilean counselor to Chile's negotiating team, Santiago, 1986.

14. *La Nacion* (Buenos Aires), August 22, 1978. Author's translation.

15. Goñi Garrido, *Crónica del Conflicto*, 74.

16. *Aquí Está* (Santiago), June, 1979, p. 49.

17. Confidential interview with Chilean counselor to Chilean negotiation team, Santiago, 1986.

18. Goñi Garrido, *Crónica del Conflicto*, 72.

19. Interview, Montes, Buenos Aires, 1986. Author's translation.

20. Many Chileans scoffed at the idea of air raids. For one, they said, many Argentines found the blackouts nothing out of the ordinary given recurrent electric power shortages. Moreover, Chilean Foreign Minister Hernan Cubillos pointed out in a 1986 interview that the Chilean air force did not have the range to go from Chile to Buenos Aires and back.

21. Goñi Garrido, *Crónica del Conflicto*, 88.

22. Interview, Cubillos, Santiago, 1986.

23. Foreign Minister Montes resigned October 28 amid controversy over the conduct of foreign affairs. By some accounts, he complained that it was impossible to have a coherent foreign policy with the way the country was being governed.

24. The following account derives largely from interviews in 1986 in Santiago with Hernan Cubillos, Chile's foreign minister at the time.

25. Interview, Héctor Riesle, Chile's ambassador to the Holy See; Rome, 1986.

26. Interview, Hernan Cubillos, Santiago, 1986.

27. *La Prensa* (Buenos Aires), November 15, 1978.

28. *La Razon* (Buenos Aires), November 9, 1978.

29. Villegas, 1982, *La Propuesta Pontificia*. Author's translation.

30. *La Nacion* (Buenos Aires), December 6, 1978; *Opinion* (Buenos Aires), December 6, 1978.

31. *La Nacion* (Buenos Aires), December 15, 1978.

32. Interview, Cubillos, Santiago, 1986.

33. George Landau, speech, December 4, 1985, Americas Society, New York.

34. According to James Nelson Goodsell, both Peru and Bolivia have long vowed to recover the land they lost in 1879, Peru having made repeated promises to take it back before one hundred years were up. February 14, 1979 would mark the one hundredth anniversary of the start of the war. He also notes that troops had mobilized in both Peru and Bolivia in October 1978 and that the military leaders from both countries engaged in a good deal of saber-rattling. *Christian Science Monitor*, October 30, 1978, 15.

35. *Washington Post*, November 3, 1978; *Christian Science Monitor*, October 30, 1978, 15.

36. *La Prensa* (Buenos Aires), December 16, 1978.

37. Interview, George Landau, New York, 1986.

38. By several accounts that came out some weeks later, on December 21, Argentina also drafted a declaration of war. Reported in *Que Pasa* (Santiago), December 3, 1984, 15.

39. Confidential interview, Vatican City, 1986.

40. Goñi Garrido, *Crónica del Conflicto*, 119.

41. Fogg, *Soberania Argentina*, 84.

42. Interview, Hernan Cubillos, Santiago, 1986.

43. Ibid.

44. Ibid.

45. *La Opinion* (Buenos Aires), December 30, 1978. Author's translation.

46. Ibid.

47. Amuchástegui Astrada, *Argentina-Chile*, 184. Author's translation.

48. Goñi Garrido, *Crónica del Conflicto*, 121. Author's translation.

49. *La Opinion* (Buenos Aires), December 30, 1978. Author's translation.

50. *La Opinion* (Buenos Aires), December 30, 1978. Author's translation.

51. Lanús, *De Chapultepec al Beagle*, 529.

52. Amuchástegui Astrada, *Argentina-Chile*, 205. Author's translation.

53. Ibid., 215.

54. Interview, Hernan Cubillos, Santiago, 1986.

55. Montalvo, 1984, Introductory speech. Author's translation.

56. *L'Osservatore Romano*, November 12, 1979, 14. Weekly English edition.

57. Ibid.

58. Ibid.

59. Sainz Muñoz, address, 1980.

60. Ibid.

61. Radio Vaticana, press release, Vatican City, Information Service of the Holy See (UISS), January 30, 1980. Author's translation.

62. Radio Vaticana, press release, Vatican City, UISS, May 16, 1980. Author's translation.

63. Sainz Muñoz, address, 1980.

64. From interviews with individuals from all sides, it is clear the cardinal was revered for, among other things, his great patience and perseverance.

65. By one account, the parties, recognizing that the mediation was not progressing, requested that the pope step in. They asked that he give them his suggestions as a means of enabling their respective governments to point to such ideas as being those of the mediator, not necessarily of the negotiators. By another account, the mediation team concluded that the mediation process was bogged down and needed impetus. Moreover, because movement was not being had in the day-to-day sessions and the positions of the two sides were, by now, perfectly clear, all that remained was to put out a papal proposal that met all the criteria of a just, equitable, honorable, complete, and definitive solution. Confidential interviews, 1986.

66. I use the capitalized Spanish word here to distinguish it from all the other minor suggestions, or proposals. The *Propuesta* (Proposal), as will be described, became the only formal papal proposal, and from this point on it was always the

basis for future discussions. It was, in effect, the "single negotiating text"; see Raiffa, *Art and Science of Negotiation*, 211–17.

67. *L'Osservatore Romano*, December 29, 1980, 2. Weekly English edition.

68. Cardinal Samoré interviewed by Paolo Salvo of Radiogiornale, distributed by Radio Vaticano. December 13, 1980. Author's translation.

69. *New York Times*, December 27, 1980.

70. Pittman, "Geopolitics in the ABC Countries," 903.

71. *Los Angeles Times*, April 5, 1981.

72. It should be noted that in the papal mediation, the controversy between the two countries was never referred to as the "Beagle Channel dispute." This connoted recognition of the Laudo, the arbitral award that Argentina had rejected. Instead, "diferendo austral" (the "southern conflict"), or less loaded phrases were used.

73. Radio Vaticana, press release, Vatican City, UISS, June 7, 1981. Author's translation.

74. The first official recognition of the fact that the Propuesta would continue to be the basis of negotiations was apparently only in August, 1984. This was given in a statement of the Office of Mediation. Radio Vaticana, press release, UISS, August 6, 1984.

75. According to David Rock, as early as October 1978, Junta member, Admiral Emilio Massera, began calling for an invasion of the British-held Malvinas/Falklands Islands once it appeared the Beagle Channel dispute was going to be resolved peacefully. But the moderates, Videla and Viola, remained in power through most of 1981 and were able to head off any such military adventures (Viola became president when Videla's term expired in March 1981). Only when the country's economy virtually collapsed in late 1981 did army commander, General Leopoldo Galtieri, take over.

Galtieri was not one to make concessions, either domestically or abroad. When he was unable to build popular domestic support for his policies, he turned to foreign affairs. As noted above, in early 1982, he put pressure on Chile. Then he launched a diplomatic offensive against Great Britain, demanding acknowledgment of Argentina's sovereignty over the Malvinas/Falklands islands. This last effort proved most promising and was pursued most vigorously. According to Rock, if the Galtieri regime had escalated the conflict with Chile, it would have risked a protracted war that could have spread elsewhere in Latin America and perhaps led to an invasion by Brazil. Consequently, in early April 1982, Argentina shifted from diplomatic pressure against Britain to military action and invaded the Malvinas/Falklands islands. Rock, *Argentina 1516–1982*, 370–76.

76. *New York Times*, January 2, 1983.

77. *Latin American Weekly Report*, April 23, 1982.

78. *Latin American Weekly Report*, June 25, 1982.

79. Montalvo, 1984, Introductory speech. Author's translation.

80. *L'Osservatore Romano*, May 24, 1982, 4–5. Weekly English edition.

81. Montalvo, 1984, Introductory speech. Author's translation.

82. "1978: Cuando el Termómeter se puso al rojo vivo," *Que Pasa* (Santiago), December 3, 1984, 15. Author's translation.

83. *L'Osservatore Romano*, January 23, 1984, 6. Weekly English edition.

84. Radio Vaticana, press release, Vatican City, UISS, January 23, 1984. Author's translation.

85. *New York Times*, January 24, 1984.

86. Montalvo, Introductory speech. Author's translation.

87. "But What About the Falklands?", 36.

88. Isaac Rojas interviewed in "Y se sembro la paz entre dos pueblos hermanos." Author's translation.

89. Ricardo Echeverry Boneo interviewed in "Y sembro la paz." Author's translation.

90. "But What About the Falklands?" 36.

91. More precisely, this choice is best thought of as a choice of a locus of points on several dimensions important to intermediary intervention. These dimensions can include the third party's ability to offer concrete incentives to come to agreement, its interest in the issues in dispute, decision-making authority, and technical expertise. For my present purpose of laying out the choice of a dispute resolution process as a bargain in its own right, however, these three points— negotiation, mediation, and arbitration—suffice.

92. Unlike in many negotiations, in a negotiation over process, one side's choice of its best alternative affects both parties. Here, if Chile went to the court and won, Argentina would suffer the international condemnation. And, of course, if Argentina had invaded the islands, Chile would had to have dealt with the consequences. Thus, the notion of best alternative to a negotiated agreement is unlike that in many negotiations where, when one party elects to take its no-agreement alternative, the other necessarily takes *its* alternative. Here, the calculation of one's reservation value must, therefore, incorporate the possibility of the other side taking its alternative.

93. For discussion of how these factors plus how an expected shift in the balance of power can contribute to leader's propensity to seek foreign successes, see Lebow, "Deterrence Deadlock."

94. Kelman and Warwick, "Bridging Micro and Macro Approaches," 27.

95. The models are based on Pruitt and Gahagan as described in Pruitt and Rubin, *Social Conflict*; and on Jervis, *Perception and Misperception*.

96. In his analysis of the geopolitics of the two countries, Pittman comes to a similar conclusion: "In the Chilean perception, it is Argentina who is the rich, powerful, but frustrated, neighbor, who is prepared to use economic power, diplomatic pressure and threats of armed force to achieve her geopolitical goals at the expense of a smaller, weaker neighboring nation which has already suffered extensive territorial losses in the past, when the 'price of peace' with Argentina was the cessation of Chilean-claimed territory on the continent. Now, the Argentine goals have been extended to the sea and the Antarctic." Pittman, "Geopolitics in the ABC Countries," 974.

97. Jervis, *Perception and Misperception*, 58.

98. Villegas, *La Propuesta Pontificia*, 99.

99. Pruitt and Rubin, *Social Conflict*, 92. In the several times I have presented this case in class or in discussion groups, I am regularly implored to reveal who was

"wrong" and who "won." Because Argentina usually comes across as the "bad guy" (for a number of good reasons), it is very difficult to get people to see Argentina's view, and, hence, they miss Pruitt and Rubin's point.

100. This explains, in part, the frequent failures of international organizations, such as the OAS and the OAU, that take as their "mediating" role the job of deciding which side is right. I explore this further in the next case and in chapter 10.

101. One may argue that this was little more than a convenient position for Chile to take, given its military vulnerability and its legal advantages after the Laudo. This may be true, but it was my experience in conducting interviews in the two countries that the legalistic characterization also fit the stereotype for Chileans (as did the militaristic for the Argentines). Given that Chilean President Pinochet gave his negotiators considerable negotiating authority, this seems to be a significant difference between the two sides, contrary to what the simple aggressor-defender model would suggest.

102. Kelman and Warwick, "Bridging Micro and Macro Approaches," 29.

103. Ibid., 37.

104. Although this may explain why the decision makers accepted papal mediation, it does not explain why they acceded to Cardinal Samoré's last-minute inclusion of a withdrawal of forces provision. Samoré's threat (probably implicit) was that the whole thing would be called off if the parties did not accept the withdrawal provision. Because Chile welcomed force withdrawals, the threat was really only directed at Argentina, particularly, the hardliners. Samoré may have been bluffing (he had no way of making the threat credible), and Chile's foreign minister, Cubillos, may have known it (recall the incident in Cubillos's home in which Samoré challenged Cubillos and threatened to return to Rome). But Argentine leaders may not have suspected that he was bluffing or, at least, they could not risk calling his bluff. After failing to reap the benefits of an assertive foreign policy, the only remaining expected benefit was to go along with the papal mission, as discussed previously. In short, Samoré's fait accompli tactic may have succeeded because the Argentines did not know Cardinal Samoré would bluff or because they could not risk what little remaining political advantages they could obtain from the dispute.

105. Improving church-state relations was, of course, not an insignificant concern, given the nature of those relations and the importance of Latin America to the Catholic church hierarchy. This may have been an "indirect interest" as discussed in chapter 2, but it offered the Vatican few bargaining opportunities. That is, the state of relations was such that neither the Vatican nor the parties could offer or deny each other much. If anything, maintaining the status quo was probably the predominant concern. To the extent the Vatican did have indirect interests and that it had something to offer (say, better relations, fewer demands for local church autonomy, warm receptions in Rome) and something to deny (worse relations, cool receptions in Rome, excommunication), the Vatican was indeed not a pure "neutral mediator." As will be seen in the next chapter, the Quakers best approximate this "ideal type." But as discussed before, this is not to say that Quakers are "ideal" mediators. The Vatican was able to exploit its position of being in the middle and having negligible bargaining resources to effect changes in the parties' interactions.

106. Of course, Kissinger did try initially to get an overall agreement, and his efforts were frustrated by a complex set of factors. What I am arguing here, however, is that, to the extent he sought to promote direct interactions—and it seemed he did not as he insisted on directing all communication through him—he was unsuccessful.

107. *L'Osservatore Romano*, December 29, 1980, 2.

108. A more extensive view of the institutional roots of Vatican diplomacy is Princen, "Mediation by a Transnational Organization: The Case of the Vatican."

109. My interpretation of the Vatican's reasoning on these matters derives from confidential interviews with officials involved directly and indirectly with the Beagle Channel case.

110. Interestingly, although this no-withdrawal stance of the Vatican may have contributed to the parties' reluctance to withdraw unilaterally and, hence, to the enhancement of the mediator's relative influence over the parties, it may have been double-edged. That is, because the parties knew the mediator would never cease its efforts, their certainty could also have undercut the Vatican's occasional threats to cut off the mediation if movement was not forthcoming. One can surmise that they were convinced of this by their appreciation of the mediator's costs of failure.

111. Raiffa, *Art and Science of Negotiation*, 23–24.

112. I should clarify that although this discussion is couched in terms of concessions—what both parties tended to do in interviews—it is not meant to suggest that the mediation team and the parties failed to see the potential of more creative, more integrative solutions. In terms of domestic consumption, especially in Argentina at this time, it is likely that both public and official reaction to any plan brought home by the negotiators would be couched in such terms.

If there is a lesson here, it seems to be that even if negotiators can appreciate the potential of integrative solutions, publics tend to evaluate outcomes in simple, win-lose, distributive terms. That they do so is often, in part, a product of leaders' attempts to gain support by so portraying the nature of the conflict. The tendency to evaluate outcomes in distributional terms will be exaggerated as the intensity of the conflict, domestic uncertainty, lack of political unity, economic decline, and so forth, increase.

113. The same kind of pressures that Argentine negotiators felt in the early attempts in 1977 and 1978 to settle the conflict likely continued until Raul Alfonsin was elected president in late 1983.

114. The Malvinas/Falklands episode was only the most dramatic of these events. As noted in the case, amid continuing social and economic crisis, the moderates, Videla and Viola, struggled to hold onto power and to withstand the aggressive designs of the hardliners. Making concessions in a matter of foreign affairs was probably out of the question under these circumstances. Moreover, after the Galtieri coup in December 1981, the new Junta was looking for a foreign victory, not a compromise settlement. In the Beagle Channel dispute and the Vatican's attempts to get a solution, it was, in some sense, fortunate that the Argentine Junta directed its efforts toward Great Britain, not Chile. If Chile had been the target in 1982, the Vatican likely would have been left helpless trying to mediate a "hot" conflict.

115. For a discussion of the "diplomatic revolution" and the role of the press and public opinion in twentieth-century diplomacy, see Craig and George, *Force and Statecraft* as well as discussion in chapters 1 and 10 in this volume.

CHAPTER NINE

1. The primary sources for this account are Stremlau, *International Politics Nigerian Civil War, 1967–1970*; Yarrow, *Quaker Experiences*, "The Nigerian Civil War," chap. 4; and an extensive interview with Adam Curle, London, 1989.

2. As early as March 1967, Ojukwu sent representatives throughout Africa to win foreign support for his interpretation of the Aburi Accords. Ojukwu then called for a summit meeting of Nigeria's leaders in the presence of four of Africa's most prominent statesmen. He apparently hoped to convert the wide sympathy generated by the October massacres in the North into international political pressure for greater autonomy. It was a tactic he played in various forms throughout the conflict. See Stremlau, *International Politics*, 51.

3. Yarrow, *Quaker Experiences*, 191.

4. Stremlau, *International Politics*, 99.

5. Ibid., 99.

6. Stremlau (pp. 82–106) argues that this attempt failed in part because of the anticipated visit of the OAU's Consultative Committee and in part because of Biafra's declining military position in late 1967. In addition, as discussed further in this chapter, Biafra's primary concern was not to talk but to reduce Britain's support for the federal government, especially its arms shipments.

7. The only way to get into Biafra at this time was via transport planes coming from Lisbon via Guinea. The planes flew only at night and without radio communication to avoid the federal government's antiaircraft batteries. Once inside Biafra, they descended in a tight corkscrew spiral to land. On more than one occasion for Curle, the planes had to turn back under threat of fire. Personal interview, Curle, London, 1989.

8. In meetings with the Commonwealth Secretariat in London in early January 1968, Nigerian officials discounted the possibility of outsiders policing a cease-fire. In fact, when the secretary general, Arnold Smith, pressed the Nigerians on the question of Ibo safety in the event of a cease-fire, they could only say that they planned for a federal occupation once rebel forces had been disarmed. If there was to be a foreign presence, it could only be token. The federal government might accept an observer team but definitely not a peace-keeping force. Stremlau, *International Politics*, 154–55.

The difference between what Gowon was saying to the Quakers and what his representatives were saying in London may only have been a difference in degree. Or it may have reflected differences of opinion within the federal government. Nevertheless, the apparent concession appears significant in that it came directly from Gowon and was intended for direct communication to Ojukwu.

9. These reactions were recalled by Adam Curle in a personal interview in London, 1989.

10. Stremlau, *International Politics*, 146.

11. Ibid., 149, interview with Arikpo.

12. Ibid., 155.

13. Sir Louis Mbanefo, Opening Address, May 23, 1968, quoted in Stremlau, *International Politics*, 167.

14. Quoted in Stremlau, *International Politics*, p. 178.

15. Ibid., 178.

16. As it turned out, the Quakers made several more trips between capitals and nearly succeeded in convening secret talks between the two sides. In the end, in January 1970, the Biafrans surrendered.

17. Notice that in the following I do not cite the parties' decisions to go to London, Kampala, Addis Ababa, and elsewhere for talks as indicators of flexibility. Most of these decisions are too easily explained in terms of appeasing a benefactor (the federal government's main motive for accepting a British role) or of seeking a world forum (Biafra's main motive for going to the conferences). Rather, the instances cited here are more difficult to explain as anything other than leaders' genuine attempts to seek multiple paths for settlement.

18. Stremlau, *International Politics*, 142.

19. N. U. Akpan, *The Struggle for Secession*, 137, quoted in Stremlau, *International Politics*, 179.

20. Negotiators' statements to this effect can also be interpreted as tactical moves designed to resist pressures for concessions. The effect, nevertheless, is the same: negotiators were in no position to concede, to explore alternatives, to disaggregate or combine issues, or to look for interim steps toward ending the violence.

21. Stremlau, *International Politics*, 100.

22. Ibid., 101.

23. Ibid., 102.

24. Radio Biafra, November 25, 1967, quoted in Stremlau, *International Politics*, 105.

25. For discussion of diplomacy in the classical era and its differences from the modern era, see chapters 1 and 10, this volume.

26. These perceptions are not unlike those of Israel and Egypt in the 1970s with respect to the United States. In this regard, it is entirely possible that the British could have pressured the Nigerians into concluding a cease-fire, if not a total concession to Biafran demands. The essential difference is that in the Middle East, agreement on the fundamental issues of recognition and troop withdrawals was already established by the parties themselves, making U.S. sweeteners effective in concluding a treaty. In West Africa, the parties were negotiating over issues of survival and national and ethnic identity; no amount of aid or security guarantees could have rearranged payoffs sufficiently for either side to buy into concessions.

That the British did not pressure the Nigerians can be attributed in part to the lack of a leader like Jimmy Carter and his single-minded moral commitment and inattention to domestic consequences. But it is also owing to the fact that the federal government had alternative arms suppliers, notably the Soviet Union. A British threat to Nigeria to make concessions or face an arms cutoff would have been questionably credible because the British were seriously concerned about an increased Soviet presence in Nigeria and the region.

27. For examples and discussion of unofficial diplomacy, see Berman and Johnson, *Unofficial Diplomats*; and McDonald and Bendahmane, *Conflict Resolution*.

28. The analysis offered here is based in part on confidential interviews conducted in 1988 and 1989 with Quakers who have been active as mediators in other conflicts. The analysis thus draws on refinements in their approach taken since the Nigeria-Biafra conflict and is presented as a general characterization of Quaker mediation. For more on Quaker mediation see Yarrow, *Quaker Experiences*; Curle, *In the Middle*; and Berman and Johnson, *Unofficial Diplomats*. The interpretation presented in this chapter of what Quakers do and how they do it—especially how they constrain parties' choices—is not necessarily shared by the above authors.

29. I should note that, in their limited message-carrying capacity, the Quakers avoid imposing their religious or moral values on the parties; they do not proselytize. Their aim, as they explain it, is not to convert the parties to peaceful ways but simply to help them find alternative means of meeting their own objectives. They avoid condemning a person, but they do stress that their primary objective is to reduce the violence.

30. It is probably fair to say that most mediators are used in exactly this way; their very expendability makes them unsung heroes. Of course, this is to suggest that *most* mediators are not Henry Kissingers and Jimmy Carters but a variety of small actors playing small roles and having a small but, possibly, critical effect.

31. For simplicity, here I am framing the leader's choice as between continuing violent struggle or communicating effectively to reach a negotiated outcome. To be consistent with much of the above discussion, in most cases, the choice is really between a single path—namely, fighting—and multiple, often simultaneous paths—namely, fighting *and* talking. Although leaders may believe that one can only fight or talk, not both, in practice, the two often occur together. The fear of talking comes from the view that talking is viewed as conceding. It is not, of course, if fighting is viewed in the Clausewitzian sense of being fundamentally a political act just as is diplomacy. From a conflict resolution perspective, the difficulty arises when the talking must be subject to public scrutiny, which diplomats did not have to contend with in Clausewitz's time. Quiet, behind-the-scenes diplomacy, especially low-risk efforts like this, plays an essential function in, at a minimum, legitimizing leaders' need to talk while they fight in order to end the fighting.

32. In fact, Curle describes how a particular Nigerian official, a British expatriate, deliberately thwarted their efforts until he, and others, were convinced of their usefulness. This official then became extremely helpful. Personal interview, Curle, London, 1989.

33. Ibid.

34. Smith told Curle that he could neither get permission nor transportation to Biafra. Moreover, it was simply out of the question that such a high-level official would secretly "stow away" on a transport plane as did the Quakers, let alone do so in secret. Interview, Curle, 1989.

35. Stremlau, *International Politics*, reaches a similar conclusion comparing third parties: "There were several private initiatives that ran parallel to the efforts

by the Commonwealth Secretariat. The most important of these was a bid by John Volkmar and Adam Curle on behalf of the Quakers, which facilitated an indirect exchange of views between Gowon and Ojukwu during February and March 1968. This communication was couched in such general terms that it did not constitute an exploration of any formulae for a settlement. Although Quaker offers to mediate were tendered discreetly, public calls for a negotiated settlement by the World Council of Churches and the Vatican had even less chance of success.

Chapter Ten

1. See, for example, Princen, "Quaker Model of Reconciliation."

2. This point is developed further under "narrowing the negotiation-hostilities gap."

3. Of course, there is a large literature critical of power politics, especially deterrence, both as theory and as policy. The difficulty of measuring accurately the calculations, motivations, or fears of each side make empirical verification and policy advice very difficult. Thus, although a power politics view of international conflict and of conflict management may be more parsimonious than the view assumed in this study, it does not lend itself to a differentiated theory that accounts for different kinds of conflicts and intervenors. For discussion , see George and Smoke, *Deterrence in American Foreign Policy*; Jervis, 1989, "Rational Deterrence." Jervis, Lebow, and Stein, *Psychology and Deterrence.*

4. Throughout this book I have not drawn a hard-and-fast distinction between settlement and resolution. A more comprehensive treatment would have to distinguish when an intermediary intervention contributes to merely a signed agreement and when to a comprehensive, mutually acceptable resolution. Settlement in the form of a signed agreement may detract from, not contribute to, a comprehensive resolution, that is, one that leads to an ongoing peace process and that is durable and internally sustainable. It is tempting to think that principal mediators are better at getting signed agreements (for example, Kissinger's Middle East agreements) and neutrals better at contributing to comprehensive resolution (for example, the problem-solving workshops of John Burton or Herbert Kelman). But neither is necessarily superior in either objective. An interim settlement may be the necessary precondition of a comprehensive resolution whereas effective interactions may be the necessary precondition to get a settlement. From a policy perspective, this suggests that an overall conflict management strategy would encompass a variety of overlapping or sequential third-party efforts as discussed under "Principal-Neutral."

5. Analytically, agreement is a good first-cut assumption regarding intermediary objectives as discussed. Measurement implies a policy objective in the analysis, and so I argue here that the appropriate criterion is not agreement—at least not a final settlement—but incremental agreements or steps toward a final agreement.

6. For discussion of a negotiator's two-way bargaining, see Iklé, *How Nations Negotiate*; Putnam, "Diplomacy and Domestic Politics"; Winham, "Negotiation as a Management Process."

7. Of course, in many of these conflicts, what starts as a limited use of force

becomes an unmanageable, protracted engagement. The dynamics of escalation involve domestic pressures for all-out victory. Both Argentina (in the Beagle Channel and Falklands/Malvinas episodes) and Japan resorted to force, so they argued, only when their opponent failed to negotiate in good faith. The point here is that, regardless of changes in intentions, when leaders do wish to negotiate, they often cannot.

8. This is not to say that the belligerents actually *preferred* at all times to negotiate and were somehow thwarted. Leaders may be expected to choose rationally their preferred courses of action and to make changes as the calculation changes. In practice, leaders, once they relax a single-minded approach, seek to expand options and then waver among them. It is the wavering between contentious and cooperative approaches that provides the opportunities for intermediary interventions.

9. This resistance to change comes not out of ignorance or stubbornness or delusions of grandeur. It is simply a product of the norms of interaction that prevail in conflictual situations. Herbert Kelman puts it this way: "A central characteristic of social interaction, under 'normal' conditions, is that its participants try to take into account, not only each other's behavior, but also each other's purposes, perceptions, and intentions, and the structural constraints within which these are formed. As interaction proceeds over time, each participant becomes aware of changes in the other's situation, ideas, and actions—and, indeed, of the possibilities of influencing these through his or her own actions. These normal processes and consequences of social interaction are impaired by the special dynamics that mark interaction between conflicting parties. . . . The norms that govern interaction between representatives of conflicting parties require each to express their own grievances and to proclaim their own rights as firmly and militantly as possible" (Kelman, "Interactional Approach to Conflict Resolution," 106–7).

10. In addition, as discussed in chapter 2, intermediaries who are not simultaneously in a bargain with the disputants will be more likely to elicit such information. Thus, neutral mediators are more likely to be effective in pinpointing the onset of mutual readiness to negotiate. Principal mediators may, nevertheless, be more effective at the other end—that is, commencing negotiations and enforcing a cease-fire or guaranteeing mutual security of the parties.

BIBLIOGRAPHY

Allison, Graham. 1971. *Essence of Decision: Explaining the Cuban Missile Crisis.* Boston: Little, Brown.

Amuschástegui Astrada, Armando. 1980. *Argentina-Chile: Controversia y mediación.* Buenos Aires: Imprenta se los Buenos Ayres S.A.

Aquí Está (Santiago), June 1979.

Axelrod, Robert. 1984. *The Evolution of Cooperation.* New York: Basic Books.

Barros, Jose Miguel. 1978. *Chilean-Argentine Relations: The Beagle Channel Controversy.* 2d ed. Geneva: Printed by the Government of Chile.

Bercovitch, Jacob. 1984. *Social Conflicts and Third Parties: Strategies of Conflict Resolution.* Boulder, Colo.: Westview Press.

———. 1986. "International Mediation: A Study of the Incidence, Strategies and Conditions of Successful Outcomes." *Cooperation and Conflict* 21:155–68.

Berman, Maureen R., and Joseph E. Johnson, eds. 1977. *Unofficial Diplomats.* New York: Columbia University Press.

Bingham, Gail. 1986. *Resolving Environmental Disputes: A Decade of Experience.* Washington, D.C.: Conservation Foundation.

Brecher, Michael, and Jonathan Wilkenfield. 1989. *Crisis, Conflict and Instability.* Oxford: Pergamon Press.

Buchanan, James M., and Gordon Tullock. 1967. *The Calculus of Consent: Logical Foundations of Constitutional Democracy.* Ann Arbor: University of Michigan Press.

Burton, John W. 1969. *Conflict and Communication: The Use of Controlled Communication in International Relations.* London: Macmillan.

———. 1987. "Track Two: An Alternative to Power Politics." In John W. McDonald, Jr. and Diane B. Bendahmane, eds., *Conflict Resolution: Track Two Diplomacy,* pp. 65–72. Washington, D.C.: Foreign Service Institute.

"But What About the Falklands?" *Economist,* December 8, 1984, 36.

Carter, Jimmy. 1982. *Keeping Faith: Memoirs of a President.* New York: Bantam Books.

Christian Science Monitor, October 30, 1978; May 1, 1979.

Cormick, Gerald W. 1982. "Intervention and Self-determination in Environmental Disputes: A Mediator's Perspective." *Resolve* (Winter): 1, 3–7.

———. 1982. "The Myth, the Reality, and the Future of Environmental Mediation." *Environment* 24:14–17, 36–39.

———. 1989. "Strategic Issues in Structuring Multi-Party Public Policy Negotiations." *Negotiation Journal* 5 (2): 125–32.

Cot, Jean-Pierre. 1968. *International Conciliation.* London: Europa Publications.

Craig, Gordon A., and Alexander L. George. 1983. *Force and Statecraft: Diplomatic Problems of Our Time.* New York: Oxford University Press.

Curle, Adam. 1971. *Making Peace.* London: Tavistock Publications.

———. 1981. *True Justice: Quaker peace makers and peace making.* London: Quaker Home Service.

———. 1986. *In the Middle: Non-official Mediation in Violent Situations*. New York: St. Martin's Press.

Dayan, Moshe. 1981. *Breakthrough: A Personal Account of the Egypt-Israel Peace Negotiations*. New York: Alfred A. Knopf.

Dominquez, Jorge. 1971. "Mice that Do Not Roar: Some Aspects of International Politics in the World's Periphery," *International Organization* 25:175–208.

El Mercurio (Santiago), February 10, 1978; May 24, 1978; December 24, 1978.

Esthus, Raymond A. 1988. *Double Eagle and Rising Sun*. Durham and London: Duke University Press.

Fahmy, Ismail. 1983. *Negotiating for Peace in the Middle East*. Baltimore, Md.: Johns Hopkins University Press.

Fisher, Roger. 1981. "Playing the Wrong Game?" In Jeffrey Z. Rubin, ed., *Dynamics of Third-Party Intervention: Kissinger in the Middle East*, pp. 95–121. New York: Praeger.

Fisher, Roger, and William Ury. 1978. *International Mediation: A Working Guide*. New York: International Peace Academy.

———. 1981. *Getting to Yes: Negotiating Agreement Without Giving In*. Boston: Houghton Mifflin.

Fogg, Guillermo J. 1983. *Soberania Argentina en el area austral*. Buenos Aires: Editorial Pleamar.

George, Alexander L. 1979. "Case Studies and Theory Development: The Method of Structured Focused Comparison." In Paul Gordon Lauren, ed. *Diplomacy: New Approaches in History, Theory, and Policy*, pp. 43–68. New York: Free Press.

George, Alexander L., and Richard Smoke. 1974. *Deterrence in American Foreign Policy*. New York: Columbia University Press.

Goñi Garrido, Carlos M. 1984. *Crónica del conflicto Chileno Argentino*. Santiago: Ediar Editores LTDA.

Gulliver, P. H. 1979. *Disputes and Negotiations: A Cross-Cultural Perspective*. New York: Academic Press.

Hebblethwaite, Peter. 1986. *In the Vatican*. Bethesda, Maryland: Adler and Adler.

Hoffmann, Stanley, ed. 1987. *Janus and Minerva: Essays in the Theory and Practice of International Politics*. Boulder, Colo.: Westview Press.

Holsti, K. J. 1970. "National Role Conceptions in the Study of Foreign Policy." *International Studies Quarterly* 14 (3): 233–309.

Holsti, Ole R. 1967. "Cognitive Dynamics and the Image of the Enemy." *Journal of International Affairs* 21:16–39.

Iklé, Fred Charles. 1964. *How Nations Negotiate*. New York: Harper and Row.

Janis, Irving L. 1982. *Groupthink*. 2d ed. Boston: Houghton Mifflin.

Janis, Irving L., and Leon Mann. 1977. *Decision Making: A Psychological Analysis of Conflict, Choice, and Commitment*. New York: Free Press.

Jervis, Robert. 1976. *Perception and Misperception in International Politics*. Princeton, N.J.: Princeton University Press.

———. 1985. "Introduction: Approach and Assumptions." In Robert Jervis, Richard Ned Lebow, and Janis Gross Stein, eds., *Psychology and Deterrence*, pp. 1–12. Baltimore: Johns Hopkins University Press.

————. 1989. "Rational Deterrence: Theory and Evidence." *World Politics* 41 (2): 183–207.

Jervis, Robert, Richard Ned Lebow, and Janice Gross Stein. 1985. *Psychology and Deterrence.* Baltimore, Md.: Johns Hopkins University Press.

Kahneman, Daniel, and Amos Tversky. 1974. "Judgment under Uncertainty: Heuristics and Biases." *Science* 185:1124–31.

Kayani, Amer. 1987. "The Kashmir Conflict: Soviet Mediation at Tashkent, 1966." Pew Program in Case Teaching and Writing in International Affairs, Case no. 15. Graduate School of Public and International Affairs, Pittsburgh University.

Kelman, Herbert C. 1979. "An Interactional Approach to Conflict Resolution and Its Application to Israeli-Palestinian Relations." *International Interactions* 6:99–122.

————. 1982. "Creating the Conditions for Israeli-Palestinian Negotiations." *Journal of Conflict Resolution* 26:39–75.

————, ed. 1965. *International Behavior: A Social-psychological Analysis.* New York: Holt.

Kelman, Herbert C., and Stephen P. Cohen. 1976. "The Problem-solving Workshop: A Social Psychological Contribution to the Resolution of International Conflicts." *Journal of Peace Research* 13:79–90.

Kelman, Herbert C., and Donald P. Warwick. 1973. "Bridging Micro and Macro Approaches to Social Change: A Social-Psychological Perspective." In Gerald Zaltman, ed., *Processes and Phenomena of Social Change*, pp. 13–59, 419–49. New York: John Wiley and Sons.

Keohane, Robert O. 1984. *After Hegemony: Cooperation and Discord in the World Political Economy.* Princeton, N.J.: Princeton University Press.

————. 1989. *International Institutions and State Power: Essays in International Relations Theory.* Boulder, Colo.: Westview Press.

Keohane, Robert O., and Joseph S. Nye. 1977. *Power and Interdependence: World Politics in Transition.* Boston: Little, Brown.

Keohane, Robert O., and Joseph S. Nye, eds. 1972. *Transnational Relations and World Politics.* Cambridge: Harvard University Press.

Kolb, Deborah M. 1983. *The Mediators.* Cambridge, Mass.: MIT Press.

————, ed. "Profiles of Master Mediators." Harvard Law School, Cambridge, Mass. Typescript.

Kolb, Deborah M., and Jeffrey Z. Rubin. 1989. "Mediation through a Disciplinary Kaleidoscope: A Summary of Empirical Research." *Dispute Resolution FORUM.* Washington, D.C.: National Institute for Dispute Resolution.

Krasner, Stephen D., ed. 1983. *International Regimes.* Ithaca, N.Y.: Cornell University Press.

Kuechle, David. 1974. "Note on Mediation." Harvard Graduate School of Business Administration Case no. 9–675–022. Boston: HBS Case Services.

La Nación (Buenos Aires), August 22, 1978; October 17, 1978; October 27, 1978; November 5, 1978; November 7, 1978; December 6, 1978; December 12, 1978; December 15, 1978; December 17, 1978; December 19, 1978; December 20, 1978; December 21, 1978.

La Opinión (Buenos Aires), October 22, 1978; December 6, 1978; December 30, 1978.

La Prensa (Buenos Aires), October 21, 1978; October 30, 1978; November 15, 1978; December 16, 1978.

La Razón (Buenos Aires), November 9, 1978.

Lakos, Amos. 1989. *International Negotiations: A Bibliography*. Boulder, Colo.: Westview Press.

Lanus, Juan Archibaldo. 1984. *De Chapultepec al Beagle. Política Exterior Argentina: 1945–1980*. Buenos Aires: Emecé Editores.

Latin American Weekly Report, April 23, 1982; June 25, 1982.

Lauren, Paul Gordon, ed., 1979. *Diplomacy: New Approaches in History, Theory, and Policy*. New York: Free Press.

Lax, David, and James K. Sebenius. 1986. *The Manager as Negotiator: Bargaining for Cooperation and Competitive Gain*. New York: Free Press.

Lebow, Richard Ned. 1985. "The Deterrence Deadlock: Is There a Way Out?" In Robert Jervis, Richard Ned Lebow, and Janis Gross Stein, eds. *Psychology and Deterrence*, pp. 180–202. Baltimore, Md.: Johns Hopkins University Press.

L'Osservatore Romano, weekly English edition, November 12, 1979; December 29, 1980; May 23, 1982; May 24, 1982; January 23, 1984; August 20, 1984.

Los Angeles Times, April 5, 1981.

Luttwak, Edward N. 1987. *Strategy: The Logic of War and Peace*. Cambridge, Mass.: Harvard University Press.

McDonald, John W., Jr., and Diane B. Bendahmane, eds., 1987. *Conflict Resolution: Track Two Diplomacy*. Washington, D.C.: Foreign Service Institute, Center for the Study of Foreign Affairs.

McMullen, Christopher J. 1980. *Resolution of the Yemen Crisis, 1963: A Case Study in Mediation*. Washington, D.C.: Institute for the Study of Diplomacy, Georgetown University.

————. 1981. *Mediation of the West New Guinea Dispute, 1962: A Case Study*. Washington, D.C.: Institute for the Study of Diplomacy, Georgetown University.

March, James G., and Herbert A. Simon. 1958. *Organizations*. New York: Wiley.

Montalvo, Gabriel, Monsignor. November 29, 1984. Radio Vaticana, press release. Appendix: Introductory speech. Vatican City: Information Service of the Holy See (UISS).

Moses, Russell Leigh. 1989. "Mediation and Private Contacts in the Iran Hostage Crisis, April 1980–January 1981." Pew Program in Case Teaching and Writing in International Affairs, Case no. 316. Graduate School of Public and International Affairs, Pittsburgh University.

Neustadt, Richard E. 1960/1980. *Presidential Power*. 4th ed. New York: Wiley.

New York Times, December 27, 1980; December 27, 1981; January 2, 1983; January 24, 1984; March 6, 1984; March 9, 1987.

Nicolson, Harold. 1950. *Diplomacy*. 3d ed. London: Oxford University Press.

"1978: Cuando el termómeter se puso al rojo vivo," *Que Pasa* (Santiago) December 3, 1984, 15.

Okamoto, Shumpei. 1970. *The Japanese Oligarchy and the Russo-Japanese War*. New York: Columbia University Press.

Oye, Kenneth A., ed. 1986. *Cooperation under Anarchy*. Princeton, N.J.: Princeton University Press.

Pittman, Howard. 1981. "Geopolitics in the ABC Countries: A Comparison." Ph.D. diss., The American University.

Princen, Thomas. 1987. "International Mediation—The View from the Vatican: Lessons from Mediating the Beagle Channel Dispute." *Negotiation Journal* 3 (October): 347–66.

———. 1988. "Beagle Channel Negotiations." Pew Program in Case Teaching and Writing in International Affairs, Case no. 401. Pittsburgh: Graduate School of Public and International Affairs, Pittsburgh University.

———. 1990. "Security and Conflict Management in the Context of Minor Disputes." Paper presented to International Studies Association, Washington, D.C.

———. 1991. "Camp David: Problem Solving or Power Politics as Usual?" *Journal of Peace Research* 28 (1): 57–69.

———. "The Quaker Model of Mediation: A Profile of Joseph Elder." In Deborah M. Kolb, ed., "When Talk Works: Profiles of Master Mediators." Harvard Law School, Cambridge Mass. Typescript.

———. 1992. "Mediation by a Transnational Organization: The Case of the Vatican." In Jacob Bercovitch and Jeffrey Z. Rubin, eds. *Mediation in International Relations: Multiple Approaches to Conflict Management*, London: Macmillan.

Pruitt, Dean G., and Jeffrey Z. Rubin. 1986. *Social Conflict: Escalation, Stalemate, and Settlement*. New York: Random House.

Putnam, Robert. 1988. "Diplomacy and Domestic Politics: The Logic of Two-Level Games." *International Organization* 42:427–53.

Quandt, William. 1977. *Decade of Decisions: American Policy Toward the Arab-Israeli Conflict, 1967–1976*. Berkeley: University of California Press.

———. 1986. *Camp David: Peacemaking and Politics*. Washington, D.C.: Brookings Institution.

Radio Vaticana, press releases. Vatican City, Information Service of the Holy See (UISS). September 27, 1979; January 30, 1980; June 7, 1981; January 23, 1984; August 6, 1984; November 29, 1984. Cardinal Samoré interviewed by Paolo Salvo of Radiogiornale, distributed by Radio Vaticana. December 13, 1980. Trans. Thomas Princen.

Raiffa, Howard. 1982. *The Art and Science of Negotiation*. Cambridge, Mass.: Harvard University Press.

Rock, David. 1985. *Argentina 1516–1982: From Spanish Colonization to the Falklands War*. Berkeley: University of California Press.

Rubin, Jeffrey Z. 1981. *Dynamics of Third-Party Intervention: Kissinger in the Middle East*. New York: Praeger.

Rubin, Jeffrey Z., and Bert R. Brown. 1975. *The Social Psychology of Bargaining and Negotiation*. New York: Academic Press.

Sadat, Anwar el-. 1977. *In Search of Identity: An Autobiography*. New York: Harper and Row.

Sainz Muñoz, Monsignor Faustino. Address at 14th General Assembly of the Pontifical Commission "Justicia et Pax," November 12, 1980. JUSTPAX n. 18, Annex 2. Printed in English.

Schelling, Thomas C. [1960]1980. *The Strategy of Conflict*. Cambridge, Mass.: Harvard University Press.

———. 1966. *Arms and Influence*. New Haven: Yale University Press.

Schofield, Richard. 1986. *Evolution of the Shatt al-'Arab Boundary Dispute*. Cambridgeshire, England: Middle East and North African Studies Press.

Sebenius, James K. 1984. *Negotiating the Law of the Sea*. Cambridge, Mass.: Harvard University Press.

Sheehan, Edward R. F. 1976. *The Arabs, Israelis, and Kissinger*. New York: Reader's Digest Press.

Sick, Gary. 1985. "The Partial Negotiator: Algeria and the U.S. Hostages in Iran." In Saadia Touval and I. William Zartman, eds., *International Mediation in Theory and Practice*, pp. 21–66. Boulder, Colo.: Westview Press.

Silbey, Susan S., and Sally E. Merry. 1986. "Mediator Settlement Strategies." *Law and Policy* 8 (January): 7–32.

Simon, Herbert A. [1945]1976. *Administrative Behavior*. 3d ed. New York: Free Press.

Snidal, Duncan. 1986. "The Game *Theory* of International Politics." In Kenneth A. Oye, ed., *Cooperation Under Anarchy*, pp. 25–57. Princeton, N.J.: Princeton University Press.

Snyder, Glenn, and Paul Diesing. 1977. *Conflict Among Nations: Bargaining, Decision Making, and System Structure in International Crises*. Princeton, N.J.: Princeton University Press.

Stein, Janice Gross. 1985. "Structures, Strategies, and Tactics of Mediation." *Negotiation Journal* 1(4): 331–47.

———. 1988. "International Negotiation: A Multidisciplinary Perspective." *Negotiation Journal* 4(3): 221–31.

Stein, Janice Gross, ed., 1989. *Getting to the Table: The Processes of International Prenegotiation*. Baltimore, Md.: The Johns Hopkins University Press.

Stremlau, John J. 1977. *The International Politics of the Nigerian Civil War, 1967–1970*. Princeton, N.J.: Princeton University Press.

Susskind, Lawrence, and Jeffrey Cruikshank. 1987. *Breaking the Impasse: Consensual Approaches to Resolving Public Disputes*. New York: Basic Books.

Tice, Orville M. 1981. "But What Does a Mediator Really Do? The Pitch Mine Case." Seattle, Wash.: Institute for Environmental Mediation.

Touval, Saadia. 1982. *The Peace Brokers: Mediators in the Arab-Israeli Conflict 1948–1979*. Princeton, N.J.: Princeton University Press.

———. 1989. "Multilateral Negotiation." *Negotiation Journal* 5(2): 159–73.

Touval, Saadia, and I. William Zartman, eds. 1985. *International Mediation in Theory and Practice*. Boulder, Colo.: Westview Press.

Villegas, Osiris G. 1982. *La propuesta pontificia y el espacio nacional compretido*. Buenos Aires: Editorial Pleamar.

Wall, James H., Jr. 1981. "Mediation." *Journal of Conflict Resolution* 25:157–80.

Walton, Richard E. 1969. *Interpersonal Peacemaking: Confrontations and Third-party Consultation*. Reading, Mass.: Addison-Wesley.

Walton, Richard E., and Robert B. McKersie. 1965. *A Behavioral Theory of Labor Negotiations*. New York: McGraw-Hill.

White, Ralph K. 1972. "The Pro-Us Illusion and the Black-Top Image." In B. T. King and E. McGinnies, eds., *Attitudes, Conflict, and Social Change*, pp. 211–21. New York: Academic Press.

Winham, Gilbert R. 1977. "Negotiation as a Management Process." *World Politics* 30:87–114.

———. 1979. "Practitioners' Views of International Negotiation." *World Politics* 32:111–35.

———. 1987. *International Trade and the Tokyo Round Negotiation.* Princeton, N.J.: Princeton University Press.

"Y se sembro la paz entre dos pueblos hermanos." *Cosas: Una Revista Internacional* (Santiago), no. 213, November 29, 1984, 23–27.

Yarrow, C. H. Mike. 1977. "Quaker Efforts toward Reconciliation in the India-Pakistan War of 1965." In Maureen R. Berman and Joseph E. Johnson, eds., *Unofficial Diplomats,* pp. 89–110. New York: Columbia University Press.

———. 1978. *Quaker Experiences in International Conciliation.* New Haven, Conn.: Yale University Press.

Young, Oran R. 1967. *The Intermediaries: Third Parties in International Crises.* Princeton, N.J.: Princeton University Press.

———. 1975. *Bargaining: Formal Theories of Negotiation.* Urbana: University of Illinois Press.

Zartman, I. William. 1985. *Ripe for Resolution: Conflict and Intervention in Africa.* New York: Oxford University Press.

———, ed. 1977. *The Negotiation Process: Theories and Applications.* Beverly Hills, Calif.: Sage Publications.

Zartman, I. William, and Maureen R. Berman. 1982. *The Practical Negotiator.* New Haven: Yale University Press.

INDEX